# The Sociology of Speed

# The Sociology of Speed

## Digital, Organizational, and Social Temporalities

*Edited by*
Judy Wajcman and Nigel Dodd

OXFORD
UNIVERSITY PRESS

# OXFORD
UNIVERSITY PRESS

Great Clarendon Street, Oxford, OX2 6DP,
United Kingdom

Oxford University Press is a department of the University of Oxford.
It furthers the University's objective of excellence in research, scholarship,
and education by publishing worldwide. Oxford is a registered trade mark of
Oxford University Press in the UK and in certain other countries

© Oxford University Press 2017

The moral rights of the authors have been asserted

First Edition published in 2017
Impression: 2

Published in the United States of America by Oxford University Press
198 Madison Avenue, New York, NY 10016, United States of America

British Library Cataloguing in Publication Data
Data available

Library of Congress Control Number: 2016939699

ISBN  978–0–19–878285–8 (hbk.)
      978–0–19–878286–5 (pbk.)

Printed and bound by CPI Group (UK) Ltd, Croydon, CR0 4YY

Links to third party websites are provided by Oxford in good faith and
for information only. Oxford disclaims any responsibility for the materials
contained in any third party website referenced in this work.

# Contents

## Contents

### Part III. Temporalities

# List of Figures

# List of Tables

# List of Contributors

**Nigel Dodd** is Professor of Sociology at the London School of Economics, and Editor-in-Chief of the *British Journal of Sociology*. His main interests are in the sociology of money, economic sociology, and classical and contemporary social thought. He is author of *The Sociology of Money* and *Social Theory and Modernity* (both published by Polity Press). His latest book, *The Social Life of Money*, was published by Princeton University Press in 2014. Nigel is also co-editor (with Patrik Aspers) of *Re-Imagining Economic Sociology* (Oxford University Press 2015).

**Paul Du Gay** came to Copenhagen Business School (CBS) in 2008 as a *Globaliserings-professor* at the Department of Organization. Prior to that he was Professor of Organizational Behaviour at Warwick Business School, and Professor of Sociology and Organization Studies at the Open University, UK. His research interests are located on the cusp of sociology, politics, history, and cultural studies, with a key focus on questions of organization and identity. At CBS, he is Co-Director of the School's Business in Society "Public-Private Platform," and Director of the collective Velux Research Programme "What Makes Organization?" Paul also holds a part-time Chair in the Management School at Royal Holloway, University of London.

**Ingrid Erickson** is Assistant Professor in the Department of Library and Information Science at Rutgers University in New Brunswick, New Jersey. Her research centers on the way that mobile devices and ubiquitous digital infrastructures are influencing how individuals and groups work and communicate with one another, navigate and inhabit spaces, and engage in and legitimate new types of sociotechnical practices.

**Melissa Gregg** is Principal Engineer in User Experience Research at Intel Corporation. A social theorist and ethnographer, her publications include *Work's Intimacy* (Polity 2011), *The Affect Theory Reader* (co-edited with Gregory J. Seigworth; Duke 2010) and *Cultural Studies' Affective Voices* (Palgrave 2006), as well as regular columns in *The Atlantic*. Her forthcoming book contracted with Duke University Press is *Counterproductive: A Brief History of Time Management*.

**Steven J. Jackson** is Associate Professor in the Department of Information Science at Cornell University, and a member of the Science and Technology Studies and Communication graduate fields. His work centers on questions of value and power in contemporary technoscience, with special emphasis on problems of time, infrastructure, maintenance, and repair in complex sociotechnical systems. Current empirical projects include work on computational development and affective change in the sciences; vernacular creativity and improvisation in science and new media arts; and problems of computation and social change in post-colonial environments. His work has been supported by the Ford Foundation, World Bank, Intel Research, and the U.S. National Science Foundation.

**Donald MacKenzie** is Professor of Sociology at the University of Edinburgh. His current research is on the sociology of financial markets, and he is focusing in particular on research on automated high-frequency trading. His books include *Inventing Accuracy: A Historical Sociology of Nuclear Missile Guidance* (MIT Press 1990) and *An Engine, Not a Camera: How Financial Models Shape Markets* (MIT Press 2006).

**Melissa Mazmanian** is Associate Professor of Informatics at the University of California, Irvine. Her research focuses on communication technologies as used in practice, organizational change, organizational culture and control, and the nature of personal and professional time in the digital age. She is currently involved in conducting ethnographies of personal time, looking at the role of communication technologies in how families juggle busy lives, negotiate work and personal demands, and understand their lives in terms of cultural narratives around professionalism, parenting, and constant connectivity.

**Harvey Molotch** is Professor of Sociology and Metropolitan Studies at NYU. He conducts research on urban development, security, and material artifacts. His books include *Against Security: How We Go Wrong at Airports, Subways, and Other Sites of Ambiguous Danger* (Princeton 2012); *Urban Fortunes* (California 2007); *Where Stuff Comes From* (Routledge 2003); and *Toilet: Public Restrooms and the Politics of Sharing* (NYU 2010).

**Hartmut Rosa** is Professor of Sociology at the Friedrich-Schiller-University in Jena, Director of the Max Weber Centre for Advanced Cultural and Social Studies at the University of Erfurt, and co-editor of the journal *Time & Society*. His research interests cover the diagnosis of the times and analysis of modernity, normative and empirical foundations of critique of society, theories of the subject and identity, and the sociology of time. He is author of several major books, including *High-Speed Society* (Penn State University Press), *Alienation and Acceleration* (NSU Press), and *Social Acceleration* (Columbia University Press). His latest book is *Resonanz. Eine Soziologie der Weltbeziehung* (Suhrkamp Verlag Gmbh, 2016).

**Saskia Sassen** is Robert S. Lynd Professor of Sociology at Columbia University. Her work focuses on globalization (including social, economic and political dimensions), immigration, global cities (including cities and terrorism), the new networked technologies, and changes within the liberal state that result from current transnational conditions. Her major books include *The Mobility of Labor and Capital* (Cambridge University Press), *The Global City* (Princeton University Press), *Territory, Authority, Rights* (Princeton University Press), and *Expulsions* (Belknap Press).

**Sarah Sharma** is Associate Professor at the University of Toronto where she is a faculty member at the Institute of Communication, Culture, Information and Technology (Mississauga) with a graduate appointment in the Faculty of Information (St. George). Professor Sharma is also the Director of the McLuhan Program in Culture and Technology. She is the author of *In the Meantime: Temporality and Cultural Politics* (Duke 2014).

**John Urry** was Distinguished Professor of Sociology and Co-Director of the Institute for Social Futures, Lancaster University. He was Fellow of the Academy of Social Sciences and published around forty books including *After the Car* (Polity 2009), *Mobile Lives* (Routledge 2010), *Climate Change and Society* (Routledge 2011), *Offshoring* (Polity 2014), and *What is the Future?* (Polity 2016). This work has been translated into over twenty languages. He collaborated with colleagues around the world developing new understandings of mobilities, energy, environment, and futures.

**Judy Wajcman** is the Anthony Giddens Professor of Sociology at the London School of Economics. She was previously Professor of Sociology in the Research School of Social Sciences at the Australian National University. Her books include: *The Politics of Working Life* (with Paul Edwards), *TechnoFeminism, Managing Like a Man: Women and Men in Corporate Management*, and *Feminism Confronts Technology*. Her latest book is *Pressed for Time: The Acceleration of Life in Digital Capitalism* (University of Chicago Press 2015).

# Introduction

## The Powerful are Fast, the Powerless are Slow

*Judy Wajcman and Nigel Dodd*

The themes of time and speed have always been central to sociology and social theory. They were at the core of classical thinkers such as Marx, Weber, and Simmel's analyses of the development of industrial capitalism and, in a broad sense, to be modern is to live in a runaway world (Giddens 2002). Indeed, the relative speed of different societies has long been seen as one of their defining characteristics.

Yet it is in diagnoses of our contemporary times, that acceleration has taken center stage. It seems to speak to our everyday experience. For many, speed and acceleration have come to signify the zeitgeist, the quintessential experience of modernity. Concepts such as *timeless time* (Castells 1996), *chronoscopic time* (Virilio 1986), *network time* (Hassan 2009), and *instantaneous time* (Urry 2000) abound to describe a purportedly new digital temporality.[1] Whether it be high-speed trading or social media, consumption or travel, the pace of life seems to be spinning ever faster. Yet, the idea that more and more aspects of our lives—technological and economic, cultural and political, public and private—are speeding up is rarely questioned.

The purpose of this volume is to bring a much-needed sociological perspective to bear on speed: it examines how speed and acceleration have become emblematic of our times, and explores the political implications of this. Among the major questions addressed are: when did acceleration become the key measure of progress? Is acceleration occurring across all sectors of society and all aspects of life, or are some groups able to mobilize speed as a

---

[1] Or indeed posit a new epoch, the "acceleration society," see Rosa 2013.

resource while others are marginalized and excluded? Does the growing centrality of technological mediations (of both information and communication) produce slower as well as faster times, waiting as well as "busyness," stasis as well as mobility? To make sense of everyday life in the twenty-first century, we must begin by interrogating the social dynamics of speed.

This book, therefore, aims to develop new sociological perspectives on digital, organizational, and social temporalities. While speed studies have proliferated, in our view little progress has been made in terms of theory because of a lack of attention to the *materiality* of time. Most major contributions in recent years have tended to consist of either macro cultural narratives or narrow empirical studies: significant new theoretical perspectives are comparatively rare. For this reason, the field is still somewhat preoccupied with extant debates such as the impact of technology on society, the "time pressure paradox," different versions of fast capitalism, and the relationship between sociology and new media studies.[2] While the contributors to this volume are well aware of these debates, and indeed are leading figures in these fields, their brief was to focus on future developments rather than to overview ideas that have begun to outlive their usefulness and relevance.

One of the intellectual currents informing a more nuanced conversation about the interrelationship between technology and temporality has been going on under the rubric of science and technology studies (STS). While sociologists have always emphasized that time is a social entity, formed through collective rhythms of human engagement with the world, technology is rarely accorded the same treatment. Technology is too often seen as outside of, and apart from, social relations. Yet, modern patterns of time can scarcely be conceived of without the use of technology. From simple tools to large technological systems, our lives are intertwined with technology. Our actions and society itself are built on and with technical artifacts.

Although technological change, especially digitalization, is at the explanatory core of the analyses of acceleration noted above, there is a common tendency toward technological determinism. The shared idea is that speed is driven by digital technologies, resulting in a one-dimensional view of time, as if everything is speeding up. In other words, the cultural condition of digital capitalism is simply one of acceleration. By contrast, STS scholars understand time not only as fundamentally social, but also as fundamentally sociotechnical or sociomaterial. Focusing on materiality, including investigating the technical and institutional infrastructure that underpins speed, is key given the extent to which temporality today is experienced via multiple media modalities. This interest is partly driven by a concern with the politics

---

[2] For a critical discussion of this literature, see Wajcman 2015.

of technology itself, its mode of development—in other words, the power dynamics of both the trajectory of innovation and its affordances for use.

As a result, some of the most lively and productive dialogues about digital temporalities are taking place at the intersections of social and cultural theory, science and technology studies, information systems, software studies, organization studies, and media studies. While there are a growing number of substantial empirical studies on the impact of network speed or latency—covering human–computer interaction, financial markets, managerial uses of information technology, and social media consumption—there has been less work on consolidating the area in theoretical terms. Too rarely is there an opportunity for scholars from these different domains to come together, and this volume showcases just how fruitful such exchanges can be.

Two brief illustrative examples. Imagined near and distant futures have long been deemed as worthy of sociological study as aspects of the present that are consequential for future making. Yet, as writing on the sociology of expectations indicates (see Chapter 3), our very ideas of the future are now wholly infused with scientific and technological imaginaries. Perhaps this is why the gap between "singularity" and what robots can actually do does nothing to break the hold of these narratives. Or perhaps, as the science fiction writer William Gibson is quoted as saying, it's because "the future is already here—it's just not evenly distributed."

This theme—that the control of time is thoroughly enmeshed with the dynamics of power—flows through every chapter in this book and gives the introduction its title: the powerful are fast, the powerless are slow. Too often abstract discussions of acceleration neglect the extent to which speed is one of the essential properties of the powerful. Explicating differential resources and experiences of time is key to this volume. For example, the temporal story about technology is typically about new inventions, and not about the labor that maintains and repairs the system (see Chapter 11). The slow digital labor, both paid and unpaid, that maintains Internet speed and keeps Facebook "clean" in order to save us time, is hidden from view. In other words, a sociomaterial perspective points to many under-researched topics such as how is speed produced, who owns speed, and how is it paid for.

## Outline of the Book

This book began with a workshop held at the London School of Economics (LSE). Our aim was to interrogate thoroughly the social dynamics of speed by focusing on theories of acceleration, the materiality of speed, and how digitalization actually results in multiple temporalities; different rhythms and paces of everyday life. To this end, we identified a range of leading scholars who have made significant interventions in the stream of critical inquiry about how technologies designed for acceleration are reconfiguring our consciousness of time. We explicitly wanted to bring together chapters that are somewhat more theoretical and those that present rich empirical data in order to highlight the links and synergies between them. In the chapters that follow, some authors examine more organizational and institutional processes, some pieces are more historical, and some present qualitative case studies—all pertinent to this question of the imperative of speed.

We have sought to craft a collection which, when read together, offers provocative and agenda-setting insights that may inspire others to break new conceptual ground in the sociology of speed. Our colloquy over two days in London felt like a coherent conversation for a number of reasons. The sociologists among us have long been familiar with each other's work and some are closely tied through various connections to the LSE. Two of the authors met at a workshop on the subject of "busyness" many moons ago in Seattle, others met in Georgia at a workshop sponsored by Intel's Science and Technology Center for Social Computing, one subset of the contributors regularly meet at the Society for the Social Studies of Science conferences, while a number attend the Computer–Human Interaction meetings. In an increasing number of academic and cultural venues, the impact of the digital universe on human time perception, concepts, and practices is a hot topic.

Following this introduction to the volume, the book is divided into three parts, each of which reflects what we consider to be major areas of scholarship on the theme. Part I deals with how accelerated temporalities feature in social *theories* of modernity, from classical thought to contemporary analyses of late capitalism, and even into visions of future societies. Part II presents different ways of thinking about speed that emphasize its *materialities* through discussions of the technical and institutional infrastructure that underpins speed. Part III explores distinctive and multiple *temporalities*, and their link with power or lack thereof. What emerges clearly is that studies of how technological speed translates into new social realities must be situated historically and in specific political and economic contexts.

There are some fascinating interconnections between the chapters of this book. For example, there are important linkages between the work of Du Gay on power and hierarchy in organizations, Gregg on time management techniques, and Erikson and Mazmanian on temporal entrepreneurship in professional contexts. All three chapters focus our attention on the impact of technology on the administering of time in the context of employment. Similarly, there are intriguing resonances between MacKenzie and Sassen on the infrastructure of the city. Their chapters bring into focus how the temporalities of money and capital are increasingly shaped by software and information technologies.

A theoretical understanding of the social relations of technology plays a critical role throughout the book. While some of the chapters seek to bring new theoretical insights to bear on long-standing areas of social theory (see for example Rosa), others are using theory in order to get to grips with phenomena that are by their nature new and difficult to theorize (see Jackson on digital labor; MacKenzie on high-frequency trading). The notion of distinctive and multiple temporalities is a further important thread that runs through the book, encompassing how speed can be outsourced (Molotch), the collective character of time (Sharma), the temporal strategies of professional employees (Erikson and Mazmanian) and the slow digital labor of maintenance and repair (Jackson). Having drawn attention to these various interconnections, what follows is a more detailed summary of each chapter.

## Part I: Theories

The first part of the volume consists of three chapters. Chapter 1 serves to remind us that the phenomenon of acceleration was a key theme in early modern social and political theory. From Marx on, classical writers record the profound temporal transformations experienced by Western modernity, especially since the Industrial Revolution. We have chosen to foreground Simmel and Benjamin here because their reflections on the temporal dynamics of modernity speak most directly to our own sense of living at a rapid pace. As such, these writings form a necessary background for this volume. Chapter 2 is by Hartmut Rosa, probably the best-known contemporary social theorist of acceleration. Rather than seeing modernity as a process of rationalization, he argues that it is best understood as driven by processes of social acceleration. The crises of the late-modern age can then be read as structured by the contradictory logics of escalation and de-synchronization. The idea that the future is emerging ever more quickly is now taken for granted in future thinking or "futurology." In Chapter 3, John Urry argues that this genre is increasingly important to organizations and societies, and has a powerful effect on how we think about the present. It thus urgently needs more social scientific critique. His critical contribution to this volume, however, is to situate accelerating energy consumption as the basis of all other accelerations. For him too, acceleration constitutes a break with previous systems, a new geographical epoch known as the Anthropocene.

In Chapter 1, Nigel Dodd and Judy Wajcman bring a much-needed historical perspective to bear on current claims that our period is one of unprecedented acceleration. In fact, speed becomes identified with modernity in classical social theory. As early as 1900, Simmel describes how the acceleration of city life in the modern metropolis gives rise to a new temporality. His analysis of modern time-consciousness as one involving immediacy, simultaneity, and presentism is so prescient that we make the case for Simmel being the first theorist of the acceleration society. The case of Benjamin is more complex, but fascinating for the more nuanced conception of time that runs through his work, as expressed in his treatment of Baudelaire's figure of the *flâneur*, who both manifests and resists the sense of shock generated by the city's compression of time. Thus, Benjamin provides an intriguing counterpoint that both draws on and invites us to question some of the assumptions that underpin the work of Simmel.

In Chapter 2, Hartmut Rosa outlines a comprehensive theoretical framework of acceleration. The chapter begins with a phenomenological account of time pressure and the disappearance of leisure. It then moves on to identify dynamic stabilization as a defining feature of modern societies. This term refers to the fact that such a society requires (material) growth, (technological) augmentation, and high rates of (cultural) innovation in order to reproduce itself and preserve the socioeconomic and political status quo. This feature has two decisive social consequences. First, it leads to progressive logics of escalation in the realms of production, speed, and social change—that is, social acceleration. However, as not all spheres of social life are equally "speedable," it also brings the problem of "de-synchronization" to the forefront of contemporary society. Therefore, Rosa argues, the four most pressing crises of the late-modern age—the ecological crisis, the financial crisis, the crisis of democracy, and the psycho-crisis—are effectively crises of de- synchronization. Attempts to speed up life can then be read as attempts of re-synchronization. The contradictory dynamics of speed are thus central to understanding the nature of social change in our society.

John Urry's contribution, in Chapter 3, takes up the subject of the ecological crisis by first exploring some links between time regimes and multiple futures. Future orientations are everywhere and are largely presented as inevitable extrapolations of the present. By contrast, the chapter argues that the analysis of social institutions and practices is crucial, as such futures serve a rhetorical function for the powerful groups who produce them. Urry then turns directly to the Great Acceleration: the exponential increase in the burning of coal, oil, and gas since the mid-twentieth century. It is burning fossil fuels that literally enable the world to go round faster and faster, and he cautions that the energy required for this speeded up of mobile civilization may well be running out.

## Part II: Materialities

The second part of the book begins with two chapters that exemplify the strengths of a sociomaterial approach to the question of acceleration. As we noted earlier, much of the discussion about the high-speed society tends toward determinism, depicting digitalization as the driver of acceleration. Yet, ironically, it is a form of technological determinism that suffers from a lack of interest in technology, what it is really made up of, what it consists of, and so on. The Internet is often treated as a virtual cyberspace, as if it is literally "in the cloud." Yet, as Chapters 4 and 5 show, financial trading and the city itself are underpinned by materiality: physical, technological, and corporeal in nature.

Speed is thus always reliant on its technical infrastructure, as are the practices that make up organizations. Chapters 6 and 7 then focus directly on the temporality of organizations, and do so by employing an historical perspective. By recalling how the concept of speed has been interpreted within traditional organizational sociology and the history of scientific management, these chapters highlight the extent to which discourses of speed remain central to modern managerial minds.

Chapter 4, by Donald MacKenzie, describes the phenomenon of high-frequency trading: the automated, ultra-fast trading of large quantities of shares or other financial instruments. This activity has come to symbolize the ultimate speed of financial capitalism. The chapter draws on extensive and fascinating interviews with high-frequency traders in order to emphasize two issues. First, he demonstrates the importance of the material means by which speed is achieved, such that even a signal travelling through a fiber-optic cable at two-thirds of the speed of light in a vacuum can be judged "too slow." Second, he focuses on the interrelationship between the materiality of speed and the social arrangements that permit and facilitate high frequency trading. "Material sociology" is Mackenzie's way of saying that even accelerated financial trading needs to be understood as a sociomaterial rather than a directly technical process.

In Chapter 5, Saskia Sassen focuses on how the city's technical infrastructure can offer resources for neighborhood activists. However, while digital technologies potentially enable a city's people to become actors rather than merely clients, variations in the quality of access and modes of use have been insufficiently examined. This involves researching the ways in which the technical properties of these electronic interactive domains deliver their utility to users through complex ecologies. Like MacKenzie, she argues that these domains are part of larger social, political, and cultural ecologies, rather than as a purely technical condition. Her key example is the way that connectivity is taken as sufficient in itself, while the needs of low-wage workers and low-income neighborhoods are ignored. There may be an enormous range of digital apps in the city, but none of them are designed for these specific groups in their local context. Several efforts are now beginning to address this problem and the chapter goes on to describe some of these initiatives. In sum,

Sassen argues that such apps can play a crucial role in strengthening neighborhood communities and increase the sense of belonging to a collective public space.

In Chapter 6, Paul du Gay argues that "speed," or lack thereof, lies at the heart of much that has been written about bureaucracy generally, and about Max Weber's theory of bureaucracy in particular. On the one hand, within sociology and social theory, Weber is regarded as one of the chief critics of bureaucracy's inherent "dark side." In this reading, formality, precision, efficiency, and speed, taken together, allow bureaucracy to subordinate everyday life to the diktats of instrumental rationalization. On the other hand, certain sections of management and organization studies view Weber as a misguided celebrant of bureaucracy because he pays too much attention to formal rationality and not enough to its inherent dysfunctions. Instead, this literature advocates a "more human" approach, in which people can give full vent to their emotions, intuition, and creativity. Here, innovation, flexibility, and speed are on the side of the post-bureaucratic organization. This chapter interrogates these contrasting stories about bureaucracy and suggests a more complex account of the relationship between the ethos of bureaucratic office and "speed."

In Chapter 7, Melissa Gregg complements du Gay's argument by showing that time management techniques have been a key feature in the engineering of professional subjectivity over the past century. The chapter draws connections between contemporary productivity tools in the software market and traditions of self-help that developed alongside modern business culture over several generations. The central theme of the chapter is that time management instruction continues in a very similar form today when compared with its earliest formations, which date back to the home economics movement and Taylorist scientific management. Bringing this story up to the present day, Gregg describes how productivity itself has become a lifestyle, a secular athleticism. This aspirational activity produces an aesthetics of accomplishment that helps withstand and legitimate the experience of information jobs that contain few stable goals, rewards, or ends.

## Part III: Temporalities

The final part of the book draws on detailed empirical evidence in order to explore our everyday experience of temporality. While Parts I and II focus on the theoretical and infrastructural underpinnings of acceleration, what is still missing is the temporal—not in the sense of grand historical trends, but in the sense of lived time—structured in particular social, economic, and political contexts. An important common starting point for Chapters 8 to 11, then, is that there is no single story about what is happening to the pace of people's lives. In reality, our lives are characterized by a multiplicity of temporal textures and rhythms, which vary in intensity, depending on what, where, and with whom we are doing things. There are both different senses of feeling pressed for time and a range of mechanisms that trigger these feelings.

In Chapter 8, Harvey Molotch opens Part III by stressing that all time is relative. Not only do people become accustomed to one pace or another, they come to demand the one that is appropriate. In other words, time becomes a moral matter as well as an issue of efficiency. The chapter illustrates this through various intriguing examples. For instance, what we consider to be speedy service varies from one place to another. That which is expected at MacDonald's is not the same as in a doctor's waiting room. Moreover, queues are stratified so that the powerful get priority and can even delegate waiting so that their precious time is not wasted. And yet, for most of us, our temporal encounters with organizations are increasingly mediated by machines, and we constantly strategize about how to use digital gadgets to enhance our efficiency. While such automated outsourcing of tasks results in productivity gains for organizations, in the end this self-service logic involves more hidden labor time on the client's part. Like all the chapters in the section, Molotch sees the control of time as an essential property of power.

In Chapter 9, Sarah Sharma argues that much of the literature on speed culture remains trapped by a universalizing and individualizing treatment of the relationship between time and technology. Her central message is that this focus on acceleration and on the individual obscures the multiple and differential relationships to time that infuse the social fabric. By focusing on speedup, she argues, we miss the opportunity to engage more fully with the lived politics of time. Indeed, this very discourse serves to perpetuate structural inequalities at the level of time. As various institutions increasingly control our time, we are simultaneously asked to become entrepreneurs of time-control, endlessly recalibrating in order to meet the demands of complex social relationships and labor arrangements. Drawing on a range of rich examples, including privileged business travellers, taxi cabs, truck drivers, and the growing precariat in the sharing economy, Sharma powerfully demonstrates that a politics of time must begin with the recognition that time is a collective entanglement.

In Chapter 10, Ingrid Erickson and Melissa Mazmanian present a detailed account of how professional workers are responding to and artfully bending time in the context of heightened sociotechnical expectations. While the speed vortex affects everyone, these workers are intensely oriented to the dominant temporal logic in which time is regarded as chunkable, single-purpose, linear, and ownable. This logic is also embedded in the digital devices and applications they use in attempting to control time and harness their productivity. However, while some individuals respond to the constant stress by opting out and rejecting their devices, others react differently, engaging in forms of temporal entrepreneurship. Drawing on rich empirical data, the authors showcase alternative experiences of time as people push back against established temporal norms by articulating innovative and risky new ideas of time in their daily lives. These entrepreneurial practices, such as when people successfully cohabit multiple times with others at the same time, may well point the way to legitimating and institutionalizing new social norms and a more holistic version of time.

In Chapter 11, Steven J. Jackson ends the volume by exploring how maintenance and repair are the slow underbelly of modernity's stories of rupture and acceleration. Drawing on empirical sites and examples from around the world, he considers the social and material work of simply "going on" through which continuities are built and established, change is produced, and forms of value—in practices, systems, and infrastructures, but also human lives—are established and preserved. This work in turn produces distinct forms and experiences of time. Jackson's original stress on the necessity of maintenance and repair thus provides us with a very different frame through which to think about the acceleration stories that have shaped understandings of technology and social order for the past 200 years.

*　*　*

There is no way of comprehensively or exhaustively mapping all the interesting work by social scientists on the sociology of speed, and we have not sought to do this here. But, in bringing together the most astute commentators from a variety of disciplines, we hope that this collection provides a fresh starting point for analyzing and furthering our understanding of pressing questions about the nature of our contemporary times. Every one of the chapters in this volume provides a critical analysis of acceleration that goes beyond the abstract theoretical debates that have characterized the conversation to date. The nexus between digitalization and organizational and social temporalities, in particular, has been marked by too easy generalization. By contrast, each of the authors represented here offers readers a careful consideration of a substantive subject in the field, and a provocative insight to chase. In conclusion, we hope that this volume affords sociologists of speed the impetus to move their own inquiries beyond critiquing the notion that digital technology determines a fast-paced life to a more nuanced politics of temporality that can encompass the dynamics of both "speed up" and "slow down."

# Part I
## Theories

# 1

# Simmel and Benjamin

## Early Theorists of the Acceleration Society

*Nigel Dodd and Judy Wajcman*

## Introduction

Current claims that our period is one of unprecedented acceleration need to be placed in proper historical perspective. The argument that time now moves faster than ever before is, in fact, rather old. Speed first became identified with modernity in classical social theory. As early as 1900, Simmel argued that the speed of the modern metropolis, alongside the acceleration of exchange relationships made possible by the circulation of money, were giving rise to a new temporality. Simmel's analysis of modern time-consciousness as one involving immediacy, simultaneity, and presentism is prescient. It is thus quite plausible to make the case that Simmel should be considered the first theorist of the acceleration society. Benjamin, too, was an early theorist of the acceleration society, particularly in his arguments about the impact of technology on aesthetics and cultural reproduction, as well as in his work on urban forms. When compared to Simmel, however, Benjamin's treatment of time, speed, and acceleration is considerably more complex. His work is especially fascinating for the more nuanced conception of time that runs through it, as expressed for example in his extensive treatment of Baudelaire's figure of the *flâneur*, whose movements in the city both manifest and resist the sense of shock generated by its compression of time. As we argue in the chapter's third section, "Benjamin: Modernity and the Dialectics of Time," Benjamin therefore provides an intriguing counterpoint that both draws on and invites us to question some of the assumptions that underpin the work of Simmel. Taken together, these thinkers therefore have much to say in the context of contemporary debates about the "speed-up society."

## Simmel: Money, the City, and the Acceleration of Time

Money and the city are Simmel's key sites of modernity, and the focus of his thesis about acceleration. He sees money as a "dynamic mediator" that accounts for "the unrest, the feverishness, the unceasing nature of modern life, whose unstoppable wheel is provided by money and which makes the machine of life into *a perpetuum mobile*" (1991: 27). The spread of monetary transactions brings about a transition "from stability to lability." Money does not represent commodities *in stasis*, but rather the ever-changing relations between them. According to Simmel, money contributes to increasing the circulation of people and things. For example, it loosens are attachment to things by making it easier to exchange them. As the "pure form of exchange-ability," money exists in a realm of ceaseless motion, drawing an increasing range of people and objects into its seemingly unstoppable motion.

Much of what Simmel has to say about the relationship between money and speed comes in the final chapter of *The Philosophy of Money*, where he explores the impact of money on intellectual life and culture. On the one hand, Simmel suggests that money almost transcends time, because it enables us to overcome temporal constraints that would normally be imposed on us by, for example, the rhythms of nature or even the business cycle. Note that this is not a feature of money per se, however, but rather of a particular stage of development of the money economy toward maturity, because it is the con-centration of money, e.g. in banks, that enables us to gain access to it during periods of "natural" or "normal" scarcity (see Simmel 2004: 492). Simmel draws particular attention to the *liquid* qualities of money in this regard: lacking its own internal limits, money adapts itself to whatever temporal rhythms we require. It is money's insubstantial nature, its apparent *indifference to time*, that enables it to do this: "money itself is completely formless," Simmel writes, "it does not contain within itself the slightest suggestion of a regular rising and falling of the contents of life" (2004: 495).

Yet at the same time, it is this very indifference of money to time that, according Simmel, accounts for its profound impact on our actual experience of time. For example, an increase in money's supply (whether through infla-tion of the balance of trade) will directly bring about a change in the pace of life, first, by disturbing our perception of economic stability and producing a "constant state of disorder and psychic shocks" (2004: 499), and second, by increasing the tempo of economic life itself. This second phenomenon is most keenly felt where there is high inflation, wherein it is in everybody's interests "to transact his economic operations as quickly as possible" (2004: 500).

Simmel's characterization of the impact of acceleration on social life—just like his portrayal of the growth of the money economy in general—is ambiva-lent. On the one side, he gives an account of cultural alienation that bears comparison with the young Marx, suggesting that money appears to exist as autonomous exchange value, and its circulation appears guided by its own laws (Frisby 2002: xxxii). Everything substantial and stable in modern culture is being rendered more fluid and unstable through money, rendering modern life "feverish" (Simmel 1991: 27). But more importantly from the perspective of this book, Simmel doubts the analytical value of focusing on speed and acceleration per se. Nowhere is this clearer than in the following passage, where he warns against prioritizing form over substance in our appreciation of speed—a position he likens to technological determinism:

> It is true that we now have acetylene and electrical light instead of oil lamps; but the enthusiasm for the progress achieved in lighting makes us sometimes forget that the essential thing is not the lighting itself but what becomes fully visible. People's ecstasy concerning the triumphs of the telegraph and telephone often makes them overlook the fact that what really matters is the value of what one has to say. (2004: 482)

This point is echoed throughout Simmel's writings on money, where the deeper problem he deals with is not just the circulation and acceleration in economic life as caused by the development of the money economy, but rather the relationship between objective and subjective culture that money helps to transform—for better *and* for worse. According to Simmel, while a "fundamental re-orientation of culture towards intellectuality . . . goes hand in hand with the growth of a money economy" (2004: 152), this is by no means necessarily a bleak and unidirectional process of change. Money may enable a cleaner separation between the individual personality and his or her economic activity (1991: 21), but at the same time, its increasing (and increasingly rapid) circulation enables a widening of the social circles we feel part of, and creates a strong social bond between members of these circles in its own right. Money establishes "incomparably more connections among people than ever existed in the days of feudal associations," he concludes (1991: 20).

Simmel associates acceleration not only with money but the metropolis, too. Cities are "the seat of the most advanced economic division of labour," where what, hitherto, was a "struggle with nature for the means of life is transformed into a conflict with human beings" (2002: 17). This gives rise to a narrow specialism, as well as an atmosphere of individuation and eccentricity as people strive to make themselves noticeable. More crucially it gives rise to a social scene that is characterized by ever briefer, rarer, and "to the point" interactions, as opposed to longer associations. What emerges from this, inevitably according to Simmel, is a certain kind of restlessness within the individual, whose mental energy is increasingly consumed by their exposure to a rapid telescoping of changing images, pronounced differences within what is grasped at a single glance, and the unexpectedness of violent stimuli. Simmel sees here "a deep contrast with the slower, more habitual, more smoothly flowing rhythm of the sensory-mental phase of small town and rural existence," which rests on feelings and emotional relationships and the "steady equilibrium of unbroken customs." With its incessant fluctuations and discontinuities, the metropolis requires us to develop an intellectualism that protects us: our reactions to the fast-moving urban environment are thereby "moved to a sphere of mental activity which is least sensitive and which is furthest removed from the depths of the personality" (Simmel, 2002: 12). The city dweller is a "new human type," which in Simmel's hands is emblematic of the developmental discrepancy that arises between subjective and objective culture in modern life more generally. According to Simmel, objective culture—i.e. language, the law, and techniques of production in art and science—has grown at a far faster rate in the modern era when compared to subjective culture, i.e. the spiritual and ideal life of the individual. The increasing lag between these forms of culture—rapid development on one side, regression on the other—is, for Simmel, the most worrisome aspect of the acceleration society (2002: 18–19).

Time matters in this environment more than ever before, and in very specific ways. The complexity of urban life is such, for example, that punctuality becomes crucial to social—and economic—order: "If all the watches in Berlin suddenly went wrong in different ways even only as much as an hour, its entire economic and commercial life would be derailed for some time" (2002: 13). On the other hand, nothing typifies the mental life of the city dweller more than the blasé outlook. Simmel characterizes this as indifference toward the distinctions between things: these are distinctions that are certainly perceived, but due to the sensory overload the city exposes us to, experienced as meaningless. Everything floats "with the same specific gravity in the constantly moving stream of money" (2002: 14). Simmel argues that by focusing our attention on the transient, and the transient alone, both money and the city transform our experience of time itself. Once everything that was stable turns into dynamism and flux, time's flow no longer occurs against a stable background. This is a time that merely "flows away": it is devoid of memory. Indeed, for Simmel this is essentially "no time at all, but rather an undimensional now" ("Philosophie der Kunst," cited in Frisby, "Preface to the Third Edition," in Simmel 2004: xxv). We therefore inhabit a permanent "now time." Note, here, the parallels and contrasts with Benjamin's conception of time as "dialectics at a standstill," which we explore later in the chapter.

The money economy is endlessly dynamic, destroying all fixed values other than itself—not so much by eroding or undermining them, but by rendering them fluid and dynamic. This is how Simmel tries to capture the relationship between money and acceleration. Through money, motion becomes absolute, which Simmel associates with objective culture. In the Rodin essay (1923), he argues that this phenomenon of acceleration and increased mobility finds its expression in art, as "rigid and stable" phenomena are "destroyed in oscillations" ("Rodin," cited in Frisby, "Preface to the Third Edition," in Simmel 2004: xxiii). Crucially, art does not merely represent mobility, but becomes more mobile in its style, as movement triumphs over matter:

> All that is substantial and secure in the empirical viewpoint is transformed into movement. Furthermore, no form is endowed in the slightest measure with stability and durability and all apparent solidity of contour is nothing but the vibration and oscillating play of the exchange of forces. ("Philosophie der Kunst," cited in Frisby, "Preface to the Third Edition," in Simmel 2004: xxiv)

For Simmel, money expresses this sense of "eternal presentness" because it captures only the image of commodities in exchange, and nothing more lasting or substantial. For this reason, modernity is nothing more than a sequence of present moments, or snapshots of "now time." This, in turn, yields a very different sense of eternity, defined by the timelessness of pure motion. This is what we experience in the city, and through our immersion in the money economy. Analytically, Simmel posits a close relationship between time and individuality, because the more we are sucked into the ceaseless flux of commodity exchange, and thus the more we experience time as always flowing away from us, the less we experiences ourselves as discrete individuals: "The more strongly individuality is emphasized so all the more powerfully is time emphasized," he writes ("Philosophie der Kunst," cited in Frisby, "Preface to the Third Edition," in Simmel 2004: xxv).

## Benjamin: Modernity and the Dialectics of Time

Having sketched out Simmel's characterization of modernity as a society of acceleration, we turn to Walter Benjamin. Benjamin was influenced by Simmel in a number of ways. For example, he suggests that the notion of "origin" that underwrites his notion of Messianic time was derived from Simmel's study of Goethe (see Benjamin 1999b: N2a, 4). There are also strong conceptual affinities between Benjamin's work and that of Simmel, such as their use of the notion of "now time." However, we want to argue here that Benjamin's is the more nuanced and multifaceted approach, which we admire not least for his thoughtful treatment of technology and its impact on capitalism, the city, politics, and everyday life experience.

Almost from the outset of his writing, Benjamin wrestles with the notion of time. Ultimately, his conception of time will be dominated by the distinction that runs through *The Arcades Project*, and which is contained in the following sentence from "On the Concept of History" (1940): "History is the subject of a construction whose site is not homogeneous, empty time, but filled full by now-time [*Jetztzeit*]" (Benjamin 2003c: 395). Each of these terms—*empty, homogeneous time* on the one hand, and *now-time* on the other—appears in Benjamin's writing under various guises. In addition, he uses a number of other constructions for describing time that are relevant to this distinction but cannot be mapped directly on to it.

Benjamin writes about speed and acceleration—and about time more generally—in several different ways: first, in relation to technological change and the idea of capitalist or industrial civilization as a runaway society heading toward an abyss; second, in relation to our experience of the city, which he partly explores through Baudelaire's figure of the *flâneur* who removes himself from the fast-moving world while simultaneously immersing himself within it; third, in relation to his distinction between historical and Messianic time, which informs his understanding of revolution; and fourth, in relation to his rationale in constructing the "image-citations" of *The Arcades Project*, which "arrest" the flow of historical time through "dialectics at a standstill." While all four themes are relevant to the discussions in this book, the first two resonate most strongly with the chapters that comprise it.

Benjamin's reflections on the temporal order of modern capitalism recur throughout his work. They are usually represented by two interrelated ideas: first, the notion of time as "empty" and "homogeneous." This suggests a chronological ordering in which events take place in sequence along a single continuum with no differentiation between them. Second, the idea of time as an additive sequence, a process of building toward something—even though the exact identity of the goal may not be clear. This form of time is *empty* because it consists merely of quantitative transitions, i.e. additions of facts laid out on an infinite temporal continuum. It is *homogeneous* because it is used—by those Benjamin refers to as history's so-called "victors"—to homogenize the subjects of history by passing off the cumulative events of history as the history of humanity as a whole. This is the broader, conceptual framework in which Benjamin's remarks about speed and acceleration need to be understood.

This idea of empty, homogenous time is one that Benjamin obviously found wanting, as most clearly set out in his "On the Concept of History" (1940, see Benjamin 2003c). Here, he uses Klee's picture, *Angelus Novus*—which Benjamin himself owned—to portray history and time in a highly distinctive way. In form (aphorism) and tone, the theses reflect the sense of urgency, anger, and despair that Benjamin clearly felt following the signing of the Molotov–Ribbentrop Pact (between Hitler and Stalin) in August 1939 (Löwy 2006: 18). The Angel forms the pivotal image of the piece, in Thesis IX. In Benjamin's eyes, the angel is positioned with its back toward the future: it is gazing into the past, toward something Benjamin describes as both an origin and a goal. And yet the angel is being propelled in the opposite direction (the direction he does not want to travel) by a storm driving him—and, by extension, us—"irresistibly into the future" (Thesis IX). The message behind the image is clear enough. For Benjamin, what we have come to think of as "progress" is anything but: if we are moving toward anything, it is catastrophe, as represented by "wreckage upon wreckage" being hurled at the angel's feet.

The deeper, philosophical argument that Benjamin is having here, however, is not simply against modern notions of progress, but *any* linear—chronological—concept of time. He rejects classical (that is, chronological or narrative) historiography for two key reasons. First, he resists its underlying notions of progress and decline (1999b: N2, 5); and second, he disagrees with its emphasis on the continuity of time. Regarding the latter, he suggests that the very notion of historical or chronological time acts like a narcotic in relation to our consciousness of history, and thereby to our sense of the present:

> since the different epochs of the past are not all touched in the same degree by the present day of the historian (and often the recent past is not touched at all; the present fails to "do it justice"), continuity in the presentation of history is unattainable. (1999b: N7a, 2)

Against conventional ideas of history as progress, Benjamin argues that the temporal order of capitalism is characterized not by acceleration, by rather by endless repetition. It is, he suggests, a disaster on repeat: just consider that image of the wreckage being hurled at the Angel's feet, always on the same spot. Benjamin portrays this idea in a somewhat unconventional but rather brilliant way in an early fragment, "Capitalism as Religion" (1996). Here, Benjamin portrays capitalism as an economic system that is fuelled not simply by the production of goods but by an ever-expanding burden of debt. Repetition is key to this analysis: in the era of compound interest, debt grows automatically—every month—purely as a function of the passing of time.

Benjamin's conception of historical time—and its corollary, universal history—is closely linked to his understanding of myth. The connection between myth and time is encapsulated by the motif of *eternal repetition*—also referred to as "eternal recurrence" or the "eternal return"—which recurs throughout his writings. Eternal repetition essentially refers to an image of history in which everything remains the same: as a permanent catastrophe, by Benjamin's reckoning, as we saw just now. Benjamin's treatment of the idea of eternal recurrence draws not only on Nietzsche but also the work of the French political activist Louis-Auguste Blanqui—whose *L'Eternité par les Astres* (1872) "proclaims the idea of the eternal return ten years before Nietzsche's *Zarathustra*, with hardly less pathos and with truly hallucinatory power," Benjamin writes (2003f: 93)—and Charles Baudelaire. Time is represented by these thinkers as the "ever same," in a condition whereby history is being constantly replayed within its own confined space: "the same drama, the same setting, on the same narrow stage," he writes in *The Arcades Project* (see Benjamin 1999b: D6a, 1, D7, D7a).

Of particular interest here is Benjamin's use of Baudelaire, for whom the commodity was the allegorical expression of the ever-sameness of capitalism: the commodity represents both the devaluation of things as they are all measured by exchange value, and (echoing Simmel) the sheer relentlessness of production and exchange in the modern money economy: "This devaluation of the human environment penetrates deeply into the poet's historical experience. What results is the 'ever-selfsame'" (2003g: 96). In Blanqui, the idea of eternal recurrence takes the form of an obsessional idea that Benjamin likens in "Central Park" to the mass-produced article, which "appears in the household of the neurotic mind as the eversame" (2003a: 9, 166). The idea of eternal return "transforms the historical event into a mass-produced article" (2003a: 9, 166).

At the heart of Benjamin's discussion of Baudelaire lies the figure of the *flâneur*, and here we find some intriguing differences in the arguments of the two thinkers we are discussing in this chapter. Whereas Simmel writes about a modern city dweller who is characterized by restlessness and distraction, Benjamin presents us with a contrast between, on the one hand, the thoroughly modern character who is hurried and routinized, and on the other, the casual, aimless *flâneur* who has a very different relationship to time and acceleration. While the former lives according to the rigors of modern clock time, the latter appears to transcend time—to live in a condition of timelessness or indifference to time.

Crucially for Benjamin, it is the *flâneur* who has a privileged perspective, and is able to see textures and details in the cityscape that the modern type is too harried to notice. Benjamin sees here, moreover, a heightened experience of modern life that can have radical potential, insofar as the *flâneur* is able to break down or see through the surface of the rationalized, commodified experience of bourgeois life. Benjamin contrasts the *flâneur*'s lassitude with Taylorism, or so-called scientific management, with its slogan, "Down with dawdling!": "A pedestrian knew how to display his nonchalance provocatively," he writes, adding:

> Around 1840 it was briefly fashionable to take turtles for a walk in the arcades. The flâneurs liked to have the turtles set the pace for them. If they had had their way, progress would have been obliged to accommodate itself to this pace. (2003e: 31)

*Flâneurie* was seen by Benjamin as a protest against the acceleration society, especially the speeding-up of the production. Loitering, he suggested, was "a demonstration against the division of labour" (1999b, M5, 8). Benjamin's sympathies here are clear, as they are when he cites Goethe's 1825 letter to Zelter in which he writes: "Wealth and speed are what the world admires and strives for... in order to over-cultivate itself and thereby to stick fast in mediocrity" (1999c: 186). In "Central Park" (1939), Benjamin states that the tempo of the *flâneur* is "a protest against the tempo of the crowd" (2003a: 31, 181). He immediately draws an analogy with production: "Boredom in the production process arises as the process accelerates (through machinery). The flâneur protests against the production process with his ostentatious nonchalance" (2003a: 31, 81). Later, Benjamin compares the *flâneur* to "the sort of idler that Socrates picked out from an Athenian marketplace to be his interlocutor. Only, there is no longer a Socrates, so there is no one to address the idler. And the slave labour that guaranteed him his leisure has likewise ceased to exist" (2003a: 37, 186).

Benjamin contrasts the relationship of the *flâneur* to the crowd with a description by Engels of the crowd—who was clearly dismayed by it—as "repulsive" (2003b: 322). The *flâneur* has "skill and nonchalance" has he moves through the crowd. For the Parisian it was "natural" to move in a mass of people. Even if wants to keep a distance from the crowd, he is evidently "coloured" by it. For Baudelaire, "the masses were anything but external to him; indeed, it was easy to trace in his works his defensive reaction to their attraction and allure" (2003b: 322). Indeed, the crowd is so much a part of Baudelaire's work, so integral to it, that he rarely describes it explicitly.

There are some important connections between Benjamin's concrete writings about city experience, and his more abstract and politically engaged reflections on history, time, and revolutionary consciousness. He sometimes uses the metaphor of dreaming and awakening to capture this: not in the obvious sense of being woken up from a dream, but through the richer and more complex idea that to awaken from a dream is to be able to reappropriate it, to reach into it or pass through it in order to make contact with a distant past that has been obscured for us by the constant shocks and distractions of modern existence. This sense of awakening *through* rather than *from* a dream is a similar idea to the "alternative temporality" that informs Benjamin's construction of dialectical images in *Passagen-Werk (The Arcades Project)*.

Benjamin began work on *The Arcades Project* in 1927. It was originally planned as a fifty-page text, which he worked on intermittently until his death in 1940, principally during 1934–40, and which, when edited text, was first published in German in 1982, amounting to 1,000 pages. The various sections of the text consist of citations, i.e. extracts from a variety of sources (books, newspapers, manuscripts, etc.), and short pieces (remarks, observations, etc.) written by Benjamin himself. His aim was to have the historical meaning of his material emerge through its montage-like arrangement: "This work has to develop to the highest degree the art of citing without quotation marks. Its theory is intimately related to that of montage" (1999b: N1, 10). By definition, grasping this meaning would entail something akin to an awakening, or a heightened state of historical consciousness. These groups of citations operate as images; Benjamin calls them "dialectical" images because they convey historical tensions (and even contradictions) within their very arrangement. To borrow Wittgenstein's language, they "show" history rather than "tell" it: "I needn't *say* anything. Merely show ... the rags, the refuse—these I will not inventory but allow, in the only way possible, to come into their own: by making use of them," he remarks (1999b: N1a, 8). This notion of historical fragments being allowed to "come into their own" suggests that history cannot be explained, theorized, or narrated. Underlying this point is a crucial argument that Benjamin makes about the nature of historical time itself.

Technology plays an important role in Benjamin's understanding of time, but raises somewhat different issues than most of the chapters in this book. Technology mattered to Benjamin because it changed the way in which the world could be represented *in* time. Photography, for example, intrigued him because it seemed capable of capturing involuntary memories and unconscious traces—aspects of history, in other words, that had hitherto not been conscious. These had to be "read," of course, and he likened Baudelaire to the developing agent that is needed to bring photographic negatives to life. Benjamin sought to capture the transient and ephemeral in various ways, for example through gathering throw-away items (old newspapers, ticket stubs, etc.) and rearranging them: this was a means of "showing" rather than "telling" history, he argued. *The Arcades Project* was never finished, of course, but given the philosophy of history and time that lies behind it, one can but wonder what its completion might have amounted to.

Whereas Simmel's analysis of mental life in the metropolis gets to grips with the subjective urban experience as the quintessential expression of modern life, *The Arcades Project* was intended to grasp what Benjamin called the *pre-history* of modernity. Reinforcing his opposition to the emptiness of "historical time," the images deals not with the narrative history of modern society, but rather with its "origin." Essentially, Benjamin wants the nineteenth century to be "legible" to his own time. This is the form of representation he seeks by constructing montage-like arrangements (he sometimes calls them constellations) of citations. As an approach to historiography, this hinges on the contention, *contra* historical materialism, that history has no final goal. This is a form of "dialectics at a standstill." Just as the *Angelus Novus* sees not historical progress but repeated disaster, so Benjamin argues that the historian must try to "freeze" history in order to grasp its meaning. He defines this meaning as an *origin*, but his use of this term is highly idiosyncratic, owing more to Goethe's notion of the *Urphänomen* than to any conventional approach to historiography (see Dodd 2008). Benjamin describes the dialectical image as an *Urphänomen*. His debt to Goethe is made clear in the "First Sketches" for *The Arcades Project*: "Formula: construction out of facts. Construction with the complete elimination of theory. What only Goethe in his morphological writings has attempted" (1999b: O, 73).

Benjamin's use of citations to construct "dialectical images" in *The Arcades Project* can be viewed as a form of de-contextualization wherein context means chronological time. What he seeks to convey in these images is not a sequence of events but an immediate, almost visceral, relationship between events now and in the distant past. Dialectical images are meant to awaken the reader to "a not-yet-conscious knowledge of what has been," which will in turn achieve "the dissolution of "mythology" into the space of history" (1999b: N1, 9). This idea of "awakening" can be enriched with reference both to surrealism, as we have already mentioned, and to Proust. In Proust's *À la recherche du temps perdu*, Benjamin discovers both the capacity of remembrance to unsettle—"The true reader of Proust is constantly jarred by small frights" (1999a: 242)—and to disrupt the continuity of clock time. According to Benjamin, remembrance in Proust's hands does not preserve history, but modifies our relationship with it. Likewise, in *The Arcades Project*, Benjamin seeks to bring about a modification of our relationship with the past in order to bring about a modification of the present. He aims to "expose" the nineteenth century to the light of the of the present day (1999b: N1a, 2). This is what historical materialism aims for too, of course, but according to Benjamin, is prevented from achieving by virtue of its attachment to chronological time.

One might say that the fundamental idea behind Benjamin's project, especially in the *Arcades*, is thus to radicalize historical consciousness—which he calls an awakening—by bringing about a rupture in our *understanding of time itself*. This entails disrupting our experience of discontinuity, challenging our sense not only of acceleration but of *any* forwards momentum. This sets his work apart from Simmel in its radical intent; even though Simmel, too, seeks to grapple with the eternal in the now—or as he puts it in *The Philosophy of Money*, to find "in each of life's details the totality of its meaning" (2004: 55). Tellingly, both Simmel and Benjamin seek to clarify the aims behind their work by positioning themselves in relation to Marx. Simmel claims to "construct a new storey beneath historical materialism" (2004: 56), and one way of reading this is that he was seeking to situate historical forms of money in universal metaphysical forms, that is to say, to view money as "the result of more profound valuations and currents of psychological or even *metaphysical pre-conditions*" (2004: 55, italics added). Benjamin, too, seeks something universal within the historical when tries to define his own approach to "materialist historiography." But in his hands, the outcome such approach is not philosophical and eternal, but political and immediate:

> Materialist historiography . . . is based on a constructive principle. Thinking involves not only the movement of thoughts, but their arrest as well. Where thinking suddenly comes to a stop in a constellation saturated with tensions, it

gives that constellation a shock, by which thinking is crystallized as a monad. The historical materialist approaches a historical subject only where it confronts him as a monad. In this structure he recognizes the sign of a Messianic arrest of happening, or (to put it differently) a revolutionary chance in the fight for the oppressed past. (Benjamin 2003c: 396)

In modern philosophy, the monad is closely associated with Leibniz: it is what he calls an "atom of nature," and contains within itself a reflection of the whole world. In Benjamin's hands, the idea of the monad can be placed alongside his use of the idea of "origin" and *Urphänomen* from Goethe: these are his attempts to capture history in its entirety: he calls it the "telescoping of the past through the present" (1999b: N7a, 3). This is history conceived not as a narrative, but as a momentary and flash of recognition. This is what he means when he says that every second of chronological time is "the narrow gate, through which the Messiah could enter." For Benjamin, chronological time is pregnant with ever-present possibility of its total destruction. By contrast, the totality that Simmel claims to find in money is the object of philosophical, not historical, arguments and investigations.

## Conclusions

In this chapter, we sought to use Simmel to historicize current claims about the acceleration of time, while introducing Benjamin as a counterweight to Simmel in order to suggest that the relationship between modernity, speed, and acceleration in classical social thought is more complex than we might assume. In addition, we hope to point to some contemporary uses of Simmel and Benjamin, as well as examining some ways in which themes we find in their work are reflected—but also, no doubt, extended still further—in the other chapters collected in this volume. What fascinates us about these thinkers is the way that each responds to his own sense of time's acceleration in modern society by attempting, through analysis, to slow it down: either by seeking the eternal within time's unceasing flow as Simmel does, or by attempting a radical disjuncture in the manner of Benjamin.

# 2

# De-Synchronization, Dynamic Stabilization, Dispositional Squeeze

## The Problem of Temporal Mismatch

*Hartmut Rosa*

## Introduction: Speed and the True Nature of Time Pressure

To attribute the chronic shortage of time in contemporary late-modern societies to the availability and speed of technological devices and digital transmission clearly amounts to a brute categorical mistake. For any given task, the introduction of faster technology amounts to the saving and gaining of temporal resources which are then at our free disposal for other activities. Thus, technological speed-up logically results in the reduction of temporal pressure, which is why technological acceleration is attractive for social actors in the first place—unless the background conditions of our lives change, too. Such changes in background conditions, however, can never be attributed to technological developments per se.

   Let us have a closer look at this. What do we mean when we complain about being short on time, suffering from time-pressure, or even time-famine (Robinson and Godbey 1999: 33) and time-squeeze? Obviously, this ubiquitous sense refers to a perceived mismatch between the temporal resources allocated to a given task, or a given number of tasks, and the time needed to do them properly. Thus, we often feel that we should walk or drive a given distance in less time than it would take if we walked or drove "normally," or that we should do the shopping or writing, cooking or caring in less time, i.e. at a faster pace, than we used to take in the past, etc. Hence, this is the nature of time pressure: the time needed to fulfill the tasks listed on our *to do list* properly exceeds the time we actually have at hand, and hence the time we can allocate to the individual entries.

In this sense, time-pressure increases with the mismatch or disproportion between these two temporalities, it decreases with their leveling. By consequence, the introduction of faster technologies is an obvious means for attempts to reduce the gap. If the time actually needed to do the travelling or cooking, for example, decreases, the mismatch between the temporal requirements of our aggregated *to do list* and the time resources at hand gets reduced. If, on the other hand, the perceived time-pressure *increases* with the speed of technology, then the causes must lie elsewhere. Either the multiplication of entries on our *to do list* has reasons that are entirely independent of technological developments—for example, it is caused by economic competition or sociopolitical conditions—or we need to analyze the effects of the new technologies *not on the pace of action* but on *cultural practices which produce those lists*. "It is our own concrete social practices that generate those qualities of technologies we usually consider as intrinsic and permanent," Judy Wajcman (2015: 3) concludes in her penetrating analyses of the *time-pressure paradox*. By consequence, she suggests using a "social shaping approach" (2015: 4) to the study of the temporal effects of technology. I find myself to be in agreement with this perspective so, in this chapter, I want to present, so to speak, my own social shaping approach to the question of how technology contributes to the explosion of our *to do lists* and to the acceleration of the daily pace of life.

Thus, the question I want to start with is this: Why do we never reach the point when the day's work is done? Why is there, for most of us, always more to do than can be done? What is the mechanism that enlarges the gap despite all technological speed-ups?

On a phenomenal level, the problem social actors face in their daily lives is rooted in the fact that the number of *legitimate claims* that can be made on their time-budget seems to rise incessantly. Just to illustrate my point by an arbitrary example, let us take the convenient case of an ordinary university teacher, let us call her Linda—an analogous story, of course, can be told of more or less any other professional, too. Linda's day might start with a teaching class. As soon as it starts, our teacher feels guilty: she should have read today's assignment more closely. She should have paid more attention to the students' papers uploaded on the intranet a few days before, and she should have prepared the lesson more properly. The students *have a right* for the teacher to be prepared. She swears that next week, she will do so. When the class is over, Linda serves on an appointment committee. "Damn," she thinks, "I did not really read through all of the 72 applications carefully." This is inexcusable. The decisions taken here will severely affect the lives of the applicants, and of her university, too. She feels terribly guilty after the committee as she walks over to the department meeting. But things do not get better over there: all the documents about research-plans and teaching-assignments, schedules and programs, plans and decisions to be taken have been sent out a week ago—she did not find the time to make up her mind on any of them. Thus, in fact, she feels she is lacking in professional ethos. When the meeting is over, probably it is way into the afternoon, she sits in her office. *Too bad*—she did not really progress with the manuscript she is supposed to turn in for publication. *Publish or perish*; she will perish if she does not devote more time to her publication-record, and this will be entirely her own fault. An email pops up: deadline for the application for research-money is next week. Her Dean expects her to create some funding. She clearly does not suffice her job. She runs to pick up her kids from school. She is late. She should have cared more about their needs; in fact, she should spend more time with the kids. Not enough time for cooking. Not enough time for her lover. Not enough time for household work. No time to go for a workout. She does not do enough for her health, her doctor tells her. At the end of the day, she is guilty because she is too stressed, not relaxed enough; *she does not get her work–life balance right*. How did she get here? How is the digitalization of life connected to the problem Linda is facing?

## The Disappearance of Leisure

The time squeeze Linda is experiencing obviously is not so much a consequence of her insatiability and greed, but much more a result of the fact that all the claims made on her time-budget appear to be legitimate, well-justified claims. It is neither unfair nor inappropriate that the students require her teacher to be prepared, nor is it unfair or unjust of the applicants to expect that their applications are read carefully, and certainly, the kids, the lover, and the body deserve attention, too. But when we add up the time needed to properly fulfill all the entries on the list, we arrive at an illegitimate, even an impossible, amount of time which probably exceeds the twenty-four hours of the day by far—not even considering the fact that Linda herself has legitimate claims and expectations to do things she *loves to do* without anyone making claims on her time-budget, too. All those claims emanate from particular contexts, and they are legitimate in light of those contexts. As a result, the multiplication of contexts and arenas of our daily lives through the process of progressive functional differentiation is one reason for the aggravating mismatch that results in an habitual or dispositional squeeze. What is the role of technology in this?

Clearly the validity, i.e. the legitimacy and plausibility of claims on our time-budget (made by ourselves as well as by others) depends on availability, responsibility, and opportunity. No one can expect you to answer the phone or your email messages when you are in the middle of nowhere without a mobile connection. Imagine Linda takes a week off and settles in a tiny hut far out in the mountains, perhaps even without electricity. When the sun sets, she experiences something people in almost all cultures all over the world have experienced in the past: the day's work is done. There is nothing that can be expected from her that evening, and she herself does not have any immediate expectations toward the world. This is what the German term *Feierabend* (leisure-time after work) was meant to signal. Leisure in this sense is an inner attitude, a disposition toward the world in which, for the time being, there are no valid claims made on us, and no claims toward the world we have ourselves, that demand for any kind of action. Peasants and farmers used to experience exactly this state of affairs quite regularly after dark, when the cattle (and kids) were taken care of.

The fact is that, in our late-modern Western civilization, this form of leisure has disappeared from our lives altogether. Surely, we sometimes, at the end of a long day, firmly decide that *we have had enough*—no matter who will knock or call, we are not going to accept or do anything. Linda might have felt and decided like this the evening before the day we followed her. But this does not in the least prevent her from feeling all the legitimate claims impinging on her: she knows that there are still messages waiting in the inbox, that the texts and documents for the next day are neatly filed and stored on her computer, that she could and should do some workout or jogging, etc. Thus, *doing nothing*, or deciding not to do anything, is categorically different from leisure in the sense of *Muße* (otium) or *Feierabend*. And, technology plays a crucial role in converting all the hypothetical claims into real, valid, and legitimate expectations. She actually *could* do all the work, or watch all the movies she ever wanted to watch on TV or on her computer, because technology allows her to do so.

Technology thus plays a twofold role in piling up our *to do lists*: first, it vastly increases the imaginable opportunities and, second, it converts all the hypothetical possibilities into real options. (Before the telephone, let alone the internet, chatting with our friends once we were at home was not an option—and hence there was no legitimate expectation on either side.) In this way, technological innovation and acceleration serve to change the nature of our temporal experience altogether. The whole mode of our being in time is transformed. Late-modern actors gradually become aware of this fact. They seek places like the tiny hut high up in the mountains which are deprived of most of the technological amenities of late-modern life such as an airport close by, Internet, TV, for a temporal refuge, and they consider this as the highest form of luxury and indulgence: a condition of life that is characterized by all the insignia of utter backwardness and deprivation (cf. Rosa 2014).

One important thing we can learn from this is the fact that increasing flexibility and time-sovereignty does not reduce, but increases the time-squeeze.[1] When you work on a nine-to-five shift, no one can legitimately expect you to do anything else (like caring for your mother, answering private messages, or checking train schedules) during that time. And no matter how badly you might be rushed by the schedule and the amount of your task-load at work, no legitimate claims emanate from your workplace *after* five o'clock. The to-do entries from your private life make only "hypothetical" claims on you while at work—they are, so to speak, set in a *standby* mode, while the entries from work are converted into non-actualized claims after shift's end. In a 24/7 world, by contrast, claims emanating from any context are perceived as legitimate at any time, and thus the mismatch between the two temporalities is no longer just an abstract fact of life, but an acute dilemma any second of our lives.

All of this does not sufficiently explain, however, the explosion of the absolute volume of our *to do list*. While it might be true that technology provides the *opportunities*, this does nothing to explain how those opportunities are turned into felt claims or pressures. Before I go on to sketch out my answer to that question, I would like to pause for a moment and ask whether the story outlined so far is plausible for more than a tiny jet-set elite of society. Are social actors unequivocally and equally affected by the mismatch observed on Linda's *to do list*?

## The Temporalities of Social Class

Linda's situation is quite different from the daily routines experienced by a truck driver, or a factory worker, or a nurse in a hospital, or from a shop assistant. For all of them, the legitimacy of claims is context-bound. But whereas for Linda the claims are made to temporal resources she disposes of *outside* the given work-context, the time-pressures experienced by the latter group of employees normally arise out of the very situations they are involved in. Thus very often, the truck driver is supposed to deliver his load at a deadline he can hardly (or never) make by sticking to the speed limits in ordinary traffic; the factory worker is assigned a workload by his boss that exceeds his capacities, and the shop assistant is expected to serve several highly impatient customers simultaneously. For the nurse, the situation is even worse, for he or she is cross-pressured by two different sets of incompatible, but legitimate expectations: patients and their needs require (a lot of) care and attention, while bosses and regulations allocate much less time to each

---

[1] At this point I actually disagree with Judy Wajcman (2015: 61–84) who, in my understanding, uncritically accepts the common belief that greater sovereignty or autonomy over one's schedule and time-resources reduces the perceived time pressure.

treatment. In this way, the mismatch is built into the very structure of routine work itself. Small wonder nurses suffer from a particularly high rate of burnout.[2]

In work, underprivileged employees have very little time-sovereignty, pressure is put on them by the boss or by external authorities who regulate their time-budget. It is them they can directly locate as the source of pressure. For Linda, the source of pressure is outside the situation, it is herself she needs to blame. Outside work, work-pressures cease for the former, but everyday time-pressures might weigh even heavier for them, because they cannot easily alleviate it by exchanging money for time, e.g. by taking a cab or a fast train or using professional cleaning services—or high-speed technologies at that. Consequently, there is some justification for saying that for the well-educated and highly qualified elites working in white-collar jobs, the locus of pressure is to a significant extent internalized, while for many less qualified, poorly paid blue-collar workers, the locus is very often external, i.e. it is their boss or some externally created synchronization problem.

For those who are excluded from the hamster wheels of work by unemployment or disease, the situation is yet again different. Very often, they suffer from the fact that there are no or few direct claims on their time-budget—social exclusion in its most depressing form often is characterized by the fact that no one expects anything from you—while they lack the means and hence the opportunities to form concrete, realizable expectations on time-use themselves. (When you are out of work, isolated and without money, neither the shopping malls nor the musical theater or the gym feel an impact on your time budget.) Hence, the socially excluded are outside the accelerating system of demands and opportunities, or outside the machines of allocation. But this state of affairs is highly problematic too, since it implies that the available time is radically devalued. Therefore, social exclusion leads to a time-problem of a different sort: the gap between the abstract list of claims that should be met to lead a respectable life (including all the requirements on capacities and possessions, resources and capabilities, and even documents needed to get a job) and the means to meet them enlarges by the day. The chances to catch up with those who run inside the treadmills of late-modern life decrease progressively if you lack the economic, cultural, social, and bodily capital to even start the race. If those who start from a privileged position run as fast as they can to stay in the game, it becomes a completely rational form of behavior for those who find themselves far behind from the beginning and without the necessary resources to catch up to never even start to run.

---

[2] See Aiken, Clarke, and Sloane's (2002) cross-national study on hospital staffing, organization and quality of care, as well as Nil et al. 2010.

In conclusion, even though the working and living conditions of social groups—and their capacities to use and command time-saving devices and technologies—differ to a highly significant degree, the mismatch between the temporal requirements on the *to do list* and the resources at hand reappears in different forms with all of them. The imperatives of speed are not uniform, but they do affect all social groups, milieus, or classes as well as sexes.[3] The social speedgame and its imperatives toward optimization appear to be quite pervasive.

## The Driving Wheels of Acceleration: The Mode of Dynamic Stabilization

Let me return to the question formulated earlier. What, if it is not technology, is responsible for the exploding volume of our *to do list*? How can we explain the growing mismatch between that list and our everyday time-resources in the face of all the spectacular time-saving effects of technology? At this point, I am afraid, we have to turn from the micro-level of everyday life to the macro-level of the institutional structures of modern society.

As a first step to develop my argument, I want to modify slightly the approach to modernity developed in my book on *Social Acceleration* (Rosa 2013) by shifting the focus from acceleration to dynamic stabilization.

In the social sciences, debates about the defining criteria of what constitutes modernity or what defines modern societies abound. A core problem of most definitions is their intended or unintended inherent normativity and ethno-centricity. Whether one follows the suggestions of "modernization theories" in the vein of Talcott Parsons or the more philosophical definitions of the "project of modernity" provided by authors like Jürgen Habermas or Charles Taylor (and often centered around conceptions of the enlightenment), a normative and/or Eurocentric bias appears to be inevitable. Furthermore, most conceptions of modernity appear to be ill equipped to grasp the vast differences between the social and cultural fabric of say, eighteenth-century societies on the one hand and late-modern culture on the other. Yet, while conceptions of "multiple" or "entangled" modernities that have been formulated to answer these problems are often successful in pointing out the vast differences and diversities over time and space (Eisenstadt 2002), they appear to be incapable of defining any essence or commonality of the (unifying) "modern" behind the difference. Against this, I would like to suggest the following, modest, and simple definition: *a society is modern when it is in a*

---

[3] For an empirical analysis of differences in time-use and perceived time-pressure arising from class, age, or gender divisions, see Wajcman 2015, particularly chapters 3 and 4.

*mode of dynamic stabilization, i.e. when it systematically requires growth, innovation, and acceleration for its structural reproduction and to maintain its socioeconomic and institutional status quo.*

On first sight, this definition seems to be haunted by an apparent contradiction. How can we talk of keeping the *status quo* through innovation, acceleration, and growth, i.e. through *change*? What changes—and what stays the same? What is dynamic—and what is stable? By structural reproduction and reification of the status quo I mean, first, the stabilization of the basic institutional fabric of society, in particular the competitive market-system, the political and legal framework, and educational and welfare institutions. Second, I refer to the basic structures of socioeconomic stratification: the reproduction of class-hierarchy and class-fractions. And third, most importantly, the status quo is defined by the operational logics of accumulation and distribution: the logic of capital accumulation and the very processes of growth, acceleration, activation, and innovation. Obviously, political, economic, educational, etc., institutions change their shape, form, or composition over time. What does not change, however, are the systemic imperatives for augmentation.

This answer, however, raises another serious question. Is modern society simply equivalent to capitalist society? Do I simply mean: *capitalism* when referring to the basic structure of modern society?

Certainly, the systematic need *to grow, to speed-up*, and *to increase (the rates of) innovation* in order to maintain the structure and to keep the socioeconomic status quo can most easily be found in capitalist economies. Without constant innovation and escalation, jobs are lost, companies close down, and tax revenues decline while welfare expenditures grow, states go bankrupt, and the political system suffers de-legitimation. All of this can be well observed in contemporary Greece, in fact. While this need for growth and augmentation results from several interlinking factors, like the logic of (extra) profit and competition, the competitive drive to increase productivity, the credit system, etc., it is nevertheless indubitable that no known form of capitalism could do without it. In the end, it might well boil down to the simple logic of money—commodity—money as the driving motor of economic escalation. Thus, the self-valorization of capital, as Marx has it, can still be interpreted as the real subject of change and as the dynamic motor of modern society.

Interestingly, however, the logic of dynamic stabilization also holds sway in other segments of society. In the reproduction of science, for example, the logic of novelty and increase has completely replaced the older notion of knowledge as something treasurable that needs to be preserved and handed down from one generation to the next. Knowledge—and in particular the most essential and most highly esteemed form of knowledge—is no longer something that has been revealed in an original act, or something that is rooted in the wisdom of the ancient, and needs to be restored, but it is recreated dynamically in a process of incessant progression. No one could achieve scientific merits or gain research money without presenting his or her achievement as something that goes beyond what was known before.

Exactly the same shift can be observed in the nature of law, too: modern society does not seek to restore and preserve the "eternal" or "holy law" given by the Gods or by the Ancestors, it does not even seek to find and establish *the best set of laws* for mankind, as Plato did. Instead, legislation is considered to be a perennial task; laws as well as the legislating bodies are legitimized by the very idea of dynamic stabilization, that is to say, by the idea that law is something that has to be improved and adjusted (and often extended) incessantly (cf. Scheuerman 2004). Similarly, our whole conception of *art* has changed, too. Modern society takes innovation and originality to lie at the very heart of artistic activity (Groys 2013: 23–42)—this stands in sharp contrast to forms of artistic aspiration known from other (pre- or non-modern) cultures for whom artistic achievement was defined by ideals of mimesis or imitation.

Finally, a similar logic can also be found in political modernity. Democracy is by definition operating in a mode of dynamic stabilization, i.e. it is based on a repetitive cycle of elections, which stands in sharp contrast to all known forms of monarchic regimes aspiring to preserve the existing political rule. Moreover, political programs and political competition invariable follow the logic of overbidding and outpacing competitors, of promising increase and augmentation (cf. Luhmann 1981). By consequence, parties, universities, and artists alike cannot survive and reproduce their institutional structures without promising and achieving "progress" in the form of innovation, augmentation, growth, or acceleration. Collectively, then, they follow a logic of escalation. In all these cases, society no longer aims at the preservation of the given or the realization of some preconceived goal, but at its constant *transgression* such that the arts, the sciences, and the economy could no longer exist without it. Or put differently, substantive innovation and augmentation is a requirement for institutional and structural preservation.

Please note at this point that I do *not* claim that previous or non-modern societies operated in a mode of *static* stabilization. No social formation or institutional system can remain stable, or can even survive, over a longer period without the capacity to adapt to external changes and challenges, and to internal contingent developments. Thus, the historical and cultural alternative to the mode of dynamic stabilization certainly is not static stabilization, but adaptive stabilization: an operational mode which allows (at least to some extent) institutional systems to grow, accelerate, innovate, or change when it is needed or desired, but does not enforce increase or augmentation as a "blind" requirement to reproduce its structure and the institutional status quo.

In order to come back to the initial question of what pumps up the volume of demands on our individual time-budgets, the crucial point here is that the logic of increase is a defining cultural moment in individuals' pursuit of the good life and the best course of action. Social actors strive for an increase in wealth, but also for an increase in the range of options and contacts. In a society whose central mode of allocation (not just for wealth and money, but also for positions and privileges, life-chances, contacts and friends, status and recognition) is competition, this strategy eventually is turned into a necessity for the reproduction of the individual status quo. Standing still for subjects (with respect to knowledge or relationships, money or health, tools or fashions, etc.) inevitably entails sliding back or falling down with respect to their position in the social order.

One could claim that this whole array of dynamic stabilizations is simply the consequence of the unleashed logic of capital(ist) reproduction. This is the Marxist or materialist interpretation of modernity and society. But one might just as well claim that this epochal shift in the logic of social stabilization and reproduction has cultural roots; that it is ignited by a process of cultural reinterpretation which is closely connected to the ideas emerging in the age of the enlightenment. As we know from the long-standing debates between, for example, Hegelians and Marxists, Taylorians and Foucauldians, Habermasians and Adornites, it is impossible to decide who is right or wrong. I tend to go along with Max Weber and observe that there seems to be an "elective affinity" between these material and cultural developments. Thus, I am agnostic with respect to the question whether or not dynamic stabilization is caused by capitalism (and by capitalism alone)—in any case, dynamic stabilization is the current mode of stabilization in all relevant spheres of contemporary social life, and it will certainly not be replaced without a fundamental change in the economic fabric of modern society.

In sum, then, we can call this co-evolutionary shift toward dynamic stabilization in the dominant spheres of society *the escalatory logic of modernity*. The crucial point for the purpose of this chapter is that *time* is the one factor or dimension in social life that cannot be increased or augmented—it can only be condensed or compressed (Harvey 1990). Thus, we can increase the *number of goods* we produce, distribute, and consume (the average European or North American household today contains about 10,000 objects vs. a few hundred in 1900)—the *number of options* for action and the *number of contacts*—almost indefinitely,[4] whereas the time we can apply to all these goods, options, and

---

[4] Thus, American psychologist Kenneth Gergen in his book on the saturated self calculates that the average North American commuter (from, say, Connecticut to New York) encounters more people on his way to work on an average day than a traditional village-dweller did in the whole of a month (Gergen 2000: 62). Gergen includes in this calculation the people encountered in and through the radio, TV, and the local newspaper. If we consider that by 2016, we also have to

contacts virtually remains the same (namely twenty-four hours a day or 365 days a year). Therefore, the escalatory logic of modernity necessarily results in an ever-increasing time-scarcity. Time can only be compressed, and this is what we all try to do in our lives—up to the point where we try to reduce, intensify, or multi-use sleep (Crary 2013).

Therefore, it is in the dimension *of time* that the limits to the mode of dynamic stabilization become more and more noticeable and pressing. But in order to understand this properly, we need to first establish the claim that growth and acceleration can be read as two sides of the same coin. Basically, my argument is this: acceleration can be defined as *quantitative growth* or *increase in quantity per unit of time*. This is exactly the definition I arrived at in my books on social acceleration (Rosa 2013: 63–73, 2010: 13–26). Thus, in the realm of transport, e.g. acceleration figures as an increase of kilometers covered per hour, with respect to communication, it might refer to the number of signs transmitted per microsecond, and in production, acceleration refers to the material output per hour, day, month, or year. Thus, the very phenomenon of increasing productivity is just as much a phenomenon of social acceleration—it is defined as increased output per unit of time. Moreover, the phenomena of accelerated *social change* can be interpreted as instances of this form of acceleration, too: if people change jobs or partners at higher rates, this amounts to an increase in the average number of jobs or spouses (or newspapers, or bank accounts, or cars, or telephone-numbers, etc.) per lifetime. Or if the temporal validity of legal orders or bureaucratic regulations shrinks, this can be read as a rise in decay rates. Put the other way round: rising rates of innovation per definition amount to an acceleration of social change. Finally, the acceleration of the pace of life, I have argued, amounts to an increase in the number of episodes of experience or action per unit of time (be it a day, a month, a year, or a lifetime). It can easily be seen how this form of acceleration results from an augmentation of our *to do list*. By consequence, all forms of growth can be interpreted or experienced as forms of acceleration and vice versa. Thus, when I describe modern society as dependent on growth, acceleration, and innovation, this only serves to distinguish experientially, or phenomenologically, three aspects of the same underlying phenomenon, which perhaps is best grasped by the term of "dynamization."

With this account of dynamic stabilization, we now arrive at a clear-cut explanation of the mismatch between the volume of the *to do lists* of social actors on the one hand and their time-budget on the other hand: while the former grows in an escalatory fashion, the latter cannot be increased at all, but

include the contacts established through social media like Facebook, Twitter, and WhatsApp, we might come to the conclusion that the real explosion of contacts has happened only after Gergen's observation. This is yet another apt illustration of what I mean by the logic of *escalation*.

only compressed. Conversely, the alleviation on our time-budget by the saving of budgeted time-resources through time-saving or time-accelerating technologies is at best linear and modest, but it cannot match the *escalatory* logic of the former—to which those very same technologies actually contribute by increasing the range of options and changing the patterns of social expectation.

## Social Acceleration and Social De-Synchronization

Now, the basic problem of endemic and escalatory dynamization is this: faster systems or actors systematically put pressure on the slower ones—and risk de-synchronization at the "interfaces." Whenever there is a temporal juncture or "fit" between two systems, actors, or processes, and one of them speeds up, the other one appears to be too slow; it figures as a break or hindrance, and synchronization is strained. As we have already seen, this helps to explain the deepening of social stratification. In fact, those who are well equipped with economic, social, and cultural capital successfully use these as resources in the speed-game: they start the accumulative race for their children even before they are borne—while those who lack these resources are "left behind," with the gap widening. However, de-synchronization also lies at the heart of the four major crises of late-modern societies in the twenty-first century. If we loosely follow a "systems-theoretic" approach,[5] we can envision the "social system" as being placed in the middle between the overarching ecological system(s) and the individuals' psychosomatic "systems." The speeding up of society places stress and pressures of de-synchronization on both these other systems. Furthermore, even *within* society, some processes or subsystems are more "speedable" than others: economic transactions, scientific progress, and technological innovations can easily be accelerated, while the workings of political democracy and cultural reproduction cannot—thus, democracy in particular is in increasing danger of being "de-synchronized" (and perhaps this is true for education, too). And finally, even within single social subsystems, the problem of de-synchronization reappears. For example, while financial markets can be accelerated to almost the speed of light with which transactions and profits can be made, the "real economy" of material production and consumption is much slower. Hence, potentially harmful de-synchronization lurks even within the economic realm itself. Let us take a closer look at this one by one.

---

[5] I take this idea from Fritz Reheis' seminal book *Kreativität der Langsamkeit* (1996).

## Macro-Level: The Ecological Crisis

Surprising as it may sound, I claim that virtually all aspects of what we call "the ecological crisis" can be reinterpreted as a problem of de-synchronization. Thus, on the hand, it is not at all a problem that we cut trees and catch fish—but it *is* a problem that we cut the trees in the rain-forest and catch the fish in the oceans at rates too high for their natural reproduction. Obviously, the temporal discrepancy vastly increases when we look at the rate with which we use up oil and other carbon-based energy supplies and the time needed for nature to reproduce them. Similarly, most of what is considered to be "poisoning" the environment by emissions is only a problem because we produce these substances and emissions at speeds that are higher than nature's capability to dispose of it. Finally, even the problem of "global warming" can be read as a form of physical and material de-synchronization: heating the atmosphere literally means making the molecules in these layers of air move faster; thus, the physical heat produced through technological acceleration on earth leads to atmospheric acceleration in the sky. Put differently, the process of material dynamization driven by the consumption of physical energy leads to a "de-synchronization" in the earth's atmosphere that results in earth's warming (see Chapter 3).

## Inter-Social De-Synchronization: The Crisis of Democracy

Alas, the speed of socioeconomic life is not just too high for our natural environment, but it also creates problems for the slower spheres of society itself. As I have argued at length elsewhere (Rosa 2013: 251–76), the current weakness of Western democracy—which can be seen from both the failing attractiveness it provides for non-Western states in Africa or Asia and the decline in support and credibility it earns in its core countries (cf. Crouch 2004)—basically arises from the fact that the democratic processes of will formation, decision making, and implementation, by their very nature, are inevitably time-consuming. In fact, the more pluralistic and post-conventionalist society gets, and the more complex its networks, chains of transaction, and contexts of action and decision become, the *slower* democracy proceeds. Thus, while the speed of cultural and economic life and technological change increases, the pace of democracy slows down—and hence, we observe a frightening extent of de-synchronization between politics and the social systems it tries to control or steer.

Thus, in the twenty-first century, democratic governments no longer appear to be a pace-maker of social change; rather, they have shifted to a role of "fire extinguisher" and to a mode of "muddling through," at best; reacting to the pressures created elsewhere rather than shaping our shared world. Nowhere could this be seen more clearly than in the recent financial crises, when political decisions always came too late and too slow for the markets—and yet too fast for the legislatures to even have a say. Parliaments, it seems, are reduced to *ex post* yay- or nay-sayers, and this leads to increasing frustration or alienation on the part of the voters—who then tend to elect xenophobic or populist parties or to abstain from voting altogether. The de-synchronization between politics and the economy, or its markets, thus results in a state of affairs where citizens have lost faith in political self-efficacy; for them, political institutions no longer "answer" their needs and aspirations.

### Intra-Social De-Synchronisation: The Financial Crisis

Yet, this is not all there is to de-synchronization. In addition to acceleration producing problems between the natural and sociotechnical processes and between the different spheres of action, temporal pathologies can arise *within* single spheres of action, too. Even after 200 years of technological acceler-ation, producing cars or houses is a time-consuming process, and so is, to some extent at least, the production (and designing) of clothes or computers. Furthermore, it is not just the production, but also the *consumption* of these commodities that is time-consuming. Compared to the cost of production, and hence to its price, it takes ages to really "consume," i.e. *read*, a book, to give just one example; and the ratio for the other consumer goods mentioned is not much better either. But the need for growth and speed in competitive global markets is insatiable. Hence, it is small wonder that the financial economy discovered ways and means to dynamize the speed of flows for capital and the creation of profits way beyond these material speed-barriers: by buying and selling "financial products," and thus by "virtualizing" pro-duction and consumption, the transaction process could be accelerated close to the speed of light.

In fact, to quite a significant extent, the speed of financial transaction has become too high for human agents to understand or steer it at all: it is left to computer algorithms that make profits from exploiting fluctuations within microseconds (see Chapter 4). Alas, this necessarily led to a serious de-synchronization between the financial markets and the "real" or material economy up to a point where these two had little connection with each other. In this way, the financial "bubble" which created the financial crisis of 2008/9 was a temporal bubble, too; and its burst implied dramatic conse-quences that are not solved yet.[6] Re-synchronization seems inevitable even to economists, but it comes at a high price: obviously, the world economy is still

[6] "The relationship between money and society [ . . . ] has been damaged [by the financial crisis]," Nigel Dodd consequently states in his seminal book *The Social Life of Money* (2014: 4f.), in which

seeking a temporal balance not just between the financial industry on the one hand and the "real industries" on the other, but also between markets and governments or politics. And it might well be that such a re-synchronization is only possible at the price of a significant slowdown of the (financial) economy.

## Micro-Level: The Global Burnout Crisis

If the mode of dynamic stabilization entails the incessant speed-up of material, social, and cultural reproduction of society, this cannot leave the structures of the individual psyche (and body) and the character of the human subject untouched. Thus, the question arises of how much speed individuals can take before they break. And here indeed, too, the evidence for pathological forms of de-synchronization appears to be mounting. Take just one indicator. While on the one hand, drugs that slow people down ("downers" like heroine, LSD, or alcohol) are on the decline, "speed," amphetamines, and other drugs that promise "synchronization" (like Ritalin, Taurin, Modafinil, etc.) are on the rise. In fact, most forms of "human enhancement" have to do with increasing the speedability of human bodies and minds—from repairing the "retards" to transhumanist fantasies of reconciling the speed of technology with the speed of social actors (cf. Savulescu and Bostrom 2011). But unless they succeed, the signs of growing pathological de-synchronization in the form of burnout and depression are alarming. In fact, the World Health Organization now acknowledges that—alongside other pathological stress reactions like eating- and sleeping-disorders and chronic anxieties—depression and burnout are the fastest-growing health problems on a world-wide scale.[7]

One of the most striking features of both burnout and depression, is the complete lack of dynamics. For those who fall into the trap of a burnout or depression, time is standing still, the world and/or the self appear to be "frozen," devoid of motion and significance (Bschor et al. 2004). This has led researchers like Alain Ehrenberg (2010) to suppose that depression is a stress reaction of a de-synchronized psyche to the speed requirements of modern life. The fact that all over the world, journals and magazines regularly double their sales by reporting on stress, burnout, depression, and exhausted selves on their cover page could serve as an amber light signaling an impending state

---

he thoroughly investigates the multiple and complex ways in which this relationship has been and can be envisioned in social thought.

[7] Wittchen and Jacobi (2006) calculate that there are five to six million adult Germans (aged 18–65) and more than twenty million Europeans affected by depression every year.

of de-synchronization even for those who are skeptical of the diagnosing practices of our medical services.

## Conclusion: De-Synchronization, Technology, and the Time-Budget

Let us now turn back to the initial question of this chapter: Why are we so short on time, and what is the role of technology in this shortage? In a way, we can reinterpret the growing mismatch between our *to do list* and our time-budget as a form of de-synchronization between our social existence and our individual capacities. There is an accelerating increase in the number of claims and demands on our temporal resources—and we try to answer it by turning to time-saving devices and technologies. The microwave oven helps to reduce the time needed for cooking, the car and airplane help to reduce the demands on our time-budget for transport, digitalization vastly reduces the time to communicate as well as to produce an incredible amount of goods and services, etc. Similarly, we try to use technologies to alleviate the problem of de-synchronization in the other three spheres too. With the help of innovative technologies, we try to reduce the speed with which we use up natural resources and simultaneously to increase the speed of nature itself—for example, by using fertilizers, artificial light which simulates a twenty-three-hour day, or genetic engineering to reduce reproduction time and increase the speed of growth and adaptation. Similarly, the digitalization of financial markets was an answer to the increasing speed of economic transaction, and the creation of Internet votes and Internet fora are a reaction to the de-synchronization of democracy. This explains why new technologies are inevitably attractive in modern society. In fact, I claim that this is what is driving technological revolutions from the industrial to the digital revolution and beyond in the first place.

However, it appears that in virtually all of these cases, the attempt to solve (temporal) problems by using *more of the same* in the end aggravates the problem: those very technologies come with the side effect of providing the means for speeding up the primary social systems even further, and at an escalatory rate; and they tend to explode the horizons of possibilities and expectations. In fact, growth, acceleration, and innovation which are needed to stabilize the social fabric and which create the problem of de-synchronization in the first place, are achieved exactly through those very technologies. Thus, the apparent solution to the temporal problem eventually aggravates the problem on the next level. What is known from the ecological realm as the "rebound effect"—i.e. the effect that any saving of (energy) resources or reduction of emissions leads to a new round of escalatory consumption at both ends (Sorrell and Dimitropoulos 2008)—is mirrored in the realm of time. We can very well talk of a *temporal rebound effect*, too. Yes, the car helps you to save time, but it vastly increases the horizon of the world within your reach for a possible workplace, in the evening, and at the weekend, and therefore it explodes the list of effective claims on your time-budget (and on your *to do list*), and the same is true for your smartphone. Perhaps no other device has the power to illustrate this rebound effect more clearly than this: while the smartphone does help you to save time on many occasions of your daily life, it also leads to a situation where the list of legitimate claims on your time-budget is effective even while you sit in the bathroom or read in your bed. Thus, as I have tried to show in this chapter, the logic of dynamic stabilization even leads to an *escalation* of temporal rebound. It is not the inherent logic of technology that drives the acceleration game—it is the institutional fabric of a capitalist modernity that can only operate in a mode of dynamic stabilization, and that can only meet the temporal requirements of dynamic stabilization through acceleratory technologies.

# 3

# Accelerating to the Future

*John Urry*

In 1994 *New Scientist* devoted a special issue to the subject of *Futures* and observed that the future is a foreign country, they do things differently there (*New Scientist* issue 1947, October 5, 1994). While according to John F. Kennedy: "Change is the law of life. And those who look only to the past or present are certain to miss the future" (Kennedy, June 25, 1963).

And now the future has most definitely arrived; it is hard now to miss the future; it is less a foreign country. Futures are everywhere but what exactly they are remains a mystery, perhaps the greatest of mysteries. Futures seem so unpredictable, uncertain, and often unknowable, the outcome of many known and especially "unknown" unknowns.

Thinking the future has become essential for most organizations and societies. Many believe the future to be a better guide to what to do than the past. States, corporations, universities, cities, NGOs, and individuals believe they must not miss the future. Such a future orientation is big and significant business undertaken by companies like Rand or Shell, environmental organizations such as the IPCC or Forum for the Future, government bodies like Foresight in the UK or ESPAS in the EU, military organizations such as the Pentagon, and very many others. That foreign country of the future is everywhere (see Son 2015; Urry 2016).

Such futures are often based upon specific methods that are developed, circulated, and marketed. Future studies became a specialized discipline with its own journals, key books, iconic figures, and founding texts. Much of this literature reflected Cold War debates, the founding figure of Hermann Kahn has been said to be the model for Dr Strangelove (see Menand 2005). Much futures thinking was tied into powerful military and corporate agendas funded outside the academy and developed within private think tanks, such as those of Alvin Toffler (1970), Jeremy Rifkin (2009), or Al Gore (2013). There have also been many imagined future worlds involving spectacular technologies, time travel, personal flying machines, roads and trains in the sky, robots, walking upon water, off-earth communities, vacuum powered propulsion, equal utopias, and so on (Urry 2016).

Futures are contested and saturated with conflicting interests. Over two centuries ago Edmund Burke argued that a society should be seen as a "partnership not only between those who are living, but between those who are living, those who are dead, and those who are to be born" (Burke [orig 1790] quoted in Beinhocker 2006: 454). Burke points to the interests possessed by unborn members of a society and how they need a powerful "voice" without which societies and lives will be based around the interests of the present. Recent environmentalism has developed something of an intergenerational global commons, as in the Brundtland Commission's Report on *Our Common Future* (1987). Environmentalism deploys generational rhetoric to argue for the interests of children, grandchildren, and those not yet born (see Hansen 2011).

However, most processes within societies principally involve molding futures to the current generation and their interests. Those yet to be born often possess no voice in the "parliament of generations." There may though be moments when there is contestation about this and efforts are made to form "imagined communities" stretching across generations seeking a "common future" (see Dayrell and Urry 2015, on recent moments).

Analyses of "social institutions, practices and lives" need to be central to this issue of thinking through futures. The first feature to note here is to deconstruct of a singular notion of "time." Adam and colleagues show that there are varied forms of time with different societies and social institutions being built around contrasting time regimes (Adam 1990, 1995; Abbott 2001). A social theory of time is significant in elaborating how time is socially variable and temporal regimes greatly matter to people's lives as experienced within different societies.

Relatedly, it is shown that there is no single future as such but multiple futures that partly relate to different time regimes. Possible futures are, according to Adam and Groves, told, tamed, traded, transformed, traversed, thought, tended, and transcended (2007). Especially significant in thinking futures has been utopian thinking ever since Thomas More's *Utopia*. Bauman maintains that the capacity to think through utopian futures is emancipatory, enabling people to break with the overwhelming dominance of what seem normal patterns of life (1976). H. G. Wells thought sociology should examine the utopian since: "Sociology is the description of the Ideal Society and its relation to existing societies" (1914: 200).

Moreover, social science shows that the future cannot be predicted or extrapolated from what is happening within the present as many techno-optimists tend to claim. To know the future means that the past must be interrogated, and it is necessary to develop ways of understanding how past, present, and future are intertwined. Anticipating the future involves knowing much from the past and especially ways in which systems can be path-dependent.

At the same time though, variations in the nature of time and of futures stem from the many ways in which social systems are characterized by accelerating social change and unpredictability. Prigogine argues from the perspective of complexity science that futures are populated with multiple unstable, complex adaptive systems with thresholds and tipping points (1997). There are many social and political implications of this "end of certainty," as elaborated in Al Gore's *The Future* (2013).

Future economic and social innovations are rarely the outcome of linear processes but involve unpredictable combinations of potential elements (Arthur 2013). Such systems are in "process" and not predetermined in their organization or effects. System innovations may not develop as rapidly as advocates maintain. Indeed "old" technologies may not disappear but combine with the "new" in some unpredicted cluster, such as the enduring importance of paper within "high-tech" offices (see Edgerton 2006, on the shock of the old). Kurzweil interestingly argues that: "most inventions fail not because the R&D department can't get them to work, but because the timing is wrong—not all of the enabling factors are at play where they are needed. Inventing is a lot like surfing: you have to anticipate and catch the wave at just the right moment."[1]

Further, some futures are built into contemporary societies, such as the idea of "smart cities" which can rapidly bring them into being, they are performative.[2] Powerful actors seeking to realize the future often deploy complex rhetorical imaginaries and visions of a future "heaven." Those seeking to perform or produce that future often denigrate those opposing it as "Luddites," as somehow stuck in the slow lane and not speeding up to the future (see Law and Urry 2004, on enacting the social).

An example of such performativity is that of "predict and provide" models deployed in planning and financing major transport infrastructures. Analysts conduct research on levels of congestion and predict increasing demand for roadspace; this is provided through a costly new infrastructure, justified since it will save "valuable" time; this soon results in more traffic filling up the; and this leads to the further predicted demand for more roadspace which is provided and so on. The prediction appears confirmed (Lyons 2015).

Especially important here is the power to produce futures. A key question is who or what owns the future, this capacity being key in how power now works

[1] See <http://crnano.org/interview.kurzweil.htm> (accessed June 2016).
[2] See <http://smartcities.media.mit.edu/> (accessed June 2016).

within societies. Lanier strongly disputes that the future is a commons and describes the power of the large international computer companies, the "server sirens" with "ultra-influential" computers where information is turned into wealth (2013). He writes: "You can't see as much of the server as it can see of you," and hence it often knows a person's future before they themselves (Lanier 2013: 63). The question of who owns the future is crucial, with the Occupy movement recently coining the slogan "Occupy the Future."

Further, many commentators argue that the future is emerging ever more quickly, such acceleration first analyzed in Toffler's *Future Shock* (1970). He documented exponentially increasing rates of technological and social transformation. And over recent decades the operation of Moore's Law meant that world computing power (the number of transistors in an integrated circuit) doubled every two years. Today's smartphones possess the computing power once found in large mainframe computers, as well as containing "magical" affordances housed within small "ready-to-hand" machines which no one knew they had "needed."

Specifically, financial "products" are increasingly based upon computerized high-frequency trading that takes place in millionths of a second and soon to be further speeded up (see Conway 2011). Actions happen beyond the speed of thought and involve movements of money and information which cannot be grasped by human minds. In such an accelerating world, financial futures can be said to arrive before they have been conceptualized or even talked about by relevant actors. This is a nanosecond "future shock."

Kurzweil focuses upon the law of accelerating returns engendered through enhanced computing and technological power. He argues that exponential rates of change will result in a "singularity," a moment when human biology merges with genetics, nanotechnology, and robotics (Kurzweil 2006; the 2010 movie *The Singularity is Near*). Kurzweil describes how there will be no distinction, post-singularity, between humans and machines. Computer-based intelligence will significantly exceed the sum total of human brainpower, so creating in effect a new species. As McLuhan once said: "First we build the tools, then they build us." Exponential change brings the future so much closer. Moreover, if we see change as only "linear" then, according to Kurzweil, we miss what is already in process and which through exponential change arrives much sooner than we can imagine (see Allen 2011; Gore 2013: 240).

I now turn to the significance of such exponential accelerating change for how societies are energized now and into the future: what we can call the "problem of energy" (Urry 2014). I begin perhaps surprisingly with ice sheets. Especially significant in climate science since around 2000 have been new techniques for researching the history of the planet through what appears the very opposite of a speeded up future. This new program involves researching ice cores that are up to two miles in depth. As a result of this novel research: "the climate community was in the midst of a full-blown paradigm shift," which demonstrates the rapidity of climate change (Linden 2007: 227). Alley showed that half the warming between the last ice age and the subsequent postglacial world of around nine degrees Celsius took place in a *single* decade. There seem to be two states of the earth's climate, an ice age or a relatively warm interglacial age and where there is no gradual movement from one to the other. This research shows how there were sudden abrupt accelerating jumps as the earth responded to carbon shifts with "speed and violence" (Pearce 2007).

Research at the Antarctic also shows that the current levels of $CO_2$ in the earth's atmosphere are unprecedented in human history and temperatures are thought to be nearly as high as they have been for 420,000 years. So the idea that there are "safe" levels of future $CO_2$ levels is almost certainly wrong if it were thought desirable to keep future temperatures within limits of which humans have some "experience." Also in certain parts of the globe increases in temperature will be much higher, especially at the poles.

This research also shows how $CO_2$ levels and temperatures varied in tandem over thousands of years, suggesting a well-established and robust relationship. Rather than the thesis of relatively stable climates, Alley argues there are sudden see-sawing shifts. A "crazily jumping climate has been the rule, not the exception," he maintains (cited in Clark 2010). And hence changing levels of $CO_2$ emissions seems key to future temperatures.

This brings us to the question of energy, where E. F. Schumacher maintains: "There is no substitute for energy. The whole edifice of modern society is built upon it.... it is not "just another commodity" but the precondition of all commodities, a basic factor equal with air, water, and earth" (1973; and see Urry 2011). Energy provides "oxygen" for societies.

There has been an exceptional acceleration in the use of energy ever since the initial burning of fossil fuels that began in England in the late eighteenth century. In 1776, the year that Adam Smith published *An Inquiry into the Nature and Causes of the Wealth of Nations* which described the powerful advantages of the division of labour (1979), the diarist and biographer James Boswell visited the world's first ever factory. This "manufactory" established by Matthew Boulton was located at Soho near Birmingham. It was powered by James Watt's steam engine which burnt coal and turned the resulting heat into motion. Boswell proclaimed: "I shall never forget Mr Bolton's [*sic*] expression to me: 'I sell here, Sir, what all the world desires to have—POWER'" (Morris 2010: 491).

And power there has been in plenty since that fateful moment as fossil fuel-based energy was initiated in England. Developing coal-based power led the "west" to develop a different trajectory from the "east." Until the eighteenth century, China and India were the largest economies in the world, generating one-third of world income (Morris 2010). But the non-fossil fuel economies of India and China went into relative decline from the eighteenth century onwards. Burning fossil fuels to generate heat, power, and movement is the *most* significant feature of the modern world. There is no clean, dynamic, and accelerating modernity without very large amounts of dirty fossil fuels of coal, gas, and oil extracted from under the ground being combusted (Berners Lee and Clark 2013).

These coal-fired steam engines led to novel workplaces, new industries and products, huge factories, vast cities, and machine-based speed through the railway system. Coal-based energy was especially significant for powering human movement. Prior to the nineteenth century, movement was slow, by feet, sedan chair, riding an ox or horse, sailboat, and carriage. Coal-powered railways, the first "mobile-machines," restructured physical and social worlds. In 1901 H. G. Wells predicted that future historians would take: "a steam engine running on a railway" as the nineteenth century's central symbol (quoted Carter 2001: 8). For the first time people and objects, including coal itself, travelled faster than galloping horses. Marx thought that the circulation of commodities via new forms of transport and communications (train, mail, telegraph) represented a huge upward shift in annihilating space by time (1973: 524).

And from around 1900, when the first oil and gas was "discovered" and started to be burnt alongside coal, an exponential increase occurred (Berners Lee and Clark 2013). According to McNeill: "We have deployed more energy since 1900 than all of human history before 1900."[3] And for all the historic significance of coal, the twentieth century was really an oil century. The mobile twentieth century could not have happened without the moveable energy resource of oil. Oil was better than gold, glistening as it spewed from land or sea. Upton Sinclair described an oil gusher: "The inside of the earth seemed to burst through that hole; a roaring and rushing, as Niagara, and a black column shot up into the air, two hundred feet, two hundred and fifty—no one could say for sure—and came thundering down to earth as a mass of thick, black, slimy, slippery fluid" (2008: 25). The world's first gusher occurred at Spindletop in Texas in 1901, establishing the era of cheap plentiful oil. Oil rapidly came to be used to speed up newly developed cars, steamships, airplanes, and some railways. Virtually free energy spurting out of the ground led many to believe that there really was a free lunch, especially for Americans who initiated the early "burning" of oil within emerging "mobility-systems" of cars, planes, and ships (Urry 2007). There was (black) gold at the end of the rainbow with little energy being expended to generate more or less free energy.

---

[3] Originally accessed at <http://www.theglobalist.com/>.

Oil became central to the speeded up mobile civilization (Mitchell 2011; Urry 2013). Burning oil enables the world to go round faster and faster. It is energy-dense, storage-able, mobile, versatile, convenient, and for most of the twentieth century exceptionally cheap (still said to be cheaper than bottled water). The burning of oil provides almost all transportation energy (at least 95 percent), powering cars, trucks, planes, ships, and some trains. It makes possible friendship, business life, professions, and much family life (what can be called "romance miles" and "family miles"). Burning oil also enables the transport of components, commodities, and food around the world, within trucks, planes, and increasingly large container ships (up to 18,000 containers per ship). Almost all activities that presuppose fast movement rely upon burning oil; and there are few significant human activities that do not entail movement of some kind. Oil is an element of most manufactured goods and much packaging and bottling worldwide (95 percent). It is present in almost all food production and distribution for the growing world population through irrigation/drainage, pesticides, and fertilizers, and moving food often very fast before it went off from field to market (Pfeiffer 2006).

And from 1950 there has been an astonishing rate of increase in this burning of coal, oil, and gas, now known as the Great Acceleration. This resulting rate of increase of $CO_2$ emissions is clear from Figure 3.1. And various indicators of economic and social change show exponential rates of change more or less paralleling the pattern here for $CO_2$ emissions. And if $CO_2$ rises then almost certainly temperatures will increase (as noted earlier), and those temperatures may rise quickly, with a crazily jumping climate being the rule.

Berners-Lee and Clark summarize how societies are locked into this fossil fuel dependence: "The unremittingly exponential nature of the carbon cycle fits perfectly with the idea that society's use of energy is driven by a powerful positive feedback mechanism" (2013: 13). These feedback mechanisms are generating acceleration.

Within a couple of generations after 1950 societies had seemingly turned into a planetary scale geological force. Major earth system changes were directly engendered by changes in global economic and social systems and especially by the rate, scale, and speed of human movement. The earth seems to be in a different state after 1950, with earth system processes driven by human production, consumption, and movement (documented in Urry 2013). The resilience of this exponential upward curve indicates that the earth system moved beyond the natural variability that had been exhibited over the last 11,700 years, during the relatively stable Holocene period. This period had commenced at the end of the last ice age and had provided relatively stable conditions for humans to develop agriculture, towns, cities, and industry.

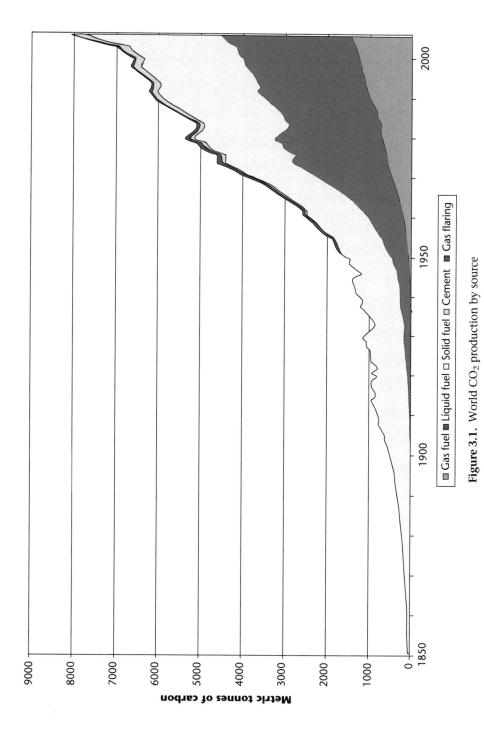

**Figure 3.1.** World CO$_2$ production by source

■ Gas fuel ■ Liquid fuel □ Solid fuel □ Cement ■ Gas flaring

But this Great Acceleration from 1950 seems to constitute a break as the earth system more clearly entered a new geological epoch, often now known as the Anthropocene.[4] Since the mid-twentieth century there were fundamental shifts in the state and functioning of the earth system that stretch beyond the variability of the Holocene. These shifts appear driven by human activities and not by natural variability. Human activities are now thought to be a "great force of nature." And further, there seems to be an accelerating rate by which geological processes themselves are evolving, with each new geological period being shorter than the previous one.

Many writers and interpreters during this century believe that massive undesirable consequences follow from these exponential increases in burning fossil fuels over the past three centuries and especially since this Great Acceleration.[5] It is anticipated that greenhouse gas levels and world temperatures will significantly increase over the next few decades; and these rises will in turn further speed up increased temperatures through multiple forms of positive feedback through unintended, perverse, and wicked problems (Rittel and Webber 1973).

There are many texts which set out a new "catastrophist" discourse within economic, social, and environmental thinking in this century (see Urry 2016: ch. 3). The key notion in much of this writing is that systems are not self-equilibrating and especially not the earth system. This Great Acceleration, this speeding up of combusting energy, generates rising greenhouse gas levels, ocean acidification, deforestation, and huge reductions in biodiversity. Even as early as 1990 it was thought that there were sixteen feedbacks, of which thirteen were positive feedback loops taking systems away from equilibrium (Wynne 2010). The most important feedbacks concern the three great ice sheets, one covering Greenland and two covering different parts of the Antarctic. They are vast, with ice compressed up to two miles high. Also there is a huge deposit of the most powerful greenhouse gas, methane, buried in permafrost in Siberia.

These are four sources of potential runaway change and if anything like the rate of increase in greenhouse gas emissions were to occur as revealed by ice core research, then most forms of life on earth would be threatened or disappear as the ice melted or the methane was released. Rockstrom and collaborators propose in "Planetary Boundaries: Exploring the Safe Operating Space for Humanity" (2009) that transgressing one or more planetary boundaries may be catastrophic because this will trigger non-linear, abrupt, speeded-up

[4] See <http://quaternary.stratigraphy.org/workinggroups/anthropocene> (accessed June 2016).
[5] See <https://www.ipcc.ch/publications_and_data/publications_and_data_reports.shtml> (accessed June 2016).

environmental change.[6] They estimate that societies have already transgressed three planetary boundaries: climate change, biodiversity loss, and the global nitrogen cycle. Planetary boundaries are interdependent, so transgressing one may shift others in a speeding up to a catastrophic future.

Along with much science fiction writing, some academic commentators now argue that acceleration has hugely undermined the resilience of various earth systems. Social scientists now wonder if human societies could disappear; could the human race become extinct (see Kolbert 2015)? It certainly seems wrong to posit that human societies are simply given and unchanging elements upon earth, as Kurzweil's thesis of the singularity of humans and machines also critiques. It may not be that "humans" are the ultimate species. A bifurcation might occur, with the catastrophic collapse of human societies if they were to pass one or more thresholds.

Tainter, in *The Collapse of Complex Societies*, argues that: "however much we like to think of ourselves as something special in world history, in fact industrial societies are subject to the same principles that caused earlier societies to collapse" (1988: 216). There are various ways that societies become more complex in response to short-term problems. Growing complexity demanded ever more high-quality energy, but such increased energy normally involved diminishing returns. An evolving combination of energy and environmental problems unpredictably reinforced each other across domains and caused some civilizations to collapse and disappear.

Like many contemporary writers, Tainter drew analogies between today's societies and the fall of the Roman Empire and the collapse of Mayan civilization in the Yucatán peninsula in central America in AD 800. Mayan civilization lasted for at least 500 years and in that period developed complex technologies, mathematics, astronomy, architecture, and culture. But then at the height of its powers Mayan civilization stopped. Monuments were no longer built, palaces were burnt, lakes silted up, cities came to be abandoned, and 90–9 percent of the population of some millions vanished (Motesharrei, Rivas, and Kalnay 2014: 91). Mayan population growth was like driving a car faster and faster until it blew up and then almost all the people seemed to disappear overnight.

Previous societies collapsed because systems were not in place to provide the continued "energizing" of their population when those societies were at the height of their powers. Societies appear to have failed at their peak and not after a long period of weakness (see Tyfield and Urry 2014). We might even speculate as to whether the Great Acceleration of western societies that especially happened from 1950 onwards will be followed at some stage by a Great Disappearance!

---

[6] See <https://www.youtube.com/watch?v=RgqtrlixYR4> (accessed June 2016).

# Part II
# **Materialities**

# 4

# Capital's Geodesic

## Chicago, New Jersey, and the Material Sociology of Speed

*Donald MacKenzie*

The development of the technologies for transmitting financial data is a clear demonstration of the central thesis of Wajcman's *Pressed for Time*.[1] "Temporal demands are not inherent to technology," she argues. "They are built into our devices by all-too-human schemes and desires" (Wajcman 2015: 3). This chapter examines one of the most dramatic increases in speed in recent times: the shift from trading conducted among human beings at a pace they could follow, to high-frequency trading or HFT (the fast, entirely automated trading of large numbers of shares and other financial instruments), which involves speeds beyond those perceptible by human beings. To be sure, this shift has been made possible by wider developments over the past three decades in computing and communication technologies, but the speed-up of trading cannot fully be explained simply by generic technological change. As Wajcman would suggest, it also results from design decisions that are quite specific, and that reflected priorities that are different from those of the wider information and communication industries.

The chapter draws upon one strand of research I have been conducting over the past five years on HFT, on the streams of data and technologies drawn on in it, and on the development of the electronic trading venues on which HFT

[1] The second section of this chapter draws upon MacKenzie (2014); I am grateful to the *London Review of Books* for permission to do so. The research reported here is part of a wider project (Evaluation Practices in Financial Markets) supported financially by the European Research Council (grant agreement no. 291733). Figure 4.1 was kindly produced by Taylor Spears, using the open-source application KDE Marble.

**Table 4.1.** The overall set of interviewees

| | |
|---|---|
| High-frequency traders (AA-BV) | 48 |
| Exchange and trading-venue members and staff (EA-FY) | 51 |
| Dealers, brokers, and broker-dealers (DA-DR) | 18 |
| Institutional-investment firms' traders (IA-ID) | 4 |
| Practitioners of other forms of algorithmic trading (OA-OM) | 13 |
| Manual traders (MA-MG) | 7 |
| Suppliers of technology and telecommunications links to HFT (SA-SO) | 15 |
| Researchers/market analysts (RA-RP) | 16 |
| **Total** | **172** |

Interviewees are identified by two-letter acronyms (specific to each category) in chronological order by the date of the (first) interview with them. E.g., AA is the first high-frequency trader interviewed (in April 2011); BV is the most recent (in June 2015).

is practiced. The research is primarily interview-based and, so far, largely US-focused (of the 172 interviews conducted so far, 61 have been in New York and 61 in Chicago); see Table 4.1 for more details, and for the two-letter acronyms used to label interviewees. (One interviewee, Stéphane Tyč of McKay Brothers, has given me his permission to name him.) The overall goal of the research is to discover how automated trading and the electronic venues in which it takes place have been and are being shaped in five main markets: shares, futures, foreign exchange, US Treasury bonds, and options.

The theoretical premise of the research is that, in order to understand financial markets, we need a *material sociology* of those markets, one that gives equal weight to each of those two words. I've explored the underlying theoretical position at length elsewhere (MacKenzie 2009), but let me summarize briefly by expressing the key point in actor-network theory terms, since that theory (for which see, e.g. Callon 1986; and Latour 1987 and 2005) is currently the most influential form taken by material sociology. The actors in financial markets are almost never "naked" individual human beings. Rather, they are assemblages of human beings (often multiple human beings) and technical artifacts: both "physical" artifacts—such as computers, calculators, and communications technologies—and "cognitive" artifacts such as mathematical models.[2]

That has always been the case, even if artifacts of the past, both physical and cognitive, look primitive to today's eyes. A basic postulate of the material sociology of financial markets is that artifacts matter: that different configurations of humans and physical/cognitive equipment form different actors and have different effects. That, for example, is a generalization of what has

---

[2] The distinction between the "physical" and the "cognitive" is for ease of exposition only. The brain is a material organ, and has limited processing and memory capacity. In consequence, as the literature on "extended" or "distributed" cognition (e.g. Hutchins 1995) emphasizes, many cognitive operations involve external equipment. For example, many of today's mathematical models in finance cannot realistically be solved by an unaided human being: they have to run on computer systems.

become the well-known thesis of the "performativity of economics": the idea that economics (understood in a broad sense, not simply as the academic discipline) is not just an external representation of markets but intervenes actively in markets, indeed is part of how markets are constructed (Callon 1998; MacKenzie, Muniesa, and Siu 2007).

It is clear that, in high-frequency trading, action flows directly from artifacts (orders to buy or sell are placed by computer systems with no direct human involvement) and indirectly from assemblages of human beings and artifacts. The firms are typically small: a staffing complement of a hundred people makes you quite a large HFT firm, possibly among the two dozen largest worldwide. (A big organization such as a bank often has an old-established, slow technical infrastructure, and banks are structured bureaucratically, frequently with an IT department separate from trading teams; the combination of slow infrastructure and organizational separation makes the flexible, responsive development of fast systems hard.) The vast majority of an HFT firm's trading is initiated by its computer systems. The direct role of human beings is often restricted to monitoring the operation of trading systems and closing them down if things go wrong, for example if trading algorithms start incurring losses and for some reason do not shut themselves off. Less directly, though, humans do of course write the algorithms, and it is quite common for human beings to be allowed to select which algorithms to employ. In some "grey box" systems (as participants call them) the human user can also choose the values of one or more mathematical parameters of an algorithm.

HFT hasn't generally speeded up the pace of human work. One consequence of the often limited direct role of human beings in HFT is that they can experience less pervasive time pressure than in older forms of trading in which humans were more central. A trading room from an earlier generation was often a busy, noisy place. Information flowed into it not just from computer screens but also via telephone calls, conversations, and shouted interjections. "Hoot-n-holler" or "squawk box" systems—involving permanently open telephone connections among multiple traders and brokers—brought near-constant interruptions when markets were busy, and reacting to customer demands or market developments involved quick use of a keyboard or a succession of rapid telephone conversations. In contrast, the trading rooms of HFT firms are usually quiet—in my visits to them, I've never heard anyone shouting; phones almost never seem to ring—and while some traders can be seen focused intensely on computer screens, others have time to chat. The typical atmosphere of such rooms resembles that of a high-technology start-up company more than that of a traditional trading floor. With machines doing the direct trading, human traders can in many cases simply keep a loose eye on them while also (as interviewee AV put it) working on "long-term projects": researching and developing new trading algorithms.

Rather, the speed-up is of HFT as a material, technological practice. What follows focuses on one very specific aspect of that material practice: the communications links between the Chicago futures markets and the computer data centers in New Jersey in which shares—and also Treasury bonds, foreign exchange, and stock options—are traded. (If space permitted, a broadly similar account could be given of other crucial links, for example those that interconnect the New Jersey data centers or the transatlantic submarine cables.) The next two sections of the chapter explore the changing material forms of those links and how, as Wajcman might suggest, those forms have been and are being deliberately shaped for speed. There are trade-offs in the design of any technical system—interviewee SO, a specialist in telecommunications links for finance, quoted an engineer's saying: "you can make it fast, cheap or reliable, pick two"—and the trade-offs made in the design of the Chicago–New Jersey links discussed in this chapter quite consciously prioritized speed. The chapter's final section then emphasizes that, though those links are shaped intimately by the physical world and our knowledge of it, they are not "mere physicality": they are also social in at least four different senses.

## Transmitting Prices from Chicago to New Jersey by Fiber-Optic Cable

It's very tempting to theorize globalization as involving time speeding up and space shrinking (see, especially, Harvey 1989). In respect to trading, however, that formulation is only half right, as is pointed out in MacKenzie et al. (2012): precisely because the material activity of automated trading has speeded up dramatically, so geography and spatial distance—where exactly places are, and the shortest route between them—have taken on a new significance. The shortest, and therefore the fastest, route on the surface of the earth between any two places is what's called the "geodesic" or great-circle route. The world's financially most crucial geodesic—the spinal cord of US capitalism—runs from Aurora, a town in Illinois that's now an outer suburb of Chicago, to northern New Jersey (see Figure 4.1).

Aurora matters to global finance because in 2012 the CME, the Chicago Mercantile Exchange, relocated its electronic trading system to a new data center there. (Earlier, its trading system and thus the start of the crucial geodesic was in a data center called Cermak, just south of the Chicago Loop.) The CME trades futures: at first, futures on eggs, onions, and other agricultural commodities, but since 1972 financial futures as well. Originally, Chicago futures trading was done face-to-face (by voice, or eye-contact and hand signal) in raucous, crowded trading pits. The CME's pit traders fiercely

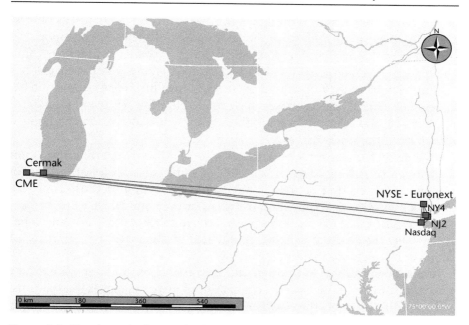

**Figure 4.1.** The six main financial data centers in the US. "CME" is the data centre of the Chicago Mercantile Exchange in Aurora, IL. The four data centres in New Jersey are where shares (and in the case of NY4, in Secaucus, NJ, bonds, foreign exchange, and options as well) are traded

resisted the coming of electronic trading: its leading advocate, Leo Melamed, received frequent death threats. By 2004, however, that resistance had crumbled, and now nearly all the CME's trading is electronic. (For discussion of the processes of change, see MacKenzie 2015.)

The CME's first fully electronic product was the E-Mini financial future, launched in 1997. It tracks the S&P 500 index, made up of the 500 leading US stocks. The buyer and the seller of an E-Mini each maintain a deposit known as "margin" on account at the CME's clearing house. Every night, the clearing house adjusts those deposits. If the S&P 500 index has risen by a single point, $50 is transferred from the seller's account to the buyer's; if it has fallen by ten points, say, $500 shifts from the buyer to the seller. If their deal is for a thousand E-Minis, the latter sum becomes $500,000. (The contract is called the "Mini" or the "little" because these transfers were five times larger for the contract that traders called the "big," the corresponding pit-traded S&P 500 future.)

Both the literature of financial economics (e.g. Budish, Cramton, and Shim 2013) and traders themselves in interview report that new information relevant to the overall value of US shares tends to show up first in orders for and in the prices of the E-Mini, and only a fraction of a second later in the underlying shares.[3] The likely reason is that the E-Mini gives greater "leverage": a modest "margin" deposit permits gains (and, of course, also losses) corresponding to buying or selling a large and expensive block of shares. So if traders think that they or their automated trading systems have an information edge, it has traditionally been to the E-Mini that they will turn first. For example, the big crises of modern US stock markets have tended to show up first in the E-Mini (or, before 1997, in its predecessor, the S&P 500 pit-traded future) and only a little later in the stock market.

Changes in the electronic order book for the E-Mini are crucial information for automated share trading (this particular game is now too fast for human players, who wouldn't be able to react quickly enough to those changes). Suppose the price of the E-Mini has fallen, or even simply that the number of offers (sell orders) has risen sharply and the number of bids (buy orders) has fallen. Over the next fraction of a second, falls in the prices of the underlying shares are more likely than increases.

The fact that changes in Chicago's futures order books and prices are closely linked to, and generally precede, changes in share prices makes the transmission of futures data to the data centers in which shares are traded a crucial matter. Originally mainly in New York, those data centers are now in New Jersey, where real estate is cheaper. For more than a decade, there have been concerted efforts to speed transmission from Chicago to New Jersey. By the time the E-Mini was launched in 1997, state-of-the-art transmission was via fiber-optic cable. That is intrinsically very fast: light signals in optical fiber travel at around two-thirds of what the theory of relativity posits as the fastest possible speed, that of light in a vacuum. For nearly all human purposes, therefore, the existing network of fiber-optic cables was fast enough, and the telecoms firms that had created that network had not been concerned with achieving further increments in speed. Rather, they chose paths (such as alongside railway lines) along which it was easy to negotiate permission to lay their cables, and shaped their networks so that they served the maximum number of large population centers. As will be discussed later, they also prioritized ease of repair over minimum cable length.

By the early 2000s, however, HFT firms were beginning to focus on the fastest possible transmission from Chicago to the East Coast data centers in which shares are traded. To begin with, it was difficult for them to get the telecoms companies even to understand their resultant concern with matters such as specific cable routes. They couldn't go to a company such as Verizon and ask for the fastest route:

---

[3] There is some suggestion in one of my more recent interviews (BU, interviewed in June 2015) that this pattern may be being replaced by more of a two-way interaction.

you could go to your Verizon salesperson, and they had no such product in their catalogue. They just sold circuits. The Verizon provisioning systems...didn't have the capacity to actually understand shortest path. They just knew you wanted a T-1 or a T-3 [or] whatever between point A and B, and they would provision on whatever [cables] happened to be available. And by the way, they would reprovision it [shift to different cables] if they needed to do some load balancing...they never actually thought that anybody cared [about the exact physical route]. (Interviewee SO)[4]

There were, nevertheless, databases of fiber-optic cable routes, including one constructed by CFN, a specialist network firm based just outside of Washington, DC. Using CFN's database, along with trial-and-error testing, a Chicago HFT firm discovered, in the early 2000s, an old cable laid several years earlier between Chicago and the East Coast by the pioneering Internet service provider UUNET.[5] From a standard telecommunications viewpoint, the cable was unimpressive. Its bandwidth (capacity) was limited, and to save money, UUNET had simply buried the cable in the soil, rather than laying it in conduits as was normal practice. However, UUNET had also sought to cut costs by choosing as short a route as reasonably feasible, largely following power lines across the countryside. That meant that the inferior, old cable was actually the fastest route between Chicago and New York/New Jersey. Eventually, the HFT firm succeeded in persuading the cable's then owner to lease it to the firm, and the resultant capacity of the firm's East Coast computer systems to receive Chicago prices faster than other systems helped it become a dominant player in share trading.

The next stage in the technological evolution of Chicago–New Jersey communications is the best documented (Steiner 2010; MacKenzie et al. 2012; Lewis 2014). It began with trader Dan Spivey's realization that existing routes were not the fastest possible (even the UUNET cable was still at some distance from the geodesic), and that a new cable closer to the geodesic was a commercially attractive proposition: any HFT firm whose algorithms depended on the fast transmission of prices between Chicago and the East Coast would *have* to use it, and would therefore be prepared to pay high fees to do so. With funding from the venture capitalist James Barksdale, Spivey's firm, Spread Networks, negotiated with dozens of local governments and landowners the rights to lay a new, more direct cable. Closeness to the geodesic brought physical difficulties—the Allegheny Mountains lay in the way (although interviewee SO reports that the extent of drilling through rock is implicitly exaggerated in

---

[4] T-1 (Transmission System 1) was the original 1962 AT&T digital-transmission specification, which was later reimplemented for optical fiber. T-2 and T-3 are higher-capacity versions.

[5] My main source here, interviewee SO, said that "couple" of firms discovered this cable, but other sources (interviewees AF and BQ) indicate that one particular firm gained control of this route.

existing accounts)—but Spread Networks overcame those difficulties, and also succeeded in keeping the project secret until shortly before its completion. The firm spent at least $300 million (one interviewee suggested it may have been as much as $500 million) laying the new cable, but its bet that HFTs would have no alternative but to pay large sums to lease strands of fiber in the cable from Spread turned out to be correct: former high-frequency trader Peter Kovac (2014: 3) reports that the fee was $176,000 per month, with a requirement to enter into leases several years long.

The new cable, which began to operate in August 2010, runs from Aurora through Chicago to Cermak, then along the south shore of Lake Michigan, across rural Indiana and Ohio, along the south shore of Lake Erie, and then across rural Pennsylvania to Carteret, New Jersey (the site of Nasdaq's data center), before finally turning north to 165 Halsey Street (the data center in Newark that is New Jersey's main telecoms hub) and then the other New Jersey financial data centers and Manhattan. This close-to-geodesic routing became its most celebrated feature. However, the prioritization of speed had other manifestations not discussed in the existing literature on the cable. First, when laying a normal telecommunications cable (see, for example, Figure 4.2), standard practice was and is for construction crews to add considerable slack (typically 5–10 percent of a cable's total length):

> [W]hen you run fibre you put slack in . . . you take the cable and you just coil it up at each of [the amplifier] centres or . . . in manholes, and the reason you do that is because every once in a while the fibre gets cut. Someone is doing construction, a train derails, a bridge abutment erodes, whatever, and the cable breaks . . . What you want is a cable that's a little loose and you can pull the two ends together, splice them together, and you're good to go. (Interviewee SO)

Spread Networks deliberately used much less slack:

> [A]t Spread there was a constant fight with the construction crews because they wanted to do what they've always done: "Why wouldn't you want slack in the network?" They didn't understand latency considerations: "Why do you care about a few microseconds [millionths of a second]?" (Interviewee SO)

Second, when optical fiber is used to transmit signals over large distances, those signals need to be amplified at intermediate points. As the Spread Networks cable runs across Indiana, Ohio, and Pennsylvania, there are eleven such points, which take the form of concrete bunkers. An HFT firm that leases a fiber in the cable needs to run that fiber through an amplifier in each of the bunkers. A telecommunications firm would place a general-purpose switch in each bunker so as to facilitate network interconnections, for example to nearby towns. Those switches, however, slow transmission, so the HFT firms

**Figure 4.2.** Fiber-optic cable being laid by a construction crew working for Skanova, a subsidiary of TeliaSonera. Courtesy TeliaSonera

using the Spread cable "would basically go just either straight optical-to-optical [amplification] or a very simple, lean electrical-to-optical and straight back, not going through a general switching fabric" (interviewee SO).

Third, modern fiber-optic transmission employs "dense wave division multiplexing," in which there are multiple channels of communication on a single fiber, which are kept from interfering with each other by the fact that a different wavelength of light is used for each. A telecommunications firm will want to maximize the bandwidth (capacity) of the fiber, so might use as many as a hundred different channels with different wavelengths. The firm will accept the fact that this dense packing causes a small amount of interference to take place, and to compensate for that will employ software that processes the messages being transmitted, adding extra binary digits to them that enable errors in transmission to be detected and corrected. This "forward error correction," as it is called, slows transmission, so HFT firms generally do not employ it. Instead, they pack many fewer communications channels (perhaps as few as ten) into a single fiber of the Spread cable.

Speed, however, was not the only imperative that imposed itself on the Spread cable: the other (perhaps surprisingly) was perceived fairness. It would have been hard to recruit subscribers if they had feared that other subscribers would still be able to have a speed advantage. So Spread devoted considerable effort to ensuring that this would not happen to a subscriber who paid for premium access.[6] The most important issue in this respect was paying close attention to the paths followed by different strands of fiber in each of the eleven bunkers, so as to ensure those paths were of equal lengths. Each bunker was only around 15 meters long, but as interviewee SO put it, "the reality is you're going up, down, and across, and so on. And if you do that eleven times it starts to add up." (The focus on this issue indicates the sensitivity of speed. Even "adding up," any path difference was likely to be only a small number of meters at most, and a signal moving at two-thirds of the speed of light in a vacuum travels 200,000 kilometers—200 million meters—in a second.) So important was fairness that even the slight physical inhomogeneity of the material making up the different strands of fiber was compensated for, with the strands that had marginally lower refractive indexes made ever so slightly longer (by a small amount of coiling if necessary) to ensure transmission times that were as equal as possible.

## When Two-Thirds of the Speed of Light is Not Enough: The Shift to Microwave

What Spread Networks could do little about, however, was the basic physical effect that slows the transmission of light in optical fiber. Spread used True-Wave® RS fiber, which was the fiber with the lowest refractive index (and thus the highest transmission speed) that could be employed without increasing the number of bunkers. Its refractive index, however, is around 1.47 (Lucent Technologies 1998; the exact value depends on the wavelength being used), which means that light travels in it at just over two-thirds of its speed in a vacuum (see Table 4.2).

There was a much older form of data transmission that did not have this drawback: radio transmission through the atmosphere, especially using microwaves transmitted along a series of towers (see Figure 4.3). The refractive index of the atmosphere varies with air pressure and temperature, but close to the earth's surface it is typically around 1.0003, meaning that wireless signals travel at around 99.97 percent of the speed of light in a vacuum. That physical fact was well known (for example to those who designed the Spread cable), but they also knew that because of the curvature of the earth, multiple towers with microwave repeater equipment were needed. This equipment introduced delays that—although imperceptible to human senses and of no consequence

---

[6] There was a second tier of subscribers who paid lower fees, but experienced a transmission time around a millisecond slower than the premium: "there was literally a cabinet that the fibre just went around and around and around until it added a millisecond in ... delay" (interviewee SO).

**Figure 4.3.** A microwave tower used by McKay Brothers. Courtesy McKay Brothers

**Table 4.2.** State-of-art one-way transmission times, Aurora, IL to Carteret, NJ (the location of Nasdaq's data center) in milliseconds (thousandths of a second). The relativistic limit is the time that would be taken by transmission along the geodesic if it took place at the speed of light in a vacuum

| | |
|---|---|
| Prior to Spread Networks | c.8.00 ms |
| Spread Networks (August 2010) | 6.65 ms |
| Limit in glass fiber (refractive index 1.47) | 5.78 ms |
| Best current microwave (2015) | c.4.01 ms |
| Relativistic limit | 3.93 ms |

Sources: Laughlin, Aquirre, and Grundfest (2012) and miscellaneous.

in the normal uses of microwaves in telecommunications—more than used up any speed advantage that microwave might have over the new cable.

At least three people, however, realized that delays in repeater equipment might simply be the result of its designers not focusing on speed. One was a Soviet-educated computer scientist, Alex Pilosov, who had emigrated to the United States, did consultancy work for various Wall Street banks, and had set up a business as a high-speed Internet provider; the others were Robert Meade and Stéphane Tyč, both physicists who had done extensive work in finance. Their enquiries to manufacturers about the speed of their repeater systems were met first with incomprehension—"they would not understand the question"—and then inability to answer: "the radio manufacturers did not even know how fast they [the repeater systems] were" (Tyč interview).

Pilosov found a small Czech company whose repeater equipment was fast by the standards of the day; as with the UUNET cable, its speed was an accidental by-product, in this case of the simplicity of its design. He paid the company to change its equipment to increase the speed further, and raised funds (by selling his house, borrowing as much as he could, and finding an HFT firm to back him) to construct a microwave link from Chicago to New Jersey. There was a plethora of existing microwave towers that could be used, but considerable work (largely done by Pilosov himself) was needed designing the network: researching feasible routes; checking that interference with other signals would not be a barrier to approval from the Federal Communications Commission; doing the structural calculations to show that the towers were strong enough to support the new microwave dishes; and persuading municipalities to give their permission to install them. By 2010, however, Pilosov had his new link up and running.

Meade and Tyč had met as physics PhD students at Harvard University, and the two closely linked firms they set up, McKay Brothers and Quincy Data, were named after Harvard's Gordon McKay Applied Science Laboratory and Quincy House. They were better resourced than Pilosov, and worked more slowly: they were aware that their new link would face eventual competition, and focused on designing it in such a way that it would be very hard for a competitor to be as fast or faster. To do so, they had to break with existing traditions of microwave network design, which had placed great emphasis on reliability and virtually none on speed:

[W]e realized . . . that networks did not have to be designed in the "old and conservative way". Microwave engineers had applied recipes which worked perfectly but which imposed constraints that we relaxed. This relaxing of engineering constraints allowed [us] to focus on the most important constraint for us which was the total path length. We ruthlessly optimized this parameter to create a long lasting network. (Email from Tyč, October 1, 2014)

Meade and Tyč placed some of their repeater stations much further apart than had been previous practice. Doing this minimized the number of stations and thus the delays they caused, but it was also necessary because a route close to the geodesic involved a lengthy crossing of Lake Erie (and in the case of signals from Cermak, also Lake Michigan) (see Figure 4.1). Their longest "hop"—the gap between towers—was around 110 kilometers. "Most microwave engineers will tell you that this is crazy stupid," says Tyč, because those engineers believed that transmission would become unreliable or even infeasible over that distance (Tyč remembers one engineer even "saying that microwave links over 50 km were not possible"). Meade and Tyč's understanding of the physics of microwave transmission, however, made them confident that their long lake-crossings were feasible.

The pursuit of speed required more than simply long hops. The US Federal Communications Commission makes a number of wavelengths available for microwave networks, including 6 GHz (gigahertz), 11 GHz, 18 GHz, and 23 GHz. From the viewpoint of the reliability of a microwave link, 6 GHz is best: as frequency increases, links become more vulnerable to disruption by rain. If, however, McKay Brothers had restricted themselves to 6 GHz they would have had to depart from the geodesic: part of the process of getting the Federal Communications Commission's permission to create a new microwave link is an analysis of whether it is likely to interfere with existing links, and there were simply too many existing 6 GHz links close to the geodesic. So Meade and Tyč's firm used not just 6 GHz but also some 11, 18, and even 23 GHz frequencies to keep their route as close as possible to the geodesic, even though they knew it increased the likelihood of disruption by rain. "[W]e had a little motif: better be first 99 percent of the time than second 100 percent of the time" (Tyč interview).

The new McKay Brothers' link, completed in 2012 but reworked almost continuously since then, has indeed remained in general the fastest (the HFT firm that had gained control of the UUNET cable built its own microwave link from Chicago to New Jersey, and it briefly surpassed McKay Brothers in speed in late 2014). The McKay Brothers' link also achieved, and indeed soon considerably surpassed, the firm's goal of 99 percent availability. Nevertheless, it (and the other microwave links between Chicago and New Jersey, including that created by Pilosov) still remain to some extent vulnerable to the physical world: to rain, to gales—which can blow microwave dishes out of alignment and make it unsafe for workers to climb the towers to realign them—and even to lightning (interviewee SL reported that his firm's equipment on one tower was "fried" by a lightning strike because thieves had stolen the copper grounding wire). Even the benign summer sunrise and sunset over the Great Lakes can be a problem for some networks: it can heat the upper atmosphere more than the lower, changing refractive indexes in a way that causes microwaves to "bend up," and "then line-of-sight is shorter than expected," which can cause a link temporarily to fail (email from interviewee SL, relayed by my colleague Alexandre Laumonnier).

## The Material and the Social

As Tyč put it, in what turned out to be the first of three interviews with him: "in the end, all [trading] firms will need to have some kind of microwave service. Otherwise they'll base their decisions on stale data. It's as simple as that, really. It's physics." As the previous two sections of this chapter have shown, the physics of data transmission along capital's geodesic is indeed important. Meade and Tyč's background as physicists also helped give them the confidence to depart from standard practices in microwave engineering. But what is at stake is not simply physics.

First, physical processes are intertwined with economic ones. Laughlin, Aguirre, and Grundfest (2012) show that the two most consequential changes in transmission technologies from Chicago to New Jersey—the opening of the Spread Networks' cable in April 2010 and of the McKay Brothers' microwave link in August 2012—had effects that can be traced in the movements of US share prices. As Laughlin and his co-authors put it, "an appreciable fraction of the entire U.S. equities market responds...to just a few bits of information emanating from suburban Chicago and travelling via various channels and between 4–10 milliseconds, to suburban New Jersey"—and the speed with which it does so increased as state-of-the-art transmission times have fallen as sketched in Table 4.2. That is an effect of "the technological" on "the economic," but traders' anticipation of that effect was of course what led to the economic investments that created the Spread cable and the various microwave links.

One of Tyč's firm's clients told him "that there is a new saying" in the markets: "when it rains, the spreads are higher in New Jersey," in other words automated trading systems in the share-trading data centers in New Jersey post less aggressive prices (bids and offers that are not as close to each other) when the microwave links from Chicago—and perhaps also the millimeter wave links among the New Jersey data centers, which because of the high frequencies they use are especially vulnerable to rain (MacKenzie 2014)—are disrupted. Of course, that is simply an anecdotal observation, not an econometric finding, but the fact that it is said, and is plausible, demonstrates the interweaving. Just as the pursuit of speed has given spatial location renewed importance, so it has created a link between financial markets and weather whose existence in the twenty-first century is striking.

Second, as I have emphasized, the pursuit of speed of transmission of price data from Chicago to New Jersey has involved conscious trade-offs (for example between speed and reliability, and speed and ease of maintenance), resulting in design decisions that were different from those typical of the wider communications industry. The resultant fiber-optic and microwave links along capital's geodesic are thus "socially shaped," to use an old expression from the sociology of technology (MacKenzie and Wajcman 1985): their design, and the priorities manifest in it, bear the imprint of the circumstances of their creation.

Third, the circumstances that have led to these substantial technological enterprises are an example of what Krippner (2001: 785) calls "congealed... struggle." The details of that struggle cannot be treated here (they will be discussed in MacKenzie forthcoming), but its core was the long-standing desire of Chicago's futures markets to trade stock-index futures. For decades, that desire had been blocked by the fact that, because an index is a mathematical abstraction, it is extremely clumsy to settle a futures trade on an index by anything other than a cash payment from the buyer to the seller (or vice versa). US law, and indeed the law of many countries, considered a futures contract that can be settled only in cash as a wager, and therefore illegal under the law of Illinois and indeed of most states of the US. Circumventing this obstacle was a tortuous and conflictual process that involved the creation of a new Federal regulatory body, the Commodity Futures Trading Commission (CFTC), via legal amendments in 1974 to the Commodity Exchange Act. The latter is a Federal act that pre-empts state law, and there is no Federal ban on gambling, which made activities within the domain of the new regulator (including trading cash-settled stock-index futures) legally permissible.

Hence capital's geodesic. Because US futures trading has been dominated since the nineteenth century by Chicago, the geodesic begins there. As noted earlier, US shares were and are traded almost exclusively on the East Coast; hence the geodesic's end-point. It is also important that this share trading falls within the jurisdiction of a different, and often rival, Federal regulator, the Securities and Exchange Commission (SEC). (The SEC and CFTC fought repeated "turf wars"—some even ending up in the courts—concerning juris-diction over products such as stock-index futures that straddled their domains.) It may seem odd that two intimately interlinked sets of financial instruments (stock-index futures and stocks) should have separate, sometimes rival regulators, but the division between the SEC and CFTC is deeply entrenched, and reinforced by the geographic separation: if it were proposed to roll the CFTC into the much larger SEC, fierce resistance could be expected from Illinois's Congressional delegation. It also matters that the SEC reports to the Senate Banking Committee, while the CFTC reports to the Senate Agriculture Committee (the origins of US futures trading lie in agricultural products), giving the two regulators separate political power bases.

The fact that futures trading and share trading fall under different regulatory regimes permits the former's leverage advantage (referred to earlier), which is what has made futures prices a strong predictor of share-price changes. Since the Great Depression, the extent to which US shares can be traded using borrowed money (a process that contributed to the 1929 Crash) has been tightly controlled, reducing the "leverage" available to those trading shares. In contrast, the "margin" deposits required in futures markets have historic-ally been much lower, so a futures contract economically equivalent to a large block of shares can be traded with much higher leverage than could be employed in trading the block directly. This economic relationship is specific to the "congealed struggle" just described. For example, the relationship between Treasury bond futures and the underlying bonds is more two-way, because high-leverage trading of Treasury bonds is possible using the collat-eralized borrowing arrangements known as "repo" (interviewee AC; Brandt, Kavajecz, and Underwood 2007). The relationship between currency futures and currencies is, if anything, the reverse of that in shares, because big banks can trade currencies with no margin deposits at all, and thus in effect with infinite leverage. So price changes in currencies tend to lead changes in currency futures, reported interviewee AV.

Fourth, the facts that changes in the order books for US stock-index futures have tended to lead changes in the markets for the underlying shares (and that futures data can be transmitted from Chicago to New York and New Jersey fast enough to make profitable trading possible) have been an important contribu-tor to a change in the very nature of share trading. Over the past thirty years, new share-trading actors (in the actor-network-theory sense) have come into being, involving different configurations of human beings and non-human artifacts: high-frequency trading algorithms. To be profitable, the latter need to be able to predict price changes, not on the basis of subtle, human phe-nomena such as a fleeting look of fear on a fellow trader's face or a change in the "feel" of a trading floor, but using relationships of a quite different sort: relationships that can be programmed not just into a computer system but in many cases into one that is simple enough to be very fast.[7] The relationship between futures and the underlying stocks is by no means the only such relationship (others are described in MacKenzie forthcoming), but historically it was the most important resource for price prediction. It was central, for example, to the algorithms of Automated Trading Desk (set up in Charleston, SC, in 1988 and in a sense the first ever HFT firm: see MacKenzie forthcoming) and to those of the futures trading firms that in the 2000s established dominant positions in share trading.

The rise of these new algorithmic actors—now to be found not just in the futures markets and stock markets, but also in the trading of Treasury bonds, options, and foreign exchange, and in Europe, East Asia, and Brazil, not just in the US—has changed many financial markets utterly. In stock markets, for example, a "topological" shift is underway, already largely complete in the US, less so in other countries. The shift is from trading as an activity conducted "inside" exchanges, to exchanges and other trading venues being "nested" within trading, in the sense that those venues now have to compete fiercely for market share, and to do that they have to provide the technical features that facilitate the operations of algorithmic actors (MacKenzie and Pardo-Guerra 2014).

This topological shift is an example of why a material sociology of markets—including a material sociology of ultrafast trading—is needed. Epochal changes are taking place in finance, and to understand them we have to examine markets as embodied, physical, and technological phenomena, not simply as "social" or "economic" phenomena (if those terms are understood in abstraction from the technological). The story of capital's geodesic is thus emblematic of wider shifts in finance that urgently require analysis, especially from the viewpoint of the sociology of speed.

---

[7] A story roughly equivalent to that of communications technology could be told for the computer technology employed in HFT, where there is an increasingly tendency to minimize the use of the main memory and central processor unit of general-purpose computer systems and to use simpler but faster hardware, especially FPGAs (field-programmable gate arrays) (see MacKenzie 2014).

# 5

# Digital Cultures of Use and their Infrastructures

*Saskia Sassen*

The technical properties of today's digital interactive domains deliver their utilities through complex ecologies that include non-digital variables, such as the social and the subjective, as well as the particular material conditions within which users work, act, or live. One synthetic image we can use is that these ecologies are partly shaped by the particular social logics of diverse domains and by the pertinent material enablements. When we conceptualize these interactive domains in terms of such ecologies, rather than as a purely technical given, we make conceptual and empirical room for the necessary infrastructures as well as the existence of diverse cultures of use. This type of inquiry, then, can extricate from the usual mix of assertions or givens the fact that such digital capabilities are socio-material events or conditions.

This mode of conceiving of the matter brings to the fore the possibility of a broad range of uses and of users as well as a broad range of absences of at least some types of uses and users. It opens up a research agenda aiming at identifying and recognizing the possibility of different modes of access and modes of using these technical facilities: it is not enough to specify that the facilities exist and that there is access. We must ask who has access, what it takes to get access, and what different users might be able to extract from existing digital domains. Further, also critical is the range of domains and modes of access, which might privilege some types of users and neglect others—the actual infrastructure might not deliver the same speed of access in all settings. None of these should be considered givens, as is so often the case when the technology and access exist. They are not givens but variables, with many diverse possible mixes of technologies and access depending on larger contexts and a range of variables.

With this type of conceptualization, the focus shifts from the fact that the technologies exist and that there is access to an inquiry as to the possible variations in quality of access and in quality of modes of access, as well as lack of access and lack of instruments for access. There is a broad range of uses and users, and these in turn vary by location. Some, like finance, get what they want out of these technical capabilities and from the entities where they are developed; indeed, over the last two decades, the financial sector has been a major actor pushing the development of particular technical capabilities. At the other extreme, there are users and potential users who do not have easy access, and more importantly, do not quite get what they need out of existing applications and modes of using these technologies.

Such disjunctures also make visible the limits of common, often unexamined notions implied by familiar representations: e.g. "everyone can benefit from these technologies because they exist and many people are already using them" (e.g. Houlne and Maxwell 2013; Bauer and Latzer 2015). Recognizing that these are socio-material conditions opens up a research agenda as to access and use (e.g. see Wajcman 2015). It is not simply about the fact that such digital capabilities exist. These capabilities are made and so are their infrastructures and software, and since societies contain vastly different opportunity as well as marginalization structures, we must allow for the fact that not all potential users and potential types of uses are necessarily in play. Some types of potential uses may not be sustained by existing software, and some users may lack access.

The next three sections examine these types of issues by focusing on three diverse domains, giving most of the attention to the first and less so to the second and third.[1] One is the insufficiency of applications that meet the needs of low-wage workers and low-income neighborhoods: there may be both connectivity and an enormous range of apps in the city where they are, but none of it meets their specific needs.

The second section focuses on high finance: here the aim is to examine to what extent the logic of finance has often little to do with these digital capacities, even if the latter are a critical instrument for doing what finance does. This entails a sort of dis-embedding of finance from its digital encasements, and to show that just because these technologies are critical to finance we cannot presume to understand finance through these technologies. Again, there is here a larger socio-material condition at work.

The third section focuses on mostly immobile local activists who have gained a sense of global connection to others around the world doing their type of activism: the effort here is to capture the fact that communication is

---

[1] All three cases are part of larger research projects. Details of these studies found in Sassen 2005, 2012, and 2013.

but one property of interactive digital networks, and that in many cases activists gain a sense of connection and membership just from the fact that they have that access, even if they rarely use it. One effort here is to interrogate the dominant understanding of the nature of "communication" in discussions of digital interactive spaces. In each case there is far more in play than technical capacities or exchange of information. Wajcman and Dodd's notion of a socio-material configuration fits these three cases.

I will begin with the absence of adequate software for low-wage workers at their workplace and in their neighborhoods.

## Misalignments: When Connectivity Is There but Not the Apps

One angle for a critical socio-material analysis of digitization is the fact that the availability of digitization does not ensure the existence of digital apps that meet the needs of particular types of social groups. I examined this specific type of misalignment in a recent study on low-income workers, their workplaces, and their modest/poor neighborhoods where I found a serious lack of apps geared toward their specific needs (Sassen 2015). The larger context for that study is the US, especially New York City—in short, places where one can, in principle, access all the digital capabilities in existence. Further, this is also a context marked by the deployment of a broad range of apps developed for scientific settings and for high-level professional settings; in the case of the latter, the apps are mostly available both at the workplace and at home (e.g. Schawbel 2014; Kvochko 2014; Hislop 2015). In short, professional workers can count on a vast array of apps to benefit from existing "global connectivity" (e.g. Anderson and Rainie 2014).

Against this background, a focus on population groups and settings not well provided with apps that meet their needs can contribute yet another angle into a critical socio-materialism about digital technologies.

In the US, most digital applications available in consumer markets are geared to the middle classes and high-end workers and households; the world of science, technology, finance, and other such sectors is a whole domain unto itself, and not the focus here. But very little has been developed to meet the needs of low-income workers, their families, and their neighborhoods. At the same time, data collected by the Pew Center indicate that most of these low-income workers and their families have access to digital apps, and are willing to spend some money on acquiring apps, but these are mostly confined to what can be bought in regular consumer markets, notably music and other entertainment apps. Further, the data also show that digital access among low-income people is overwhelmingly through their phones—especially Android phones, rather than through computers or iPhones. This turns out to be another constraint that leaves many low-income potential users of digital apps at a disadvantage insofar as there are far more apps developed for iPhones than for Androids. In short, there is a shortage of innovations that meet the needs and constraints of low-wage workers.[2]

We can conceive of this as yet another instance of shortcomings in generalizing accounts about digitization. This shortcoming becomes visible through a socio-material approach to digital applications: the fact that these apps exist does not mean that the needs of the full range of potential classes of users are addressed. Against this set of conditions, I focus on how digital innovations can address the needs of one specific class of potential users: low-wage workers, their families, and their neighborhoods. I will focus on new applications geared toward low-income people and neighborhoods mostly developed by non-commercial entities (notably doctoral students!).

Among high-end workers: digitization has become a way of restructuring not only their workspace but also the living space of these workers. It is increasingly inconceivable today that the high-end worker can or does simply leave it all behind when closing the door of her *office* for the day—on those few days every week when s/he might actually work in the office.

We can say the obverse for the low-wage worker: it is a fiction to expect s/he can simply leave it all behind when s/he closes the door of her *home* and goes to work. This asymmetry between the situation of professional and low-income workers is yet another way of showing the limits of generic categories such as "global connectivity."

My core hypothesis in the larger research project on low-wage workers is that what would most enable low-wage workers is the digital connecting, even if partial, of the spaces of work and neighborhood—I emphasize neighborhood, not home. This would be the systemic equivalent of the high-end worker who has a fluid interaction between home and work. Important for low-wage workers is that digitization can help transform the neighborhood into a *social* backup system, which might in turn be a first step in a larger trajectory of strengthening the neighborhood as a multi-function entity (Sassen 2015).

The home and the neighborhood have long been support spaces for the working class. Today, the home, the workspace, and the neighborhood are all underperforming when it comes to support, mostly due to changes in the condition of low-wage workers. Little attention, if any, has gone to exploring how digitization could help rebuild some strength in these spaces. For instance, in case of trouble (a sick child of a parent who is at work, police

---

[2] The major reasons why this matters are examined in Sassen 2014. An explanation of the asymmetries contained within the development of digital tools emphasized in this essay can be found in Sassen 2012.

violence, etc.) a digital application on all neighborhood residents' phones can be a call for quick deployment of neighbors, grandmothers, hairdressers, shopkeepers, and other somewhat stationary people. This can also become a first step in a trajectory toward greater neighborhood integration based, importantly, on practical issues (not a romantic notion of community) and expanded use of diverse digital capabilities.

I see here a strong instance of a socio-material assemblage that can be a support mechanism for low-income workers and that can strengthen the role of the neighborhood as a social backup system.

Two key assumptions organize my analysis. First, the lack of digital apps that meet the needs of low-income workers and neighborhoods is an added disadvantage for low-wage workers, their families and their neighborhoods. For instance, it reduces their capacity to connect promptly the three domains of their lives (work, family, neighborhood) when needed. Low-wage workers have their phones, but a telephone call is far more visible at the workplace (and likely to be seen as invasive by the boss in low-income work situations) than clicking on an app on their phones: it will do the work of communicating if the neighborhood is part of a network. In contrast we know that high-end workers (especially if they have small children) have a whole variety of connecting bridges to their homes (e.g. video-links to stay connected to their homes and nannies).

The second is that the sense of self-worth of workers can be enhanced by recognition from a larger social context, notably the neighborhood, and that this in turn has positive effects regarding collective initiatives at the workplace and in the neighborhood. One feature that matters is the possibility of mobilizing the neighborhoods as an active space that functions beyond workplace issues: a space of support in case of a health crisis with a child, for organizing a union strike, for *making* (as in urban agriculture, craft work, etc.). The activated neighborhood can enhance workers' sense of the worth of what they contribute to the neighborhood and to the larger society. High-end workers have long been praised for their contributions to society. But low-wage workers lack such recognition, so their community should generate it.

## Underutilization of Digital Apps in Low-Income Neighborhoods

Underutilization of digitization in the larger life-space of low-wage workers is a subject that we must address but has thus far received little attention. In contrast, digitization in the workplace has been the object of much research and attention for well over a decade.[3]

---

[3] This is not a new subject when it comes to the domain of work, see e.g. an older scholarship that dealt with these issue but never managed to penetrate the "techie" discourse (Autor et al. 1998;

I see this as a sharp contrast with the intense use of digitization in the work- and life-space of high-end workers. To remind us of familiar numbers let me quote a 2013 article.[4] These numbers have probably further increased for high-end workers, but less so if at all for low-income workers:

> In total, *30 million Americans* work from home at least once each week, which will increase by 63% in the next five years. About 3 million Americans never go to an office and 54% are happier working from home than in an office. Furthermore, *70%* of employees work from alternative locations (not just home) on a regular basis.

The key aspect that concerns me here is that this digital underutilization constructs a radical differentiation between work-space and life-space (i.e. the neighborhood) for low-wage workers. This is disabling and adds to the difficulties in their daily life at work and off work.[5] Neighborhood is here used as a somewhat generic term to capture a fairly large local area with reasonable transport and generally modest socio-economic standing of households.

The question then is what can we do with current technologies but are not doing because of diverse reasons: lack of resources, lack of motivation, lack of interest in low-income households, individuals, and localities, and so on. Important to this report, and too often overlooked, is that the types of digital applications that are being developed mostly do not address the needs/limited resources of low-income workers, their households, and their neighborhoods.

This is an especially unacceptable situation because data from diverse sources show that low-income individuals in the US *are* users of digitized devices, especially through mobile telephones, and particularly Android models. In one of their recent overviews, the Pew Center found that 45 percent of households living with less than $30,000 per year and 39 percent of those living on $30,000–$50,000 use mobile phones as their primary way to access the Internet. Email at home is rare. In a larger investigation on digital technology use by women across the world that I prepared for the United Nations Development Program, I found extensive use of mobile telephones by modest-income and poor women in poor areas of Africa: the mobile phone is what allowed these women to run their businesses, which were mostly diverse types of small-scale trading.

It is becoming increasingly clear that low-income households and low-income workers need mobile-friendly products (e.g. Graham 2014). The

---

Freeman 2002; Ellison 2004; Fountain 2005; for early studies on the social side, see e.g. Haythornthwaite and Weldman 2002; Ellison 2004).

[4] Rapoza (2013) finds that "One in Five Americans Work from Home: Numbers Seen Rising."
[5] Thus Richard Freeman finds that when the Internet took off it helped workers seeking to mobilize support: "This union is able to survive even though the probability of getting a collective agreement from IBM in the US is minimal because the Web offers it a low cost way to connect with IBM workers and the general public" (2002: 25).

use of web solutions is at this time limited, in contrast to what is the case for high-end workers both at the workplace and at home. The available evidence shows that music and other entertainment apps are those most used by low-income individuals or members of low-income households: these are standardized mass markets to which all consumers are welcome, including low-income buyers. But most available apps and most of the new apps coming online are geared to the middle classes, not to low-income individuals, households, or neighborhoods. For instance, there are long lists of apps for contacting or finding spas, high-end restaurants, and a long list of other such pricey luxuries. But there are few if any apps that give you information about a healthy food shop in a modest-to-poor-income area in a city. In short, what is absent is applications that address the needs of low-income individuals and households.[6]

### Useful Apps for Low-Income Workers and Neighborhoods

Several efforts are beginning to address some of these needs.[7] Here are a few examples of mostly recent applications geared to modest-to-low-income households and neighborhoods. Kinvolved is an application for teachers and after-school program leaders that makes it easy for them to connect to parents in case of a student's lateness or absenteeism. In many of our schools in poor neighborhoods, lack or difficulty of communication between the school and a student's home has allowed self-destructive conduct to worsen, damaging a student's chances of getting a job or acceptance to college. This app is simple and straightforward: when a teacher, or a coach, or whoever is part of the student's adult network at school, takes attendance or sees something of concern, the family is immediately notified via text messages or email updates—whichever they prefer. The low-income worker knows that if there is trouble s/he will be alerted.

Another app, developed by Propel, simplifies applying for government services, a notoriously time-consuming process. Now there is the option of a simple mobile enrollment application. Yet another such application is Neat Streak, which lets home-cleaners communicate with clients in a quick non-obtrusive way. There is also a money management app for mobiles which combines cash and loans requests, again simplifying the lives of very low-income people who need to cash their paychecks before payday, and can avoid the high interest rates charged by so called "payday sharks." But as yet

---

[6] It should be noted that there is sharp competition to develop apps and other features in specific markets—those that can generate revenues, see e.g. Waters and Kuchler 2014, or those are simply fanciful, see e.g. Takeuchi 2014.

[7] For more detail on the apps described here, see Sassen 2015; see also Aragon et al. 2009 for a different type of focus—including on children.

there are few such applications of use to modest-income workers and house-holds, compared with what is available in the high-end consumer sector.

A very different type of app from the aforementioned, far more complex and encompassing, is Panoply (presented by Robert Morris): an online interven-tion that replaces typical therapy involving a health professional with a crowdsourced response to individuals with anxiety and depression.[8] What I find significant here is that it has the added effect of mobilizing a network of people, which may be one step in a larger trajectory of support that can also become a local neighborhood network. Panoply coordinates support from crowd workers and unpaid volunteers, all of whom are trained on demand, as needed. Panoply incorporates recent advances in crowdsourcing and human computation, enabling timely feedback and quality vetting. "The therapeutic approach behind this system is inspired by research from the fields of emotion regulation, cognitive neuroscience, and clinical psychology, and hinges primar-ily on the concept of cognitive reappraisal." Crowds are recruited to help users think more flexibly and objectively about stressful events.

Another useful tool seeks to develop new ways of working together online (Aragon et al. 2009). This is something quite common among middle-class users and in certain professional jobs, but far less likely among low-income workers. And while it is not necessarily aimed at low-income workers and families, it could be extremely useful to the latter. It can enable a sense of individual worth to a network, and thereby solidarity and mobilization around issues of concern to low-income neighborhoods, families, and work-ers. Again, it can feed into individual worth ("I matter to my community") and a sense of collective strength. I would also highlight here tools for sex workers, enabling them to move online and gain strength through sharing informa-tion, and possibly organizing (see e.g. Grant 2013).

Then there are, of course, the fancier apps aimed at scientists or corpor-ations, but these should also become part of the tools (and experiences!) of low-income workers and neighborhoods. Here is one that might also be great for immigrants who have dear ones far away but need/want to be part of their education broadly understood. For instance, take a Filipino mother who is working as a nurse or a domestic worker in the US, and has her children at home, a very common fact. An MIT Media Lab project (The Communication of the Future Is So Real You Can Touch It)[9] aims at going well beyond the currently remote communication options by mobilizing one's sensorial response. Currently, remote communication (including that done in working environments) is an elementary, and in that sense incomplete, experience. The app aims at experiencing "a faraway friend's footsteps walking alongside

[8] Morris 2014.     [9] Baratz 2015.

me as we share an afternoon stroll. Different streams of interface broaden our meaning of a physical world" (see also the installation Mirror Fugue).[10]

An important long-distance option—though not as far away as the above example—is of course telemedicine, which for low-wage workers with constraints to their mobility given little home support, can be a major help. Or it can be used to argue the mobility constraints of low-wage workers, who may lack full time nannies, and may have elderly living at home, all of which reduces their options of leaving home (Sharon and Frank 2000).

## Apps that can Strengthen Collective Space

A second vector that I think should become part of the experience of low-wage workers is a sense of their worth in a general societal sense. High-end workers are often praised for adding value to our economies, for their intelligence and capacity to do complex work, and so on—recognitions, by the way, that are not necessarily always warranted. Low-wage workers should also be recognized as mattering for the larger social good. This has long been one of my research questions. Every epoch and every sector contains its own answers to this question.

There are diverse ways in which the worth of these workers as individuals can become a sort of collective good—meaningful to the workers themselves and to a larger community. One aspect that has long interested me is how even the poorest communities or groups of workers add to the public good and can experience *themselves* as adding to the public good.

The Netherlands provides a good example of such recognition of worth. Its health system is based on the principle of universal care. It includes a neighborhood system as a key part of the medical apparatus. When a patient can go back home but still needs care, the immediate neighborhood is promptly alerted and designated residents (who have time, and are not ill) organize themselves to ensure 24-hour oversight: the patient will at all times be able to use a simple app to call on the neighborhood caregivers, and the latter will also make regular visits. All these caregivers, but also the whole neighborhood, are recognized as being a sort of public actor contributing to the public good.

Positive neighborhood effects are a long-standing aspiration. Much of that was eventually lost. But it also always recurs. Thus fifteen years ago, Bailyn et al. (2001: 47–8), once again emphasized its importance. Let me quote at length:

> Communities have not been a large part of the thinking about work-family issues. Employees are viewed as being either "at work" or "at home," as if there were no

---

[10] Ishil and Xiao 2014.

larger context of social relationships and institutions outside of the family to which households and individuals belong. But it is the very "embeddedness"— or lack of embeddedness—of families and individual family members in specific communities that may determine whether employees can successfully negotiate the worlds of work and family. Similarly, it may be the embeddedness, or lack of it, of businesses in the communities in which they are located that determines their success in recruiting and retaining workers, and in selling their services or products. Employers and members of their workforces must acknowledge and contribute to the communities of which they are a part. The quality of community life is important to the survival of both employers and employees, and communities need the involvement of both to build and strengthen their capacity to offer livable environments for all.

This signals that the neighborhood can expand the knowledge-space of one's work-life. Key components of the neighborhood work-space we can think of are, among others, the use of digital technologies to work at home, to make what we now buy, to design for one's use or for sale. And it would make the neighborhood an interconnected space enabled by apps that are designed with low-income neighborhoods in mind. The key image is that even modest neighborhoods and modest-earning workers are immersed in spaces that collectivize specific needs of neighborhood residents.

The next two sections briefly examine the interactions between local and global dimensions in two major sectors—finance and civil society—as part of a critical socio-material perspective.

## Finance Depends on Digital Capacities but It Is Not About the Digital

The digitization of financial instruments and markets has been critical to the sharp growth in the value and power of the global capital market. But, it is important to recognize that high-finance is shaped by interests and logics that typically have little to do with digitization per se. This, in turn, brings to the fore the extent to which digitized markets are embedded in complex institutional settings that go well beyond the digital; this aspect is underlined in Dodd's (2014) analysis of the social life of finance which introduces yet another set of variables on this account. In other words, to a very large extent digital capabilities are mostly mobilized for specific financial logics—rather than finance being mobilized by specific digital features.

This is one instantiation that signals the importance of a larger context: the existence of digital capabilities is not enough to explain outcomes because there was and is a larger socio-material project at work, a fact documented two decades ago (see e.g. Sassen 1991/2001; Mackenzie and Millo 2003; Knorr

Cetina and Preda 2004). The mobilizing of such digital capabilities required material infrastructures but also cultural frames (Pryke and Allen 2000; Zaloom 2003; Thrift 2005; Lovink and Dean 2010), and even intersubjective dynamics (Fisher 2006). It is important to note that the raw power achieved by capital markets through digitization facilitated the institutionalizing of finance-dominated economic criteria in national policy. But digitization per se could not have achieved this raw power and this policy outcome—it took actual national institutional settings and actors (Harvey 2007; Sassen 2008: ch. 5, 2014: ch. 3).

In short, this supranational electronic market, which partly operates outside any government's exclusive jurisdiction, is only one of the spaces of global finance. The other type of space is one marked by the thick environments of actual financial centers, with their buildings and infrastructures and armies of blue- and white-collar workers. And these are places where national laws continue to be operative, albeit in often profoundly altered ways.

These multiple territorial insertions of private economic electronic space entail a complex interaction with national laws and state authority. The notion of "global cities" captures this particular embeddedness of various forms of global hypermobile capital—including, prominently, financial capital—in a network of well over forty leading financial centers across the world. This embeddedness carries significant implications for theory and politics, specifically for the conditions through which governments and citizens can act on this new electronic world, an aspect never attended to by politicians but long documented by researchers (e.g. Rosenau and Singh 2002; Latham and Sassen 2005; Sassen 2008: chs. 5, 8, and 9), though there are, clearly, limits (Wajcman 2002; Lovink 2008; Daniels 2009; Fernando 2010).

A key point to retrieve here for the larger argument of this chapter is that capital mobility requires capital fixity: state-of-the-art built environments, well-housed talent, and conventional infrastructure—from highways to airports and railways (Sassen 1991/2001; Chen and de'Medici 2010). These are all partly place-bound conditions, even when the nature of their place-boundedness differs from what it may have been a hundred years ago when it was far more likely to be simply a form of immobility, even if often partial. Today, such place-boundedness is a strategic enabler for hypermobility—one of the core features I document in my work on the global city by identifying the variety of facilities, regulations, and talents needed. But digitization also brings with it an amplification of capacities that enable the liquefying of what is not liquid, thereby producing or raising the mobility of what we have customarily thought of as not mobile, or barely so.

At its most extreme, this liquefying digitizes its object. Yet the hypermobility gained by an object through digitization is but one moment of a more complex condition that includes material immobilities. Even so, most writing about finance either implicitly or explicitly focuses almost exclusively on its hypermobility.

In turn, much place-boundedness is today increasingly—though not completely—inflected or inscribed by the hypermobility of some of its components, products, and outcomes (Sassen 2008: chs. 5, 7, and 8, 2014: ch. 3). More than in the past, both fixity and mobility are located in a temporal frame where speed is ascendant and consequential; one item often forgotten in general commentaries about finance, is the fact that the key infrastructure for mobility is not Wi-Fi but the very material and very fixed fiber-optic cables.

But this type of fixity cannot be fully captured through a description confined to its material and locational features—whether buildings or fiber-optic cables. The real estate industry illustrates some of these issues. Financial firms have invented instruments that liquefy real estate, thereby facilitating investment in real estate and its "circulation" in global markets via such instruments. The physical building itself has been transformed by the fact that it is represented by highly liquid instruments that can circulate in global markets. It looks the same, it involves the same bricks and mortar and stand there immobile, but it is a transformed entity.

Thus it is unlikely that the average resident of a global city sees the built environment of its corporate business and financial center as simply built fixity: there is most probably a projection of its globality. This is also a feature I sought to capture with my concept of the global city—the juxtaposition of such a city's vastness of immobile buildings and, at the same time, all their many diverse histories of internationalisms and emergent globalities of all sorts.

## Civil Society Goes Global but Mostly Stays in the Old Neighborhood

Perhaps the opposite kind of articulation of mobility and infrastructure from that of global finance is evident in a domain that has been equally transformed by digitization, but under radically different conditions. As with finance, it cannot be reduced simply to the fact that global connectivity became available. Unlike finance, the key digital medium is the public access Internet, and the key actors are largely immobile resource-poor organizations and individuals (for a range of instances see, e.g., Friedman 2005; Tennant 2007; Imbert 2008; Daniels 2009).

That even small, immobile, resource-poor organizations and individuals can become participants in electronic networks, began to signal already in the 1980s the possibility of a sharp growth in cross-border politics by actors other than states (Warkentin 2001; Khagram, Riker, and Sikkink 2002; Bartlett 2007). What is of interest here is that while these are poor and mostly immobile local actors, in some ways they can partly bypass territorial state jurisdictions by being part of trans-local networks, whose members they may never get to know personally. Though local, they can begin to articulate with others worldwide and thereby constitute an incipient global commons.

Their physical immobility is largely due to poverty, government-imposed constraints on their mobility, or, very often, due to the fact that their locality is the focus of their work. This produces a specific kind of activism, one centered on mostly immobile local residents in localities across the world, yet connected digitally and thereby de facto becoming a global force or event, even if one not centered in or based on communication. I consider it a crucial fact that communication may not be the most important transaction or key to becoming a global force among these types of efforts. There is a strong tendency to emphasize the communication aspect of digital technologies: I find it an important feature of the digital that there are many other capabilities in play that have little to do with communication in the narrow sense of the term—an overused concept when explaining the Internet. Many poor activist organizations barely have time or opportunities to be online regularly: the work is out there, on the ground. Similarly with speed: there is a strong tendency to see speed as one of the key features that these technologies contribute. Yet what really matters in the type of cases I focus on here is that a particular type of social tissue and ideational zone can be made through being part of a multi-sited, often global, network: "I am not alone" becomes a constitutive element in the experience of such activists, an assertion that across the world there are others as engaged and as confined to their locality. Perhaps the biggest contribution to this sense of connection and shared struggles is a sort of ideational space that is shared rather than frequent communication or speed. Nonetheless, even this ideational space is predicated on the existence of infrastructures that enable direct engagement with other groups across the world—in short, here we can also detect a socio-material condition.

We see the formation of types of global politics that run through the specificities of local concerns and struggles yet can be seen as expanding democratic participation beyond state boundaries. I regard these as non-cosmopolitan versions of global politics that in many ways raise questions about the relation of law to place that are the opposite of those raised by global finance.

## Conclusion

While the digital is an important factor present in each of these very different cases, using this generic term obscures different socio-material constraints and options, as well as differences in the importance of speed for diverse users.

Much is left out by the tendency to describe the digital in generic terms and by limiting the concept to the narrowly technical fact of connectivity and speed. We need to capture the specific ways in which each case presents distinctive modes of making the digital present in its particular logic. In the case of finance it needs the localized operations in global cities to construct, develop, and execute its global project. In the case of local activists it is the obverse: they need the global network to enable them to do their local activisms. And in the case of low-wage workers it is the need to connect to what is immediately there, their neighborhoods, in order to make a strong connective tissue that can offer needed support.

I want to conclude with a brief elaboration of finance. Electronic financial markets are an interesting case because they present themselves, from a distance, as perhaps the most extreme example of how the digital might reveal itself to be indeed free of any spatial and, more concretely, territorial conditionalities and frictions on speed. But in fact, we re-enter the domain of the socio-material because these technical capabilities, along with the growing complexity of instruments, actually generate a need for cultures of interpretation in the operation of these markets, and such cultures take time to develop. These cultures are best produced and enacted in financial centers— that is, in very territorial, complex, and thick environments because every leading financial center has strong specialized differences from other such centers, a fact typically overlooked in the generic literature on finance. Thus, and perhaps ironically, as the technical features of financial instruments and markets have become stronger, these cultures of interpretation become more significant in an interesting trade-off between technical capacities and cultural capacities (Sassen 2008: ch. 7, 2014; ch. 3).

We can then use the need for these cultures of interpretation as an indicator of the limits of the academic/technical features of derivatives and therewith recover the social architecture of derivatives trading markets. More specifically, it brings us back to the importance of financial centers—as distinct from financial "markets"—as key, nested communities enabling the construction and functioning of such cultures of interpretation. And the making of these cultures have temporal frames that are not necessarily speedy. The need for financial centers also, then, explains why the financial system needs a network of such centers (Sassen 1991/2001), and therewith the rise of global cities and their proliferation. Global cities are a more general, less narrowly technical instance of this same dynamic, including not only finance but also other specialized and globalized sectors. This need for a network of financial centers, and more generally global cities, in turn carries implications for territorially bounded authority, and signals the formation of a specific type of territoriality, one marked by electronic networks and territorial insertions. And here we are back to socio-material conditions.

# 6

# "A Pause in the Impatience of Things"

## Notes On Formal Organization, the Bureaucratic Ethos, and Speed

*Paul Du Gay*

The slowness and delay for which they like to blame us are nothing to be ashamed of. If you were to go to war unprepared, a hasty start could mean a drawn out finish. And the city we administer has always been free and always held in high regard: so this very slowness could well be called intelligent restraint. This quality has kept us, uniquely, from arrogance in success and from the surrender that others make to adversity. We are not seduced by the pleasant flattery of those who urge us to dangerous action against our judgment, and if anyone tries to provoke us with accusations, this is no more successful—we are not goaded into agreement. Our discipline makes us both brave in war and sensible in policy... We are not schooled in that useless over-intelligence which can make a brilliant verbal attack on the enemies' plans but fail to match it in consequent action. Rather we are taught to believe that other people's minds are similar to ours, and that no theory can determine the accidents of chance. It is always our principle to make practical plans on the assumption of an intelligent enemy, and not to let our hopes reside in the likelihood of his mistakes, but in the security of our own precautions. We do not need to suppose that men differ greatly one from another, but we can think that the strongest are those brought up in the hardest school.

Thucydides, *The Peloponnesian War*, 2009: 41–2

## Introduction

Strange as it may seem to modern managerial and organizational minds, there was a time when the terms "officious" and "officiousness" could commend the proper, prudent, exercise of authority, and the term "innovation" had purely negative connotations, signifying excessive novelty and speed without purpose or end (Condren 2006; Lepore 2014).[1] No longer. One of the most salient features of contemporary management and organizational discourse is the continuous reference to "change," "speed," "innovation," "disruption," and "reinvention" as indisputable ontological premises within the field (Peters 1987, 1992; Kanter 1989; Champy 1995; Keller and Price 2011; Christensen 2013; Linkner 2014). "Speed" and the other signifiers to which it is invariably attached in a "chain of equivalences" is frequently represented as an organizational imperative that trumps many other concerns (Thrift 2002; Grey 2009; Czarniawska 2013). Enhancing speed is therefore seen as a crucial feature of the business of organizing, and it is from this basic premise that organizational theory and practice is encouraged to depart:

> It may seem natural that all organizations would desire to be fast but the exact opposite is true. A majority of organizations and their corporate cultures are not fast at all; at best you could say that they instead move at "deliberate speed." Most firms don't move fast because it takes a special speed strategy in order to success-fully move fast, and many corporate leaders are risk averse, they avoid moving fast because they fear it may result in unnecessary risks and too many costly errors... [D]eliberate speed was fine until we entered... the 1990s, where intense global competition, rapid copying, and continual chaotic change now assigned some significant negative business consequences to slow organizations. And often that negative consequence is irrelevance... Firms... that are "built for speed" have grown and prospered because of that ability to move fast. (Sullivan 2013)

Certainly, this call to arms has not been ignored. No shortage of, often antithetical, theoretical, and practical approaches to "speed" and "change" have emerged within the field of organization studies, broadly conceived. Across the differences, however, "speed" is seldom specified in detail, but treated as a general and basic premise from which to theorize. Furthermore, "speed" is often treated as something that it is in itself good or bad (Tomlinson 2007; Czarniawska 2013). Accordingly, cases of "fast organization" are routinely intro-duced and analyzed as examples of general theoretical or epochalist axioms rather than as specific, concrete instances of reorganization from situation A to situation B. In other words, speed and change are typically conceived of and

---

[1] Edmund Burke described the French Revolution as a "revolt of innovation," for instance, while the Federalists were self-styled "enemies of innovation" (Lepore 2014).

represented as generic phenomena, which are more or less desirable and manageable depending on the point of view adopted.

The inclination to address speed both as an existential absolute and in a broad and general fashion seems to coincide with a declining interest in other topics in organization theory. As "speed," "change," "innovation," "disruption," "process," and "flux" have grown in theoretical and substantive prominence, traditional key concepts such as "core task," "distribution of work," and "exercise of authority" have correspondingly fallen out of favor. Such terms are increasingly considered as at best anachronistic, and at worst fundamentally misguided, being based, it is assumed, upon a nostalgic idea of the organizational world as in some sense stable and leisurely, and upon an equally quaint view of organization theory as a practical science that positively defines, describes, and evaluates this world. In much contemporary organization theory, the core object of analysis is less the organization as a distinctive entity than ongoing, multifarious, and often ephemeral processes of "organizing." Here, organizations are never fully established, but always in the process of "becoming"; tasks are not given bundles of activity to be undertaken, but the occasional result of interpretative processes; and actors are not engaged in practical, recurrent work, but in making-sense of, experimenting with, and enacting a fast, chaotic, and unstable environment.

"Change is inevitable. You need to decide. Will you drive that change or be driven away by it? Will you disrupt or be disrupted?," Linkner (2014: 1) states in his paean to speed, change, and disruption, *The Road to Reinvention*. Here, following clearly in the "visionary" religious and romantic footsteps of popular management and organization theorists such as Peters (1987, 1992), Osborne and Gaebler (1992), Champy (1995), and Christensen (2013), for example, Linkner lists a number of external forces (pretty much the same ones as the earlier authors articulated) that combine to make something euphemistically called "business as usual" an impossibility for each and every organization, no matter what its "core task" might be, and thus radical "reinvention" an absolute necessity: "fickle consumer trends, friction-free markets, and political unrest . . . dizzying speed, exponential complexity, and mind-numbing technology advances" all coalesce to produce a generalized context of panic, fear, asymmetry, and disorder in which only those willing to constantly "disrupt" can effectively survive. Or, as Tom Peters (1987) put it almost thirty years earlier (but in pretty much identically evangelical terms), organizations and managements are operating in an increasingly chaotic environment that has the capacity to destroy them if left unrecognized and unconfronted. The enemy, in the form of globalization, new technology, hard-to-please consumers, and unprecedented competition is at the gates and threatens to lay waste the promised land which has been betrayed by unwieldy organizations (most notably, of course, the formal organization, particularly its bureaucratic manifestation) and complacent, self-satisfied managements. If organizations and the persons who work for them are to survive and flourish in a "world turned upside down" they need to alter themselves and their modes of conduct completely. The old order is passing away, the traditional ways cannot work, and there is a need for radical change, increased speed, and constant reinvention. However, salvation is at hand if, and only if, you receive the prophet's spirit and "face up to the need for revolution" and "achieve extraordinary responsiveness": that is unprecedented speed (Peters 1987: 3–4).

Using this sort of evangelical rhetorical strategy (one that will be familiar to readers of Christensen, Linkner, or Keller and Price), Peters sets up a dynamic of fear, anxiety, and discontent. An atmosphere of generalized threat is articulated—what could be more threatening but less specific than the chaos of infinite speed?—whose veracity cannot be questioned or tested, but simply accepted or rejected (the founding statement that the world is now chaotic is a profoundly religious assertion). Recasting specific circumstances into general polarities that create polemical comparisons out of non-comparable terms (likewise in Christensen, Linkner, et al.), an aggressively polarized world is conjured up in which organizations are either conspicuously successful— those adept at fast change so they can "thrive on chaos" (disrupt, innovate, reinvent), or doomed to failure. There is nothing in between. The idea that forced options are often false options is never countenanced. As Ronald Moe (1994: 111) put it in relation to the enactment of Osborne and Gaebler's (1992) (Tom Peters inspired) reinvention agenda in the US Federal Government—*The National Performance Review* (NPR)—"a theological aura" permeates contemporary programs of "fast" organizational "change" in the private, public, and not-for-profit sectors. Focusing specifically on the NPR, Moe argued:

> The report largely rejects the traditional language of administrative discourse which attempts...to deploy terms with precise meanings. Instead a new, highly value-laden lexicon is employed...to disarm would be questioners. Thus...there is a heavy reliance on active verbs—reinventing, reengineering, empowering—to maximise the emotive content of what has been a largely non-emotive subject matter...The administrative management paradigm with its emphasis on the Constitution, statutory controls, hierarchical lines of responsibility to the President, distinctive legal character of the governmental and private sectors, and the need for a cadre of nonpartisan professional managers ultimately responsible not only to the President but to Congress as well is depicted as the paradigm that failed. This paradigm is the cause of the government being broken in the eyes of the entrepreneurial

management promoters. It has not proven flexible enough to permit change to occur at the speed considered necessary in the new information-driven technological world. The report argues, somewhat deterministically, that the entrepreneurial management paradigm will prevail in the future. Those who question this paradigm are not merely incorrect, they have no place in the government of the future. (Moe 1994: 113–14)

Similarly, with Christensen and Linkner's claims concerning "disruptive innovation," Lepore (2014) writes, "[D]isruptive innovation as the explanation for how change happens has been subject to little serious criticism, partly because it's headlong, while critical inquiry is unhurried, partly because disrupters ridicule doubters by charging them with fogeyism, as if to criticize a theory of change were identical to decrying change; and partly because, in this modern usage, innovation is the idea of progress jammed into a criticism-proof jack-in-in-the-box." Like Peter's millenarian "chaos," "disruptive innovation" holds "out the hope of salvation against the very damnation it describes: disrupt and you will be saved" (Lepore 2014).

The work of Peters, Moss Kanter, Christensen, Linkner, and so forth explicitly states that the contemporary "epoch" of speed—of fast and unpredictable change—requires new organization theories and new organizations. The old adages and axioms and the organizational reality devices or arrangements associated with them are simply irrelevant to the present and future. However, in this chapter I will argue that the phenomena gathered together under the contemporary heading of "speed," "change," and its associates are not absent from the canon of classical organization thinking, but addressed there in rather different ways. In the tradition of organizational design for instance, speed and change are not viewed as overarching norms (whether good or bad), but in terms of the chosen adjustments in the relations between an organization's goal or purpose, its organizing mode and its integration policies. In many classic texts on organization and management, "speed" is not represented as an abstract entity—a thing in itself, that an organization must relate to or "acknowledge"—but a relevant concern insofar it designates a specific modification of an organization's key features: its core tasks, work roles, product line, authority structure, or its allocation of resources, for example. Throughout this chapter I seek to provide some examples to substantiate the hypothesis that detailed specification of particular organizational arrangements—rather than "speed" and "change" as general and epochal assumptions or assertions—is the best, indeed the only possible starting point for organizational analysis and action. In other words, to adopt a useful and realistic stance toward organizational analysis as a practical science requires scholars and practitioners to both provide and work from precise specification rather than highly general or abstract assertions or assumptions about speed, organizations, and their relation one to the other.

## Purposive Pace

> Disciplined routines get a bum rap in today's world, where we celebrate
> spontaneity and often look for the game-changing sprint to the end zone.
> But this war was a marathon, and distance running had taught me the
> importance of pace. Moreover, it was my message to the force that we
> couldn't be rattled: In times of both quiet and chaos, we would maintain a
> calm, disciplined, even rhythm.
>
> General Stanley McChrystal, *My Share of the Task*, 2014: 162

As indicated in the previous section, contemporary discourses of organizational change tend toward being both absolutist (change is undeniable, it is
everywhere and you can't escape it) and highly abstract (its imperatives
require speed, flexibility, innovation, creativity, enterprise: the list is as endless as the practical operationalization of its imperatives remains remarkably
underspecified). While it is clear that such discourses have some intuitive
rhetorical appeal—offering, for instance, a powerful set of generalizations
that can act as a catalyst for "transformation"—it is not at all obvious how
such abstract injunctions are to be acted upon, practically, and whether their
lack of precision and specificity has some serious implications for the appropriateness of particular changes in different organizational settings. After all,
as Peter Drucker (quoted in MacDonald et al. 2006: 271) once argued: "the
function of management in a church is to make it more church-like, not
more business-like," thus raising the question as to the appropriateness of
applicability of generic "speed strategies" to the "core tasks" of different sorts
of organizations.

It was a key maxim in classic organization theory that the nature of the
management task, and the appropriateness of the management methods
deployed, can be defined only in relationship to the particular purposes, or
"core tasks" of the organization to be managed. When it comes to "speed," the
differences between organizations—their distinctive missions, their varying
obligations to differing constituencies, and their typical ways of specifying
and addressing ethical questions, for instance—are as vital as their similarities.
It is unlikely that they will experience "change" in an identical manner—as an
abstract phenomenon—but rather as a particular matter of concern, with
distinctive characteristics and practical implications related to the conduct
of concrete aspects of their activities. If this is indeed the case, then it is
unlikely that a generalized "speed strategy" would be appropriate to them
all. Indeed, without a clear sense of what an organization's core tasks are, and
equally precise concepts through which to formulate the conditions of their
attainment, generalizations about speed, and injunctions to "become fast,"
"change," and so forth are at best somewhat gestural or gratuitous, and at

worst potentially quite destructive. We can begin to specify this more precisely by introducing some cases:

## A Pause in the Impatience of Things

> If our civilization breaks down, as it well may, it will be primarily a breakdown in the administrative area. If we can make a real contribution toward preventing such a breakdown, I believe this contribution will be in the administrative area.
>
> W. B. Donham, quoted in Khurana 2010: 189

In his prize-winning trilogy charting the career of an Australian woman employed in the League of Nations in Geneva during the interwar years, Frank Moorhouse (1993) has some interesting things to say about the various different ways one might come at the relation between formal organization, especially bureaucracy, and speed.

The story of Edith Campbell-Barry, a would-be ideal-typical bureaucrat, is told against the rise and fall of the fortunes of the League, which is, itself, for Moorhouse it seems, a model of the ideal-typical public organization. At an early point in *Grand Days*, the first book in the series, soon after her arrival in Geneva we find Edith stealing in and out of the office of the Secretary-General of the League. Edith is not the official leader of the institution. Rather, she is a recent and rather junior recruit. However, she is a very principled new recruit and is keen, impatient even, for the League to live up to what she considers to be it's better nature.

Edith is, in fact, impersonating the real Secretary-General, Sir Eric Drummond, by using his office, his official stationary, and his forged signature to send out letters to groups around the world that Edith thinks deserve the official support of the League. She is convinced that what she is doing, while informal, spontaneous, covert, and unofficial, is in fact ethical because it is in the cause of true principle, as she sees it. She literally cannot bear the thought that those in need of support are failing to receive it because of the (slow) pace at which the League's operations are conducted. The organization's cumbersome, formal rules and due process obligations undermine its capacity to live up to its pressing moral obligations, as she views them. She wants to bypass all this red tape and get things done ASAP.

At a crucial juncture, however, one of Edith's colleagues, Florence, who has become aware of what Edith is up to, asks her to use her access to the Secretary-General's office to send a memo out internally to some of their colleagues. Florence has none of Edith's high-minded zeal, she just wants them to concoct a humorous message under the auspices of the Secretary-General's office so that their colleagues will be impressed by their wily skills.

At this point, Edith begins to have doubts. She wonders what would happen if everyone took it upon themselves to act as she had, and, in effect, to "pursue private policies by stealth"? How dysfunctional and potentially catastrophic for the fulfillment of the League's "core tasks" or purpose this could be. Edith suddenly sees the episode from the Secretary-General's point of view. And from this perspective she gets a sense of how important it is for employees to act within the confines of their respective offices, and to be on guard against the temptations of impatience, impetuosity, and heart-led enthusiasms. She begins, indeed, to see the significance of what Weber (1994) termed "the ethos of bureaucratic office-holding":

> Formalities and procedures were the wisdom of human organization and were in themselves civilizing instruments. She knew that now. When she was younger she'd opposed all red tape. Not any more. Red tape was often just a way of causing a pause in the impatience of things so that everything could be properly checked and considered. She realized that when enthusiasm and dedication had been expended, an organization had to leave in their place a bureaucracy. (Moorhouse 1993: 178)

There is a particular lesson about bureaucracy and speed to be drawn from this tale, and about the problems that attend the institutionalization of a disposition of " restless eagerness," or "enthusiasm," and it is one which has been learned, often at some cost, time and again in any number of formal organizational settings. It is one that Weber (1994) articulated in his political writings, and one with which Franz Kafka (2015), perhaps surprisingly to some, concurred. We find it articulated in recent times, for instance, in official investigations into events surrounding the decision to go to war in Iraq conducted on both sides of the Atlantic (in the UK, the Hutton and Butler inquiries, for instance), and in official investigations into various corporate collapses in the wake of the financial crisis (the 2010 Valukas report into Lehman Brothers; the 2013 UK Parliamentary Committee on Banking Standards report into HBOS, for example). While no organizational form or technology is immutable, particular organizational stances can nonetheless continue to have some traction, some value, for the securing of particular purposes. The bureaucratic ethos and the pause it engenders in the impatience of things, including that restless eagerness, characteristic of what Walt Whitman described as "the never ending audacity of elected persons," and which Anthony Kronman (1993) associated with the "adherents of every great political simplification," is one such stance. A valuable one here and now, and probably in the future. Or so I shall argue.

In the USA, official reports into the Iraq adventure voiced considerable concern over the manner in which the threat posed by international jihadist terrorism had been invoked by the George W. Bush presidency to jump established lines of authority in various areas of government, not least in intelligence gathering and appraisal, and military interrogation, for example, in the pursuit of greater speed, flexibility, adaptation, and innovation in countering what was represented as an entirely unprecedented situation (Holmes 2009). The assumption here was that "security" could only be assured if existing machineries of government and the lines of authority they gave rise to were bypassed to accord with the urgency, novelty, complexity, and so forth of the perceived terrorist threat.

According to the Head of the CIA, the aim of many of these measures was to: "end business as usual, to cut through red tape, and give people the authority to do things they might not ordinarily be allowed to do ... If there is some bureaucratic hurdle, leap it" (Tenet, quoted in Betts 2007: 142).

Likewise, in the UK, the Hutton and Butler reports (the Chilcot Report (a public inquiry into Britain's involvement in the Iraq war and its aftermath) was reported after this chapter was written. If anything, its conclusions concerning the organization and operations of government are even more devastating) shed considerable light on to the organization of government under the premiership of Tony Blair, indicating in so doing how constitutionally surprising and administratively disabling the Blair regime's informal "style of organizing" with its emphasis on speed—of decision making, or of delivery, for instance—at the expense of structure, system, and process, had proven to be (Hennessy 2004; Quinlan 2004; du Gay 2006).

In one way, the often rather unedifying picture of a far from "joined up" administration in action that both the Hutton and Butler reports provided was neither that surprising nor particularly disturbing. Rather, insiders considered it indicative of the "fog of government" that anyone who had any intimate knowledge of the workings of Westminster and Whitehall for any length of time would be familiar with. However, that said, there were significant exceptions to that relaxed recognition. Of crucial import here was the evidence elicited by Hutton of the "remarkable informality (to use no sharper term)" of how the business of government was transacted under the Blair premiership, which, as Quinlan indicates, "was surely an uncomfortable surprise, even to cognoscenti" (2004: 125). The Butler Report also made much of what it described as the informal "sofa style" of government operating in and around No. 10 Downing Street, and voiced some remarkably adverse comment upon how the relationship had come to function between career civil servants, most especially those working in the intelligence services, and figures in the prime minister's inner circle. That report ended with what was, in its context, a dramatically critical six-paragraph conclusion about the general way in which the prime minister had organized and conducted his administration.

One key facet of this, as a number of commentators pointed out, was a suspicious and hostile attitude toward traditional relations of authority and formality within governmental administration—to bureaucracy; this attitude derived in no small part from what Peter Hennessy termed the particular "managerial pair of spectacles" through which the governing party viewed the purposes of governmental administration. Interestingly, the entire Labour shadow cabinet had been given "pre-office" training in contemporary management and organizational thinking at Templeton College, Oxford, in 1996, and the attempts to operationalize the norms and techniques introduced to them at this time—on "change," "culture," "innovation," "leadership," "performance," and "delivery," for instance—were core elements of the Blair "style of organizing." Hence the importance attached to cultivating an informal "all on one team mentality" that overrode established distinctions of office, function, and authority, with inculcating a "just do it" ethic among public servants, and with the unprecedented deployment of partisan appointments—special advisers and other "irregulars"—in key positions in governmental administration, some vested with constitutionally anomalous powers to issue orders to civil servants (thus accentuating "the problem of authentication"[2] outlined by Chester Barnard (1938/1968) in his classic *The Functions of the Executive*).

A cocktail of inexperience in government, suspicion of official machineries of administration, and a remarkably uncritical belief in the powers of their own favored forms of managerial "modernization" proved lethal to established conventions framing the conduct of governmental business, as the scene disclosed by Hutton and Butler made only too clear. Changes in the machinery of government, often reflective it was noted of *a marked impatience with due process and collective, deliberative decision-making*, appeared to have had some serious downsides, though, ones that could have been predicted in advance, if due consideration had been applied (Edith at the League, again). As Quinlan (2004: 127) argued, it was not at all clear that the changes initiated always rested upon "sufficient understanding that existing patterns had not been developed without practical reason." In that context, the revelations elicited by Hutton of the extent to which, under the Blair administration, the traditional bureaucratic practices of careful and precise note-taking and writing of minutes had fallen into abeyance were both striking and worrying. It was seen most vividly, perhaps, when Jonathan Powell, the prime minister's (partisan and thus constitutionally and organizationally "unauthenticated")

---

[2] In brief, this means that a particular member of the organization issuing an order must be known to occupy "the position of authority" requisite to the domain covered by the order; in other words, "that the position includes the type of communication concerned—that is, it is 'within its authority'; and that it actually is an authorised communication from the office" (Barnard 1938/1968: 180). Barnard says that such practices of authentication often differ within and between organizations, but that the basic structure and purpose of these practices remains remarkably consistent: "Ceremonials of investiture, inaugurations, swearing-in, general orders of appointment, induction, and introduction, are all essentially appropriate methods of making known who actually fills a position and what the position includes as authority. In order that these positions may function it is often necessary that the filling of them should be dramatized, an essential process to the creation of authority . . . that it, it is essential to inculcate 'the sense of organization' "(1938/1968: 180).

chief-of-staff, disclosed to James Dingemans QC, the senior counsel at the Hutton Inquiry, that, of an average seventeen meetings a day in Downing Street, only three were minuted:

A. No minutes were kept of this meeting or subsequent meetings we are probably going to discuss, no.

Q. Is that the normal course, that they are just discussions and no-one is bothering to write them down because they are free flowing, as it were?

A. Yes, I thought I might be asked that question because it may seem odd to people from outside, so I looked through the diary for the two weeks of the period we are talking about and the usual pattern is about three written records for 17 meetings a day is sort of the average you get to because there is no purpose served by minutes unless they are either recording people visiting from outside, the president of Nigeria, or something like that, or if they are action points that need to be taken forward, something on school funding for example.

Q. The only documents that Lord Hutton effectively is going to look at, and I think you have very kindly supplied some of these over the weekend, are e-mails that people sent to each other after meetings or before meetings following up on discussions.[3]

What Butler famously described as "the informality and circumscribed character of the Government's procedures" seriously risked "reducing the scope for informed collective political judgement." As another former Cabinet Secretary, (Lord) Richard Wilson (2004: 85) commented in relation to this point:

formal meetings and minute-taking, for instance, might seem overly "bureau-cratic" and thus very un-modern technologies, yet they play a crucial practical role in ensuring good government and provide a necessary underpinning for the realization of constitutionally sanctioned authority and accountability require-ments by ensuring a proper record of governmental decision-making existed and that agreed actions are clearly delineated.

Linked to this, both Quinlan and Wilson indicated concern with the govern-ment's near-exclusive focus on "delivery" at the expense of attention to structure, system, and due process. As Quinlan (2004: 128) put it, a singular focus on delivery can easily

slide into a sense that outcome is the only true reality and that process is flum-mery. But the two are not antithetical, still less inimical to one another. Process is care and thoroughness; it is consultation, involvement . . . legitimacy and accept-ance; it is also record, auditability and clear accountability. It is often accordingly a

---

[3] Hutton Inquiry website <http://image.guardian.co.uk/sys-files/Politics/documents/2003/08/20/August18AM.pdf> (accessed June 2016), paras. 94 and 95.

significant component of outcome itself; and the more awkward and demanding the issue—especially amid the gravity of peace and war—the more it may come to matter.

The informal and personalized ways of doing business established at No. 10 also had serious repercussions for the possibility of the Cabinet exercising the constitutionally important role of "collective responsibility" on what Butler described as the "vital matter of war and peace." As Hennessy (2004: 73) argued:

> the Butler Report suggests that the reliance on "unscripted" oral presentations from Mr. Blair and the ministers in his inner group on Iraq, without supporting papers ("excellent quality papers were written by officials but these were not discussed in Cabinet or Cabinet committee") meant that it was..."obviously much more difficult" for Cabinet ministers on the outer rim to test out the evidence and arguments of the inner circle even though the discussion ranged over 24 meetings of the full cabinet.

Wilson (2004: 85) agreed, adding that the danger of "informality" is that it can "slide into something more fluid and unstructured, where advice and dissent may either not always be offered or else may not be heard. This is certainly a matter which engages collective responsibility."

The demands of the "just do it" ethic with its focus on speed of delivery via "a see no problems, can do pair of spectacles," and the absence of thorough analysis and of the bureaucratic system for conducting it was conspicuously displayed in a number of other governmental farragoes (du Gay 2006). What Hutton and Butler suggested, though, was that this was not simply a reflection of the "normal" complexities of governing, but rather a widespread feature of a particular "style" of government; a product, in large part, of a attempts to bypass established machinery, and the rules and procedures they gave effect to, in the pursuit of its own form of what Jane Caplan (1988), in another context—the National Socialist one—described as "government without administration." In Quinlan's (2004: 127–8) words, as a result of the Hutton and Butler enquiries it looked increasingly like the Labour government had little interest in or tolerance for distinctions of function, authority, and responsibility "between different categories of actor within the Government machine (except perhaps when political defences needed to be erected, as over the purported 'ownership' of the September 2002 dossier)." Rather, "there was a sense of all participants—ministers, civil servants, special policy advisers, public relations handlers—being treated as part of an undifferentiated resource for the support of the central executive." In attempting to bypass established bureaucratic lines of authority—to "jump the line" in Chester Barnard's words—politics literally ran riot.

## Formality and Conservation: Some Concluding Comments

> I found Supreme Headquarters a fascinating place ... It was full of interesting people, not least persuasive young men interested in selling short cuts to victory, of which they held the rights of way ... Few of them had anything really new to say and the few that had, usually forgot that a new idea should have something to recommend it besides just breaking up normal organization.
>
> Field Marshall Viscount Slim, *Defeat Into Victory*, 2009: 233

So reflex has become the assumption that formal organization and the bureaucratic ethos or stance are anachronisms, fundamentally out of synch with the demands of the present and imagined future—"zombie categories" as Ulrich Beck (2002) put it—that no sooner are their potential enunciated than they are immediately problematized and what the organizational sociologist Charles Perrow (1979) dubbed the "customary view" of bureaucracy—the one we might say that led to all the trouble in the first place—is once again reasserted.

At the beginning of his classic essay, *Complex Organizations*, Perrow (1979) noted that formality and bureaucracy had largely been negatively coded by sociologists and organizational theorists, for instance, and that many of the same criticisms of them appear time and time again throughout the history of sociology, social theory, and organizational studies (Perrow 1979: 6). He pointed, in particular, to two enduring lines of criticism that are central to the "customary view" and directly impinge on the relationship between formality, bureaucracy, and speed. The first associates formal organization and bureaucracy with inflexibility, inefficiency, and, at times of rapid environmental change, with a lack of innovation and a pervasive unresponsiveness. The second, which he associates specifically with the pro-substance, anti-formality "whole person" humanistic tradition (a tradition more than well represented in sociological theorizing and analysis), represents formality and bureaucracy as stifling the spontaneity, freedom, and self-realizing, self-actualizing capacities of organizational members. He notes too, that both lines of criticism are often combined by a single author and "are echoed by the right, the left, and the unaligned" and concluded that, despite its enduring popularity and reach, the "customary view" was a busted flush: "the sins generally attributed to bureaucracy are either not sins at all or are consequences of the failure to bureaucratize sufficiently" (Perrow 1979: 5–6). For Perrow (1979: 200ff.) the bureaucratic ethos was not inherently un-adaptive. Rather, it could be seen as a many-sided, evolving, diversified stance that had proven "almost uniquely" capable of both "rule" and "response."

In his essay, Perrow (1979: 24–6, 44) offered an acute reconsideration of formality and bureaucracy as potentially positive, if often fragile, organizational achievements. In so doing, he had cause to turn at certain points to the work of Wilfred Brown, an experienced and successful business executive, minister of state, university pro-chancellor, and organizational analyst, who rose to prominence in the field of organizational sociology as a result of his involvement in the first major research project undertaken by the Tavistock Institute of Human Relations in the UK after the Second World War—The Glacier Project—but whose work is now largely forgotten.

Brown's experience of working within and empirically analyzing the operations of bureaucratic hierarchy in a number of contexts had led him to argue, against the "customary view," that bureaucracy was neither inherently pathological nor dysfunctional but rather, in contrast, something that could potentially enable an organization to employ large numbers of people and yet preserve both unambiguous work role boundaries and accountability for work conducted by those occupying those roles. In particular, Brown stressed that the very formalities, or so called "rigidities," of bureaucratic hierarchy were not antithetical to flexibility (or indeed creativity, or innovation, as so much contemporary wisdom has it), but rather its precondition (see also du Gay 2000; Stinchcombe 2001; or The Dogma '95 Manifesto). Instead of being seen as mutually exclusive, as the "customary view" within organizational theory had it, the one was seen as the condition of the other. For Brown, it was the relationship between the two that was important.

Brown could not stomach theorizing for its own sake, and was intolerant of what he described as the "extraordinary amount of dogmatically stated nonsense" on the topic of organization emanating both from academics and from people "of ample experience." For Brown, the "customary view" of bureaucracy was one such dogmatism, and he was at pains to indicate just how easy it was to slip into, and how much inner distance and self-discipline it took to avoid these sorts of trap, not least for practicing managers (Brown 1971: 114).

For Brown (1965a: 153), morally expressivist appeals to "informality" as the bedrock of organizational creativity, innovation, freedom, and flexibility—the sorts of appeals characteristic of the Blair and Bush styles of governing as well as admirers of "disruptive innovation"—were "the converse of my organizational experience." They were, rather, appeals to dis-organize; to return to what Brown saw as "a natural condition" in the Hobbesian sense. As Brown (1965a: 153–4) put it, "a deliberate policy of leaving organization unformulated is tantamount to the deliberate setting up of a situation of anarchy. I use the word 'anarchy' in its original sense, i.e. 'the want of government in a state'." Echoing Hobbes's statements about Law and Injustice, Brown argued:

> It is not absence of law, which allows creative use of discretion, but an explicit area of freedom bounded by the law which reduces anarchy and allows the individual

to make his [sic] contribution . . . A little reflection will surely enable each of us to see that we want a system of law, despite the fact that at times we find it irksome, first, because we desire to be protected from the effect of the unlimited decisions of our fellows and, secondly, because without limitations on our freedom of decision, we must carry unlimited responsibility.

Brown (1976: 289) stressed the need for an explicit acknowledgment that what he called the "executive system"[4] was "brought into being to perform the work of an organization, that its structure must be a function of such work, that it must be capable of constant adaptation to match the changes in the work, and that the total work must be divided between all the roles in the Executive System." He then posed the rhetorical question: "To what extent is this to be done with deliberation and in a statable manner," in other words, "formally," and, to what extent is it "to be left to be decided by the pressure generated by group and individual interaction," in other words, "informally?" (Brown 1976: 289). His answer is clear and precise:

> the salient result of the latter process is that the people involved in the situation lack full and consistent knowledge of who does what. The assumption made by some is that this is a situation of liberty for the individual, but is it not more accurate to say that such a situation is one where the right to do certain types of work is decided by the competitive ambitions and power positions of the individual concerned? Jones may well feel a need to carry a certain area of responsibility but, supposing that Smith equally feels that his needs can be met only by carrying that same responsibility, what then? If they are left to fight it out, that can scarcely be called a situation of freedom for either of them. (Brown 1976: 289)

Nor would it be a situation in which the efficiency of, or indeed prospects of survival for, the enterprise (and thus the securing of the purposes for which it was instantiated) was enhanced. No doubt informal groups are capable of improvising a kind of order, but what the latter is and how it contributes to the securing of an overall organizational purpose can only be known after the event, as a historical fact; there will be no prior, logistical guarantees. The latter, after all, is the provenance of "formality" (Stinchcombe 2001) and of "bureaucracy."

The antipathy toward restless eagerness ("the fast and loose"), enthusiasm, or impatience inherent in the bureaucratic ethos has its own *raison d'être*. While it is easy to see how such an ethos can be viewed by politicians, disruptive innovators, and others as a license to obstruct, it was, until comparatively recently, generally considered indispensable to the achievement of

---

[4] Brown (1965b: 307) defined an "Executive System" as comprising "the network of positions to which the company's work is assigned. It is made up of positions which shall be called 'Executive Roles.' The executive system includes all members of the operating organizations, a member being in his [sic] role while he is carrying out his job responsibility."

responsible (as opposed to merely "responsive") government, because it was seen to balance and even complement political will, making governance more effective in the long run.

As the American scholar John Rohr (1998) suggested, the bureaucratic ethos is in important respects necessarily unresponsive. The role accorded to governmental bureaus, for instance, has been deliberately devised to isolate officials from the electoral process, or from the demands of "special interests," for example, thus institutionalizing the very "unresponsiveness" which so many enthusiasts decry. And, it has been so organized to serve a positive political purpose—to help preserve a modicum of stability, consistency, and continuity, and institutional memory in the face of the vagaries and experimental enthusiasms of partisan politicians, for instance. In this specific and limited sense, the bureaucratic ethos is a conservative one, or better, a conservational one. Bureaucratic practices in governmental administration can be seen to provide some of the important "conservation standards" appropriate to the political management of the state, including the management of "change" within the state.

The bureaucratic comportment of the person therefore embodies an acceptance, which no moral zealot can really abide, of the irreconcilable diversity of human goods, and an awareness of the possible costs, moral and otherwise, of pursuing one end to the detriment of another. In this way, the bureaucrat tends to see in every controversial change to existing social arrangements the possibility of important losses as well as the opportunity for certain gains (Larmore 1987: xiv).

As a report into the "US Abuse of Detainees at Afghanistan Bases" put it, quoting a captain of the US Military Police: "It's extremely hard to wage war with so many undefined rules and roles" (quoted in Holmes 2009: 309).

# 7

# The Athleticism of Accomplishment

## Speed in the Workplace

*Melissa Gregg*

Recently the walls around my workplace started to change. Stepping off the courtesy shuttle one morning, a bus ride that links the Hillsboro fairgrounds with Intel Corporation's Oregon campus twenty miles west of Portland, I noticed a huge blue banner covering the front entrance of the otherwise anonymous building known as Jones Farm. "Moore's Law Inside: 50 years of Amazing Experiences Outside" read the sign, its electric hue hanging provocatively against the otherwise drab office exterior. Entering the vast cubicle hub that is JF-3, gracing the walls, foyers, and hallways linking various common areas, smiling employees populated posters and elevator doors, their names and full-sized body renderings superimposed over the new marketing slogan. The company blog, *Circuit*, invited us to nominate more amazing colleagues for the purpose of producing further publicity materials. Daydreaming in line for coffee, in a new campus cafeteria "inspired by Portland's food cart scene," I consider what to do if the sales and marketing team ask to use my photograph in a customized print trumpeting the benefits of having "Melissa Inside."

Most employees probably first became aware of Intel's "Let the Inside Out" campaign by way of a screensaver automatically downloaded in a regular security update foisted on our computers. For the duration of the Moore's Law anniversary month in April 2015, any company laptop left untouched for more than a few minutes reverted to a lock-screen and password request, along with the motivational prompt: "For 50 years Moore's Law has propelled us forward. Imagine what we'll do for the next 50." Through the many transitions in the course of an average day, the security screensaver doubles as a company refrain affirming the identity and integrity of the business, like an old IBM songbook or a pledge of allegiance. As an example of internal marketing, the terms of media[1] conditioning the workplace environment here are multiple, whether it is the vision and rhetoric involved in imagining the future, the projected confidence of believing that there will be fifty more years of any company, let alone Intel, and, perhaps most importantly for my own job, defining through sound bites the constitutive qualities of "amazing"—indeed, of "experience." As a "user experience researcher," my role is to take these words literally: to advise engineers on what counts as "delightful" for users, so that they can enable equipment manufacturers to turn such affective encounters in to "solutions" and ultimately products that can be built, packaged, and shipped.

"Cramming More Components onto Integrated Circuits," published in *Electronics* magazine in April 1965, outlined the phenomenal and at the time exponential growth of transistor power relative to size and cost. Based on retrospective accounting, Gordon Moore predicted computer chips would double in complexity every year, at little or no added cost, for at least ten years. A decade on, this forecast was revised to every two years, though the broader premise remained. "If Silicon Valley has a heartbeat, it's Moore's Law," Valley consultant Rob Enderle observed in a representative anniversary press feature. It "drove the Valley at what has been a historic speed, unmatched in history, and allowed it to lead the rest of the world" (Carey 2015). Enderle's repetitive and hyperbolic claim goes some way to capturing the ideological and financial stakes involved in high tech's growth narrative. "In the beginning, it was just a way of chronicling the progress," Moore himself admitted of his paper in an interview for the golden jubilee: "But gradually, it became something that the various industry participants recognized . . . You had to be at least that fast or you were falling behind" (in Carey 2015). In this sense, Moore's Law is better understood as a recursive loop in which a handful of influential companies race to confirm a hypothesis that was never intended to be permanent. This inflated athleticism—*the drive to keep up to speed with reassuring ideals of accomplishment backed by science*—is observable in three different moments of industrial production over the course of the last century. In this chapter, I turn to history to explain how ideas of speed came to be incorporated, quite literally, in the bodies of workers engaged in iconic forms of labor precipitated by new communication technologies. As we will see, the uptake of the typewriter, telephone, and transistor each contributed to an understanding of speed that became the basis for dominant notions of superior workplace performance, or what we often call productivity.[2]

[1] This chapter benefits from conversations at Leuphana University's "Terms of Media" conference, Lüneburg, June 2015. See the full conference description at <http://cdc.leuphana.com/events/event/the-terms-of-media/> (accessed June 2016).
[2] This chapter is an outline of arguments developed in greater length in Gregg (forthcoming). My focus on three specific media technologies is intended to reflect and extend Frederick Kittler's

How many workplaces claim to dictate the speed of production for an entire industry? Indeed, how many ideas that propel a company equate to a hypothesis of modernity? Intel's role in the ecosystem for hardware manufacturing and chip design is not without precedent. If Moore's Law's "tick-tock" cadence governs the temporality of Intel's fabrication plants, earlier moments of industrial capitalism reflect their own particular assumptions about the temporality of production. Fritz Roethlisberger and William Dickson's *Management and the Worker* (1939) is the much debated published version of what are known collectively as "The Hawthorne Studies": experiments at the Western Electric company in the Chicago suburb of Cicero in the 1920s and 1930s. Before the transistor's reign, the Hawthorne plant was the manufacturing subsidiary of the largest telephone company in the United States. American Telegraph and Telephone (AT&T) provided employment opportunities for thousands of Americans during the highpoint of welfare capitalism. Before the dormitory cities of present day Foxconn, or the stock benefits of CEOs and tech geeks, Western Electric hosted company picnics for workers living amid the imposing factory precinct just as it offered shares for employee purchase.[3] Headcount at Hawthorne nearly doubled between 1927 and 1929, from 21,929 from 40,272 workers (Gillespie 1991: 128). To assist with this vast expansion in operations, Harvard Business School researchers were hired to investigate retention and efficiency. What began as a simple and inconclusive "illumination study" gauging the impact of brighter lighting on output led to further exercises in various environmental and practical factors thought to affect employee performance. Amassing tens of thousands of interviews with factory personnel, the Hawthorne Studies remain the most comprehensive social science investigation of employees ever conducted in a single location for the benefit of broader consumption.[4]

The Hawthorne researchers followed and extended productivity premises established by pioneers of time and motion studies such as Frederick Taylor. Writing in an early issue of *The Efficiency Society Journal* in 1912, Henry R. Towne, president of the Yale and Towne Manufacturing Company, describes scientific management as "the effort to have the right article in the right place in the right quantity and at the right time." Like many industry captains of his era, Towne promoted the benefits of this new science, which

*Gramophone, Film, Typewriter* (1999) which, in offering a unique media history of the past century, somewhat downplays women's material contribution as assembly-line, infrastructure, and communication workers.

[3] The Harvard Business School's overview of both the Hawthorne Studies and the beginnings of Human Relations in industry is at <http://www.library.hbs.edu/hc/hawthorne/> (accessed June 2016).

[4] Today, with the growth of HR as a profession, companies are much more likely to conduct their own research of employees internally. The screen-based nature of so many jobs makes it easier to harvest employee data, with or without explicit consent.

assumes that minimizing unnecessary motions is in the interests of both worker and manager. Scientific management advanced the embryonic field of "fatigue studies" toward a more compelling synthesis of ergonomics and psychology. Workers' bodies came under greater degrees of scrutiny in the quest for what Taylor's contemporaries and sometime rivals Frank and Lillian Gilbreth called "the one best way" of competing a task (Lancaster 2004). In alliance with the stopwatch, film was the medium of choice adopted by these efficiency engineers in the early days of management consulting. For the benefit of supervisors, their methods of capturing movement and form could be used to "determine the situation" of the worker, in the sense that they provided the terms on which her performance could be judged.[5] From this moment on, the worker's capacity to manage time became a foundational principle of reward and recognition. Speed became the measure of accomplishment.

## Training Champions

Frank and Lillian Gilbreth's iconic workplace reform was reducing the brick-layer's stoop through the provision of on-site scaffolding. As a former bricklayer himself, Frank surmised the energy and effort that could be saved by placing bricks within arm's reach of the worker.[6] This principle was the bedrock for many subsequent reforms the pair would make in a range of locations. The archive of Gilbreth films provides before-and-after insight on the unnecessary motions involved in a variety of tasks, including card punch-ing, pear washing, soap packing, and produce labeling.[7] In many of the reels, a portly, officious, waistcoated Frank supervises proceedings and accompanying information slides and statistics. Productivity comes alive as both a quantita-tive and qualitative measurement in these initial forays into industrial PR, some of the first examples of promotional film (Curtis 2009). The camera's ability to track the worker's body, hands, and eye movements creates an unprecedented level of accuracy in recording the labor motions under obser-vation. Unlike the "stopwatch men," as the Taylorites were often known, the Gilbreths' films and other light-based imaging devices aimed to capture activities taking place at speeds beyond human perception. Providing an empirical basis for the physiology of labor, time and motion films summoned the spirit of more artistic chrono-photographers such as Etienne Jules Marey's

---

[5] Here I deliberately echo the determinism of Kittler's opening words in *Gramophone, Film, Typewriter*, even though my aim is to identify moments of resistance in the archaeology of media as it relates to the development of management thought.
[6] YouTube footage is at <https://www.youtube.com/watch?v=lDg9REgkCQk> (accessed June 2016).
[7] Available at <https://archive.org/details/OriginalFilm> (accessed June 2016).

mesmerizing renderings of human and animal form in motion.[8] The still images produced by the slow-motion camera enabled a new kind of awareness of the manifold movements involved in a task, a visual record of achievement. Applied to worksites, these technical systems had the benefit of removing managerial bias in capturing field data. For the first time, workers could see the activity upon which their performance would be judged. Trained to recognize and covet optimization—the principle of scientific management being to "eliminate waste"—the worker could begin to contemplate managing taskloads for himself. He could start to see the beauty and elegance in speed.

One notable demo in the Gilbreth archive shows the method involved to "train a lady to become a champion typist." Sitting at her desk and typewriter, the worker in this film calmly processes line upon line of text against the backdrop of a ticking clock.[9] Her fingers move, her left hand raises as she moves the carriage to return. The only break in output is to adjust the page and place a tick on the completed document. Departing from this set framing, a subsequent shot shows the typist's face in portrait style with particular attention focused on her eyes. The written slide explains the purpose of the film, to demonstrate "early studies of eye movements in conjunction with the motion of hands." Gilbreth's new keyboard layout minimizes both hand stretching and head turning. The wide eyes and demure smile playing across the typist's pale face convey delight at her industry as much as the modesty of an earlier era.

Next, the typist's hands become the focus for further close-up inspection. A grid of squares is transposed over footage of the busy fingers, assisting the measure of activity relative to the space occupied or touched in each square. The grid's addition is a development from the blank backgrounds of Malvey's films, producing a layer of scientific certainty to the visions on screen. Curtis (2009) explains the performativity of these Gilbrethian methods, which, through inventions such as the stereocyclegraph, made the most of photography's affordances. This apparatus involved applying tiny light bulbs to the hands of workers to photograph the smallest of motions. Capturing micro-movement for subsequent assessment generates a trace of labor otherwise lost. However accurate these representations may have been, their effect was to turn film in to a landscape of data ripe for survey and inspection. The Gilbreths enabled "one kind of image (detailed, moving)" to be transported and reified "into another (simplified, still)" so that the elements of a task could be identified. Their cinematic depictions of small-scale gestures created "a graphic image of what efficiency and inefficiency look like" (Curtis 2009: 93): a means of encouraging, by way of capturing, speed.

---

[8] A selection of these films are available at <https://www.youtube.com/watch?v=11lKItGNuiY> (accessed June 2016).
[9] Online at <https://www.youtube.com/watch?v=8iTOSgAnJ54> (accessed June 2016).

The portrait of the individual worker on camera is a new kind of labor performance, an act choreographed and directed for a witnessing audience. In *The Psychology of Management* (1904), the book arising from her PhD, Lillian Gilbreth makes an explicit link between the worker's desire to have their performance recorded for history and the ambitions of actors hoping to have their artistry captured for posterity on film. From this perspective, scientific management could be pitched as an obvious solution to workers' frustration at not having a record of accomplishment for the day's toil. The measurement of motion efficiency relative to output generates an archive of achievement, much like the actors and singers who were also "grasping the opportunity to make their best efforts permanent through the instrumentality of the motion picture films and the talking machine records." In Gilbreth's account, knowledge that the record will be compiled creates interest in the work, for with it "comes the possibility of a real, scientific, 'athletic contest'" (1904: 33–4). For the worker, attention "is concentrated on the fact that he as an individual is expected to do his very best." The psychological dimension to this is most notable:

> He has the moral stimulus of responsibility. He has the emotional stimulus of competition. He has the mental stimulus of definiteness. He has, most valuable of all, a chance to be an entity rather than one of an undiscriminated gang. (1904: 36–7)

Gilbreth writes at a time when Taylorism faced vocal criticism from workers concerned about its heartless quantification methods. She aims to assuage doubts by arguing that, "under Scientific Management, the spirit of individuality, far from being crowded out, is a basic principle, and *everything possible is done to encourage the desire to be a personality*" (1904: 48, emphasis added). In the case of the typist, working against her own previous record, embracing productivity becomes a way to match and better a previous version of herself, and, in turn, a way of being recognized. Gilbreth anticipates that individual performance will ultimately draw out new kinds of pleasures for workers that will rival the security and comfort of the group. "This chance to be an individual, or personality, is in great contradistinction to the popular opinion of Scientific Management which thinks it turns men into machines" (1904: 36–7).

The Gilbreths' introduction of motion to time-motion study is significant on multiple levels. Applied to manual work, the cinematic apparatus transforms the worker's conception of their job away from a team or gang to a personal achievement. This visual account, and the performance of productivity for a witnessing eye, coincides with the first mainstream experiences of cinematic vision. The intimacy of the close-up, focused particularly on the face and eyes, provides coordinates for appraising the worker as a particular kind of actor. The typist's gaze is offered for scrutiny, her movements open to mastery and replication given the assumed benefits of reform. Time and motion studies in this way educate viewers in the dynamics of empathy and recognition through filmic projection. Like the male gaze that would come to be associated with the pleasure of Hollywood narrative (Mulvey 1975), industrial film normalizes the manager's view of a world waiting to be optimized. Identifying with the recorded image turns work into a science, labor into information, and the worker into an individual. Improving upon one's own prior record becomes a seductive prospect as a mark of distinction. For the typist, accomplishing ever-greater productivity—becoming "a champion," in the words of the film—is a victory she alone can possess.[10]

## Mayo's Missing Women

It is precisely the principle of separating workers from each other and assessing individual contribution that we see in the Hawthorne experiments at Western Electric. In the most well-known study of the women in "The Relay Room," five assemblers and a parts assistant were chosen to work in an area shut off from the main factory floor so that their activities could be monitored. Recording outputs by way of an automated ticker, the workers' productivity was plotted on graphs reflecting their individual performance relative to each other and specific variables, such as hours of sleep.[11] Rest times, changes to starting/stopping hours, and free meal provision were just some of the measures used to test the relationship between motivation and speed. For the project's duration, the group's pay rate was calculated relative to the smaller team of contributors rather than the customary number of up to one hundred teammates on the regular shop floor. This financial incentive clearly matters to any assessment of the productivity gains among workers in the study, as is now recognized (Gillespie 1991: 55). In official records, however, these wage adjustments were downplayed in favor of the psychological and even physiological concerns of interest to the research consultants. The women varied in age from 18 to 28, and had Polish, Norwegian, and Bohemian heritage. Like the broader Hawthorne population, many were breadwinners for their first-generation migrant families. The pressure to maintain employment at a time

[10] Typing world championships were an annual event in the early 1900s, with press coverage often lamenting the limitations of human motion in relation to machine capacity. Robert Messenger's (2014) rich archive at *OzTypewriter* shows the stadium-size seating accommodating these spectacles of speed.
[11] Reproductions of the graphs can be seen in these samples from the HBS collection: <http://www.library.hbs.edu/hc/hawthorne/03.html#three> (accessed June 2016).

of growing economic instability (the study ran during the unfolding Depression in 1927–32) is a further consideration affecting the research findings, since the work itself was not obviously fulfilling. The work of telephone relay assembly "required manual dexterity, along with a willingness to repeat the same task every minute or so for almost nine hours per day, five and a half days per week" (Gillespie 1991: 51). Both hands were needed "to place pins, bushings, springs, terminals, and insulators between plates, insert a coil and armature, then screw the assembly together," equating to "thirty-two separate operations for each hand."

At the time of the Hawthorne Study, Harvard's Fatigue Laboratory was a test bed for the latest theories of employee conditioning and well-being, consolidating the emerging field of workplace ergonomics. Elton Mayo, the Harvard professor Western Electric held on a retainer, drew liberally on existing fatigue research in developing his own approach to employee productivity. His *Human Problems of Industrial Civilization* (1933) maintained that some workers were better suited to withstand the physical and mental effects of repetitive job tasks, a Darwinian principle accordant with the book's ambitious title. For Mayo, the "capacity to be unfavorably influenced by repetitive work differs between individuals in respect of, for example, what can be tentatively called intelligent endowment and temperament" (1933: 35). Not a trained doctor (he dropped out of medicine before fleeing his Australian homeland), Mayo was appointed to his first US academic post on dubious credentials (Trahair 2005: 198). His success at Harvard is typically attributed to a combination of charisma and suggestive if abstract ideas. As part of a wealthy Adelaide family, he mixed in high-class company throughout his life, networking successfully to attain his first teaching job at the University of Queensland. Mayo counted the anthropologist Bronisław Malinowski among his close friends. Intellectually, he drew from child psychologist Jean Piaget and Alfred North Whitehead alongside Freud, Jung, and other advocates of therapeutic technique. This heritage forms the conceptual frame for the vast schedule of interviews that would be conducted at Hawthorne. One-to-one dialogues carried out by specially trained managers were seen as essential to uncovering the basis of worker sentiment. Attention to the holistic social and personal life of the individual was thought to get to the heart of any grievances—or in Mayo's psychoanalytic parlance, "neuroses"—affecting performance on the job. The conviction that these details would provide suitable material for management also justified the unprecedented investigations in the Relay Room.

Records in Harvard's Baker Library show the data collected over several years of the study extended to organ health and blood count, in line with dominant ideas of fatigue studies and its relation to athletic capacity and fitness. Judgments conveyed in the records mix medical opinion, morality, and anthropological classification in assertions such as "body and ears normal" to "underwear is clean and sufficient." The information gathered about the five assemblers expanded beyond physical attributes to extensive investigations of home, neighborhood, and family life. To the Harvard researchers, any insight that could be gleaned from the outside work environment was fair game in the quest to uncover the secrets of enhanced productivity. Observations covered the content of workers' lunches, dental health, footwear choices and number of hours slept at night, in addition to more vague assessments ("she is subject to worries"). Moving the workers from the test room to a nearby clinic for medical examination added a further layer of scientific scrutiny and authority to the research program. The deliberate confusion of research, work, and medical interrogation side-stepped the power dynamics of employee/management roles and a host of consent issues: "The doctors exploited the doctor–patient relationship to ask the workers questions that the women might otherwise have been unwilling to answer," Gillespie (1991: 54–5) notes, "including the timing of their menstrual periods. A heavy paternalism suffused the relationship of the researchers to the workers and colored their perceptions."

This unique mix of physiological and psychological appraisal had distinct consequences for the women who failed to meet preconceived expectations. Adeline Bogatowicz and Irene Rybacki were two workers initially chosen for the relay assembly study whose conduct challenged the researchers' hopes for enthusiasm and obedience. Repeatedly scolded for talking too much during the workday, both girls were ultimately dismissed from the experiment for "uncooperative behavior" (Trahair 2005: 229). Hospital visits were the source of particular consternation for Bogatowicz, who was regarded as especially "antagonistic" on these occasions. Following her expulsion from the test room, she eventually left the company, leaving behind Rybacki, whose output had decreased in the lead up to Bogatowicz's marriage (2005: 230). The girls' friendship clearly impacted the speed and efficiency of the test room, even if the field notes of proceedings offer little sympathy to expand on such observations.

In his account of the troublesome pair, Mayo attributed Rybacki's deteriorating effort to a poor blood count. This retrospective diagnosis remained a favored piece of evidence used to promote the benefit of medical surveillance in workplace research. "Under medical treatment she rapidly recovered in respect of both cell count and haemoglobin percentage and in subsequent discussion disavowed her former criticisms of the Company," Mayo wrote: "She added that at the time of making these criticisms she was suffering a 'feeling of fatigue'—which was considered possibly to have been indicative of her organic disability" (1933: 114–15). As Gillespie (1991: 73) surmises, such observations reveal "a persistent tendency in Mayo's work to transform any challenge by workers of managerial control into evidence of psychiatric disturbance":

Rybacki's assertions that she would work as she liked became evidence to Mayo of fatigue and Bolshevism, and her objections to having her conversations secretly recorded were indications of paranoia.

Many years later, it still seems necessary to reiterate that this cornerstone study of productivity in the manufacturing era, a research program that influenced the theory and practice of management for decades, simply removed two workers that conflicted with its goals. Two of the five women resisted the most invasive aspects of the investigation, and did not bend to the efficiency imperative. This stance in turn prompted compensatory measures from management. The decision to allow small parties on the day of the doctor's visits—previously unthinkable privileges such as cake, ice cream, tea, and radio—was made in an effort to assuage the women's negative reactions to the indignity of scientific measurement. If such gestures were close to a form of bribery, they were also indication of the workers' determination "to influence the test room environment in exchange for their participation in the experiment" (Gillespie 1991: 59).

Of course, the removal of women deemed too talkative for the workplace is not just a familiar story, or a mere tale of silencing dissent; it confirms the burden regularly placed on women to embody dexterity and docility (Hossfeld 2001; Chang 2008).[12] Hawthorne shows that the productivity imperative failed to address all workers from the very beginning. The need for speed—the drive to enhance athleticism to lift output and improve efficiency—relied upon a neat combination of economic precarity, social subjection, and corporeal incursion. The paternalistic and coercive authority enacted by Mayo and his colleagues provided a pernicious basis for the emerging field of management and a worthy entry in the growing number of business ethics textbooks.

## The Productive Lifestyle

The forms of visual literacy and individual performance-monitoring inaugurated through these iconic productivity studies live on in today's self-quantifying technologies and computing devices. Lillian Gilbreth's intuition that worker and manager both benefit from the exercise of individual will anticipates the market for systems such as RescueTime,[13] one of many tools claiming to enhance productivity by way of an easy download. Productivity apps in this mode promise to remove the distractions and obligations of needy colleagues whose emails, updates, and instant messages demand diligent time

---

[12] As Kittler notes, writing of the typewriter: "It was precisely their marginal position in the power system of script that forced women to develop their manual dexterity" (1999: 194).

[13] <https://www.rescuetime.com/> (accessed June 2016).

management. Just like the filmic grid that isolated finger strokes in the type-writer era, Rescue Time provides personalized analytics of the minutiae of eye movement (screen use) and platform preferences through the course of a worker's day. Like the Gilbrethian camera, the app provides evidence of present performance that will prompt reformist reflections and an appetite for better future results. It epitomizes the managerial gaze while rendering it clandestine in the background of the screen. SwiftKey[14] is another, automated example of a "smart" keyboard that eliminates wasted motion by learning the keystroke patterns of phone and tablet users. Repeated spelling mistakes and word preferences are tracked and stored by the app to predict movements and generate future typing suggestions that "suit your style." The demonstration video even shows the zippy electrified lines charted by fingers as they dart around the keyboard, reminiscent of the Gilbrethian stereocyclegraphs. In the parlance of "user experience," one of the features making this app so appealing is the aesthetic of activity: the design performs efficiency by emphasizing smooth movement. It makes speed appear inevitably elegant and desirable.

Compared with the omniscient gaze of the assembly-line researcher or the minute observation of a slow-motion camera, productivity tools of this kind appear innocuous in that they are less obviously tied to power structures in the workplace. For one thing, the worker's body is no longer stuck in one place. Indeed, for users of software like SwiftKey—typically mobile, in-transit, and on-the-go—technology secures a regular and trusted interface for work against a regularly changing background. In these high-paced settings, the speed of communication is often regarded as a currency of employability: missing the right text or email could mean missing contention for the next contract or project. In this way, productivity tools today follow a wider pattern of enthusiast-driven data optics in that their adoption is *apparently* self-chosen. The option to engage in self-quantifying activities is voluntary even though there are clear social sanctions accorded to the productive lifestyle. Meanwhile, traditional regimes of efficiency and output continue to govern the hardware assembly line of material manufacturing (Sacchetto and Andrijasevic 2015) as much as "gray collar" service industries (Qiu 2009). In either case, software and logistics packages are the contemporary equivalent of the time and motion films that first taught workers to see "what efficiency looks like" (Curtis 2009). Rendering screen-based motions into data allows insight on the self we may otherwise never see given the fallibilities of human observation. Productivity tools enable the possibility of reforming workers' bad habits through enlightened instruction, a set of rituals for availability and right action. For knowledge professionals, the productive lifestyle is an

---

[14] <https://swiftkey.com/en> (accessed June 2016).

"aesthetics of existence" (Foucault 1977) that enables good practices to triumph over the many obstacles to "getting things done" (Gregg 2015). It is the end result of a series of technical innovations that allowed individuals to view themselves differently, namely, from the point of view of efficiency. The cinematic apparatus made the possibility of sensor-based self-tracking not only likely but desirable as an effort to prove one's ability to eliminate waste and excel.

As is now clear, the spirit of competition that time and motion study encouraged among workers at the turn of the century marks the beginning of a form of collegial scrutiny with dire consequences for collective labor. The "athletic contest" outlined by Gilbreth entailed a frank assessment of teammates who posed a liability to one's own speed and rewards for success. The possibility of having one's performance recorded for future revision consecrated a process of ever-more personalized measures for individual contribution. Workers were able to harness data to advance their own interests, with or without benefits accruing to colleagues. In addition, management initiatives that turned annual, bi-annual, and monthly performance objectives into self-nominated confessionals traded on the tradition established by Mayo that therapeutic encounter, dialogue, and paternal concern would ensure more thoroughgoing identification with the employer and the job (Illouz 2007). This historical context helps to make sense of the forms of intercollegial branding with which I began this chapter. For a company like Intel, simultaneously harboring the work practices of an earlier manufacturing era with the more qualitative indices of creative and symbolic work, management theories and employee incentives must operate on several levels at once. The efficiency of fab labs is secured by many of the same incentive schemes that human factors engineers identified in the early years of business scholarship. When it comes to motivating knowledge workers however—the technical and social experts who form the research, marketing, and engineering backbone for IT—the pace of production is affected by immaterial factors. Maintaining morale in a high-tech setting that is notoriously male-dominated and aggressive poses questions of identity and complicity by association when few alternative workstyles are displayed or rewarded in the organizational hierarchy. "Letting the Inside Out" allows the company to offer subtle forms of support, sanction, and encouragement for employees seeking other visions of accomplishment beyond the speed of velocity of the market. The program provides an avenue for individuals to be noticed and appreciated in the anonymous conditions of a large bureaucracy. It allows everyone the opportunity for fifteen minutes of fame, a chance to star in the broader roadshow that is Intel's ongoing success in the semiconductor industry. Nominating and celebrating colleagues' specific qualities and experiences fosters gratitude and confidence in the broad skill set driving the team. It deflects concerns about structural inequality and diversity in senior positions by enabling employees to shape the image of the company, and by association the industry, to appear more like them.

If labor politics was once premised on the idea of placing limits on work—reducing hours, resisting speed-up, guarding rights and benefits—in today's industrial settings the challenge is to adopt this politics to an environment which fails to recognize work as laborious. The privileged knowledge class is urged to love what they do, to create a "life's work" with so many services dedicated to the lucrative serendipity of dynamism and networking (Boltanski and Chiapello 2007). The post-secular visions of co-working communities like WeWork[15] address a class of "wannapreneurs" (Tiku 2015) whose privilege is to dismiss distinctions between individual calling, labor, and lifestyle. Meanwhile, in companies that continue to promote a job for life, with benefits devised to stave off competitor wooing, workers are encouraged to associate their success with that of the firm. Like the Gilbrethian typist, you too have the chance to star in the script in the performance that is your labor. And who can resist the joyous imperative to be amazing?

Identifying a collective politics to withstand the management innovations of the past century requires understanding the culture of competitive individualism that athleticism came to normalize. The politics of speed now escape the workplace to encompass the freedoms and constraints of an increasingly intensified and incorporated chrono-politics (Sharma 2014). Valuable lives attract investment to move with agility, comfort, and ease while others are left to lag, accumulate weight, and ossify. Working in tandem, '*both* reductions and investments cultivate docile and productive bodies' (Sharma 2009: 139). The growth of symbolic and communication labor alongside the service economy provokes neuroses of attention and authenticity, with accompanying industries of therapy, decompression, and cessation. Mindfulness and meditation flourish as the boutique salve for productivity's pressures, offering momentary respite from the demands of accomplishment. In these affective conditions that define contemporary labor, we seek solace internally, tending to body and mind. Our retreat from the social echoes the history of efforts persuading us to reject collective imaginings and focus on improving oneself. Observing this, we might pause to reflect on the technical means available to harness a better vision of shared accomplishments, to usher forth a work world that allows us the chance to direct a more fulfilling and sustainable script.

---

[15] <https://www.wework.com/> (accessed June 2016).

# Part III
# **Temporalities**

# 8

# "Just Time" and the Relativity of Speed

*Harvey Molotch*

Speed is relative.[1] Obvious enough, history matters: what was once fast is now slow. Speed is also relative to the nature of the medium: what is fast by boat is slow by plane. Pleasures and punishments also count. A two-hour dinner with an interesting friend goes by "too fast," while a one-hour meal with a bore is a drag. And there is national context that shapes what is right to happen: we would forgive a slow Internet in Myanmar compared to the same experience in Korea. Not only do people become accustomed to one pace or another, they come to demand the one that fits and think things amiss if time doesn't proceed as expected. It becomes a moral matter as well as an issue of efficiency.

## Baselines

Some things don't vary as much as others in terms of their speed. Certain attainments are limited by human biology, like the speed of running. Yes, more and more people do the four-minute mile, but nobody runs the mile in three minutes and it is probably safe to say nobody ever will. There is no Moore's Law in regard to human self-propulsion; its speed will not double every two years. Walking also has a range of speeds, but within limits and those limits set up possibilities for synchronization. People commonly attain close-ordered walking together. They quicken and slow to stay "in tune" as they move (Antin 1984)—an aspect of the urban "choreography" so prized by Jane Jacobs (1961). Getting it synchronic, again with the right person in the right condition, is a life pleasure rather than lost time. I doubt much has

---

[1] Thanks to Jonathan Gershuny for suggesting "Just Time" as the title.

changed over many centuries in speeds of walking or techniques of walking together (Minister of Funny Walks aside).

A still more profoundly crucial site of human sociality is ordinary talk which also has a range of velocities, but has biologically given limits and potentials. Overwhelmingly, the norm is to take turns, to speak one at a time; it is almost impossible for two people to speak simultaneously (try it). By the nature of circumstance, individuals must adjust overlaps, silences, and pauses so as to minimize gap and overlap. They massively manage to do just this, as meticulously documented by a generation of scholars in the field of conversation analysis (CA). Speakers are—regardless of language group or cultural milieu— "hypersensitive to perturbations in timing (Stivers et al. 2009: 10591). Three-tenths of a second is detectable and actionable as delay. "There is thus a universal semiotics undergirding all social life" (2009: 10591) likely with "ethological foundation," writes a group of global investigators (Stivers et al. 2009: 10587; see also Boden 1983). However "rushed" things may appear, participants actually *wait* for an appropriate entry point before jumping in. Yes, they also interrupt but even these are attuned and systemic accomplishments, happening at just the right "beat" in another speaker's turn. As with other aspects of conversation, they come through intimate attentiveness to the given tempo—a "mutual entrainment" (Campos-Castillo and Hitlin 2013: 169). Whether in a dominant role (as interrupter for example) or on the short end of the interaction stick (e.g. as interruptee) all must pay sharp attention and adjust in situ and in real time as things move along (see e.g. West and Zimmerman 1983).

Ordinary conversation, conjoined with other basic pacing systems like walks and runs, plausibly sets the metronome by which still other speeds get measured. Some activities are set up to be very fast, to equal or exceed the norms of the conversational metronome. Jazz musicians can riff "wildly" with their instruments—at least as fast as any fast-talking dyad. Their system of mutual cues, response, initiation is like conversation, itself often playful, aesthetic, and poetic (Jefferson 1996; Becker and Faulkner 2009). Players, as with precise, articulate, charming and/or fast-talking conversationalists, exult in the feeling and display. When things go well, an audience may join in with well-timed applause. People become conjoined, even with anonymity among them. They can achieve, through timing and in interaction with one another and with performers, the high of a good crowd in ensemble (Atkinson 1984).

## Getting Around

We enter into a travel trip—around the block or around the world—based on the acceptability of a given speed, a kind of bargain of the opportunity cost of time spent against the rewards that might come. Things should be neither too fast nor too slow, but just right given the purpose at hand, as per Goldilocks. Critical in our judging of any given experience is the full gamut of the rewards delivered. If I like the destination enough, I'll bear the boredom of a seven-hour flight to reach it. On the other hand, sometimes slow is what you want: a cruise ship is not supposed to be as fast as a jet plane. The "slow" clock-time performance does not disappoint on account of the meager distance covered and the feeling of hardly moving. Similarly, a leisurely drive of many hours through the changing autumn leaves of New England bears no comparative disadvantage against a freeway trip through a similar territorial expanse. As always, what counts is the specificity of the activity and its granular context.

Whatever the means of movement and associated utilities and pleasures, things can go wrong, and unpredictably so. Here's the crucial rub: expectations may not be met. There may be a highway detour. The car may run out of gas. Traffic may be horrific. The plane may take off late. So unexpected impediments intrude, even some we didn't even know could exist. A downpour in the Arizona desert holds us up. Breach of expectation—expectation based on specific ensemble of technology, purpose, and social context—shifts perception and frustrates. Anticipated velocity is thwarted. The feature of rapid speed, through the lack of it, is made noticeable. Time does not fly.

This takes us to still another speed paradox, one noted in other contributions to this volume. Speed becomes manifest through its failure to occur. It happens with a noticing of bodily aging; "don't get around much anymore" can come somewhat as a surprise. Most radically, there can be full-on interruption, as with paralysis. Interruptions consist not of a dead stop in clock time, but of a dead life stop where it is not supposed to be. Every machine and every body, no matter how fast, lends itself to such unexpected slowing down. The faster things can go, the more remarkable it is when they fall short of their customary velocity.

## Organizational Speed

People have varied speed expectations of particular types of organizations, just as organizations come to constitute themselves, at least in part, through their temporal ordering. Pacing differs in terms of how workers relate to one another and with their machines, as well as in their external relations with others.[2] In some cases the organization owes its origin and continuation to being able to beat the norm; or alternatively, its demise comes from being

---

[2] To the writing of Schwartz on this point, we can also add Zerubavel 1979, Young 1988, and Thompson 2002.

laggard. Henry Ford's assembly lines made cars very quickly. MacDonald's unleashed fast food—under the slogan "Speedy Service"—at first jolting and then altering expectations of how fast a meal could materialize. But all organizations vary in what their managers, providers, workers, and customers take to be a proper pace. Again the specifics: what is slow at MacDonald's is fast at a French bistro. A MacDonald's pace is objectionable at a Zen retreat. What is slow at Starbucks is meteoric at the doctor's waiting room. In any case, temporal pattern is a defining aspect of not just how "good" an organization is, but—in a reciprocal sense—the type of place it is.

In terms of internal speed, organizations—like jazz groups—have a norm of appropriate timings. So academic journal approval systems are based on a series of very slow reaction times, compared, for example, to the approval apparatus for a new industrial product or, more radically, the preparation of a line of high-fashion clothing. Up close, as colleagues and co-workers, organizational members get into the "swing" of things as they co-produce their enterprise. As again with Goldilocks and people walking together, coordination requires going not too fast and not too slow. Whether in a restaurant kitchen, architectural studio, or among electric vehicle engineers (Noren 2014), failure to speed-conform generates trouble and rebuke, including from frustrated co-workers. And because the right organizational pace is an embodied skill rooted in experience, those with limited access to such experience similarly lose access to jobs. They are "out of it."

Whatever the pace internal to organizations (and internal variation of who waits for whom), those on the outside—as customers, clients, or patients—experience waiting advantage and disadvantage along the usual patterns of class, race, and gender biases. As a rule of thumb, the more affluent a type of clientele, the lesser the wait imposed by organizational routine. Airports that service only private aircraft impose no waits whatever for passengers; there is no check-in and seldom even any security inspection. Luxury retail shops have more sales people at the ready than what obtains at Ikea. Welfare agencies, armies, and prisons keep people waiting as a matter of course, often in an environment kept socially and aesthetically mean (see Auyero 2012).

Within a given type of organizational setting—not just between them—the pattern persists. At commercial airports, those of premium status have shorter lines, including at security. On board, those in first class can often receive food whenever they ask for it. They also have a more favorable passenger:toilet ratio so they enjoy shorter waits to relieve themselves. On landing, premium passengers are first off, with their baggage marked as "priority." Such pacing helps define the nature of the venue and classifies the people who make it up, both to themselves and to others. The powerful have "relative immunity from waiting," says Barry Schwartz (1974: 849), so much so that they come to take for granted the fast pace of those who serve them. Schwartz offers as maxim: "Far from being a coincidental byproduct of power, then, control of time comes into view as one of its essential properties" (1974: 869). As he still more generally elaborates, "every social system must 'decide' not only how much different members are to be given from a collective supply of goods and services; there must also be a decision as to the priority in which their needs are to be satisfied... Queuing for resources is in this sense a fundamental process of social organization" (1974: 842).

Queues thus not only make stratification systems evident, they construct them. Historically and geographically speaking, black people in the US South always went to the back of the bus and, under Jim Crow, the back of the (separate) lines for any public service. At the extreme, say of an earlier India, those of low caste await members of the higher class to pass, standing aside until they do. People of higher standing hire others to do their waiting: secretaries, flunkies, agents of one sort or another. Chivalry may dictate "ladies first" but class (or caste) weighs in to at least an equal (usually much greater) degree (Elinder and Erixson 2012). When it comes to public rest-rooms, even in caste-free societies, women wait in long lines to use them while men, at glaringly obvious advantage, move rapidly into and out of the relevant facility. Women's longer wait times arise in the first place through hyper gender segregation; they can't go where men go. Separate is not equal. Inequalities are in part built in through physical layouts, which, by failing to assign sufficient square footage to meet their collective needs, systemically put individual women at a disadvantage compared to individual men (Molotch 1988). Hardware also plays a role: urinals (placed closely together) make it faster for men to come and go compared to women who receive no compensating hardware resource. Thanks to the general acceptance of this particular socio-technic regime of peeing, men typically encounter no line at all. We see again that whatever form of classification and however the ensemble arises, waiting—how long the wait and who waits for whom—displays and constitutes hierarchical position.

More generally, and without a regard for some sort of political injustice, sometimes people have anticipation of rightness and wrongness widely held to apply for all. If I'm having a heart attack, no queue should exist at all when I get to the emergency room. I expect the post office line to take longer to get through than the one to get on the bus. The queue to pay for my food at the cafeteria should not be so long that my food goes cold by the time I reach the cashier. Elevator rides are timed to be more or less constant no matter how tall the building; slower technologies are put in shorter buildings and faster ones in higher ones.

Occasionally women complain or even go into the men's room because they, like Southern US blacks who go to the *front* of the bus, have had enough.

For those who ardently support the Cuban revolution (or the Soviet regime at a prior moment), what otherwise would be slow service at bureaucracies, food counters, and visa offices may be accepted with equanimity. For others, it is a cause for redress and counter-revolution. There is always a moral loading: when norms are not met, the organization is considered specifically deficient which is why some of them, even nation-states, cease to be. Besides the low quality of goods, the long queues to get to them likely contributed to the collapse of the Soviet Union—and the contemporary clamor in Cuba for change.

Those who set up and maintain security apparatuses, like at airports and national borders, routinely impose waiting. Indeed, some might regard the presence of lines as actively signaling that authorities are indeed "on the job" (Molotch 2012). Beyond their functional need to intercept contraband or miscreants, they are performatives in a similar sense to how waiting establishes status in other contexts. As further iconographic features, security apparatuses are typically accompanied by arbitrary rules and procedures. Rather than protest, people may readily proclaim a willingness to "do their part" and actively forgive, even celebrate, what would otherwise be irritating interruption. Others acquiesce only through necessity. For them, the imposed waits are mechanisms of intimidation. As has been well argued, they are meant to further docility, a docility that the regime can generalize into other realms.

## Mundane Adaptation and Agency

Part of ordinary life practice is to logistically avoid situations, like the kind of confrontations at security that render us helpless. We actively pick and choose our restaurants, shops, airlines, and petrol stations based on how fast they should be given the task at hand. We may seek local lore on how to avoid lines, traffic, or slow offices and ask those who have gone before for tips and information. We also—and here is the socio-technical complementarity again—might use technology for good work-arounds. If we know the right app we can discover road delays in real time on various routes. With our mobile, we can restore some purposiveness to our time in the queue by taking up messages, texting and conniving with those off-site. There is music and video. New artifacts and systems come as a helper during what otherwise might be a rough patch. Still around of course to occupy us is the oldest of technologies, things to read on paper—"books."

Some organizations construct themselves to mitigate the wait. At Disneyland cartoon creatures entertain on the sidelines to break the monotony of the yellow brick road. Some market research analysts (see e.g. Taylor 1995) have looked for variations in dissatisfaction that come with different conditions of waiting. Not surprisingly, customer dissatisfaction does correlate with wait time. Managers respond by interjecting what are termed "time fillers" to ameliorate the effect which, at least in experimental settings, do work (Katz, Larson, and Larson 1991). It can be, for example, music or announcements. One less obvious example of filler occurs in doctors' waiting rooms, where patients are asked to list symptoms and prior conditions on forms. Sometimes these forms are clinically relevant. But sometimes nobody will ever look at them. Being made busy makes it seem the "appointment" has already begun, instead of an extension of the wait.

Also of relevance is the degree clients think organizational actors are in control over unfolding conditions and hence can properly be held responsible for delays. Airlines, for example, are less likely to be blamed when bad weather is happening versus pilots not showing up. Agencies, with or without benefit of social research, know to try and blame "conditions beyond our control." They also interject fillers like announcements that provide information relevant to conditions of the trip (weather ahead, arrival time, meal options, etc.). Such announcements will backfire—the research also suggests—if people deem them mere blather, not related to the task at hand (Taylor 1995). Amenity-value of the wait always counts. We may complain or never go back to those who offend through the quantity–quality of the wait.

One of the resources that people can draw on to fill time is other people. So we can strive to have the company of people we know (the right people, of course) while doing things that otherwise would force us to be alone. This helps overcome one of the costs of queues—a lack of sociality. So people arrange to wait together. When I lived in Vienna as a young student, a group of us regularly joined forces to line up for cheap standing-room tickets at the opera. Such tickets could only be had by a long wait, which was all part of the ritual of being young together; we bantered about sopranos, pastries, Vienna, and other favored topics of the milieu. The pricing system, the absence of being able to pay the cost of seats, the "technology" of the line-up—all joined in convivial ensemble. The queue was both an excuse to come together as well as a mechanism for social order and marking of our status—low in the economic hierarchy, high in aspirations (at least) for cultural capital.

While in the presence of the line, we can also do some time and motion ethnography, folk or professional. If we're in a queue we can look to see if "first come–first served" is actually being practiced or if some kind of preference (illegitimately perhaps) is being given. We can try to judge the best line to stand in—with retrospective regret or strategies for shifting, as when driving in heavy traffic as well as while at the end of the supermarket queue. We can think about which cashier or official is the most or least efficient, and whether or not there is sufficient staffing—and again, perhaps, take immediate action and switch queues. And we can size people up—as athletes, as intellectuals, or as partners for sex, sex, sex.

We may ruminate if there are aspects of national cultures on view; essentialist critique be damned. We need the material. So I can observe: British people wait their turn at bus stops. Italian people not so much. In his stream of consciousness offerings of what goes on at train stations, the British scholar/novelist/travel writer Tim Parks humorously conveys the cunning maneuvers that Italians use to get to the head of the line (Parks 2014). With various degrees of amusement, we all do such social theorizing on the spot. We may also share it with others when we arrive home or (for some of us) at the classroom ("A funny thing happened on the way to . . . "). This work of retroactive accounting is done without much by way of hard evidence or test of truth-value; it is part of the give and take of life to report observations and give analyses. It is part of minding in the line.

At Walden or wherever, we always have as default our own all-alone compulsion for sense-making and entertainment. To ease the emptiness, we may fantasize future events and encounters, richer in possibilities of projects and social interaction. Or we may daydream of happenings gone by, maybe retroactively reconstructing the decisions we took to get into a present waiting predicament—and who we told it wouldn't work or who assured us it would. But as indicated by the dire consequences of solitary confinement, creative adjustment can carry us only so far.

## Technologies Strikes Back

Our repertoires for anti-wait utilize the nice appliances to which I have already alluded, mobile phones and the like. At least at the outset, the telephone hugely enhanced capacities for sustaining—not interrupting or eliminating—human interaction (Fischer 1994). Indeed, the very first utterance on a landline was to prompt a face-to-face meet up. Alexander Graham Bell spoke them to his assistant "Watson" (actual name): "Mr. Watson—come here—I want to see you." By mid-twentieth century, mechanical interruption could interfere with such smooth hooking up. People can be put on hold, before even speaking to a person at all. The experts were able to delegate to machines the task of dealing with a caller by, in effect, not dealing with them (see Wajcman 2015). Instrumentation came to intrude between what otherwise would have been humans talking to humans. The machine, in Akrich's (1992) term, "prescribes" what we are to do including, in the case of "hold," nothing at all. All along, there is no conscious actor keeping track of just who and for how long an interference is occurring. In its plethora of expanding procedures, protocols, and orderings, the artifact and infrastructure make up its own runaway world.

With machines substituting for direct human delay, we have few clues of how long an interference will last. Nobody is there to advise or to suggest, even by innuendo. While a respite can be a good thing—a chance to gather thoughts or sip some coffee—it gets old fast. We often do not know how long "hold" will be. It is an indeterminate sentence of solitary confinement. This is *long* time. Assurance that "your call is important to us" or a crackly "Rhapsody in Blue" filler may not ameliorate. This kind of queue is devoid of sociality. One has no sense of context: Who else is waiting? How is the line proceeding? What else are "they" doing while I wait? In terms of awareness and dignity, it is terrible because it has no life within it—not even the minimal interpersonal gaze of strangers who happen to be standing together. Almost pathetically, some may invent social scenarios, like the way brokers are said to read human traits as lying behind machine-executed commodity trades (Zaloom 2010) or gamblers come to see certain tables or machines as offering better luck advantages than others (Goffman 1969; Schull 2012). Technology invites animism.

For their part, organizations deliberately attempt to imbue machines with human-like qualities, laughably and irritatingly deliberate. A first series of simulated human instruction offers options/instructions: "press one" or "press two" and so on up to as many as seven choices—to cite a recent call to my bank. It then can branch off into additional menus taking us farther away from what used to be an initial human "hello." We hear options without benefit of seeing the hand movements, posture shifts, and facial expressions that are ordinarily intrinsic aspects of sense-making. The non-person at the other end of the line similarly has no appreciation of our own physical movements, tone of voice, or rolling of eyes. Interactants cannot, as they ordinarily do, adjust pronunciation, voice volume, or speaking pace to deal with specifics of the conversation partner (language accents, age, confusion).

One clear breach of ordinary talk is in the way machines voice digits in a series—like a phone or account number. Machines (at least at this writing and in the US) sound each digit exactly the same way, something we do not do in real talk. In real talk, the ending digit comes with a downward pitch which serves notice the list is complete. It is a "list completer" in Jefferson's term (Jefferson 1991). Among other functions, it serves notice that the listener can put down their pencil, go on to another topic, or begin speaking with a new turn of their own. There are other tactics, such as adhering to speech conventions like speaking in "chunks," pronouncing—for example—three digits in a single chunk when giving out a list with a split-second pause at appropriate intervals. Such "recipient-designed" intonations and timings serve notice of a series coming and a series coming to an end. Along with many other tacit resources we deploy in conversation[3] (see Sacks, Schegloff, and Jefferson 1974), these resources help keep things moving—misunderstandings are kept at bay, requests for repeats can be minimized, and speed is enhanced. Inability to shift pitch is one example of the ways machines, at least for now, fail at mimicking the radical contextuality of ordinary interaction—the fulsome resources that come with co-presence (Boden and Molotch 1994).

In a still more flagrant way, technological communication—oblivious to context—issues insensitive requests. In no particular order, without transition or hesitations, demands come at us: for a pin number, case number, account number, product serial number, or alternative phone number. There may be a prompt for a password (almost at any point in the series), a paternal grandmother's first name, or indication of whether or not we have ever lived at a series of listed geographic addresses. The questioning resembles a kind of authoritarian nonsense. It seems akin to aggressive police interrogation, where as a matter of technique, questions are sprung without apparent rhyme or reason. The machine lacks civility; it does not hold back until, as happens in ordinary talk, there is perceptible evidence that it is OK to continue.

Meanwhile, the human has imperfections of their own that breed still other failures and lost time. Pressing an incorrect key through misunderstanding or physical clumsiness can lead into a trajectory from which there is no easy return. By way of contrast, a restaurant waiter says "no problem" when you drop your napkin or spill a drink. The machine is not programmed for such niceties. The whole sequence can abruptly end—no matter how arduous the route to get there has been—as the instrument, without grimace, complaint, or warning, just goes dead. We often blame ourselves for causing such mishaps, a blaming of the victim by the victim, something Wajcman suspects is encouraged by corporate strategists to be the outcome (Wajcman 2015).

The Internet comes with its special traps and foibles. Without password or pin number at hand or consciousness, there is no access. Each of us has been forced to cumulate different passwords across our sites and to keep inventing new ones with newly imposed criteria. Punishment follows for failing more than twice. Three tries and you're out. Password request can also happen deep within a sequence. One solution is to resort to post-it (a truly breakthrough technology) and write down passwords and stick them on the computer housing. This common practice of course undermines much of the security arsenal of the whole apparatus but is a human-made adjustment to a dumb machine system of controls.

---

[3] A founding document is Sacks, Schegloff, and Jefferson 1974. See also, e.g., Boden and Zimmerman 1993.

The Internet and the web bring on other pesky delays. As we move through successive screens, we can stumble into missing URLs, broken connections, or similar e-troubles. Analogous to the evil of robo phone calls, advertisements, pop-ups, and software notifications can further frustrate. And, of course, a file on which we are working can inexplicably disappear. The laptop battery can go dead or at least seem to do so. Seeking redress in FAQs requires user-empathy with how site designers have worded others' troubles rather than being able to articulate a trouble through one's own logic and experience. Failure to find the right formulation of one's own troubles in someone's translation of someone else's question is a time-sink. One has to judge at the outset the probability of hitting an answer via FAQ versus the lost time in seeking it.

As a general matter, digital menus, including those now offered by the phone, take the form of forced-choice questions—which have always aimed to simulate the digital even before digital was known as digital. Digital allows little wiggle room for instances of grey, of betweenness, of "it all depends" on what you mean by "pet" or even by maternal grandfather (my adopted one? The one who actually took care of me? The legal one? Legal in which country?). They rely on the ability to prefigure all possible meanings of questions and their possible answers. Ethnomethodologists have offered trenchant critiques of these types of forced-choice methods in terms of validity and reliability (see e.g. Cicourel 1964) as well as the ways they differ from competent social interaction. Depending on how well one can psyche out the survey researcher, or the exam, or the organizational technology, one can end up at a loss and attendant downward spirals.

As corporations and agencies decrease payrolls by substituting machines for labor, they erode human interface. Within organizations' accounting schemes, the substitutions show up as productivity gain. Some of it, no doubt, is also genuinely appreciated by users and eliminates tedium at both ends. People may find their chores simplified—no need to travel to an office, a shop, or a travel agent or deal with a phone operator. Genuine miracles are in the offing as Uber-logics increasingly replace not only interactions but also wait times and discomforts of not knowing who is coming and when. But the prospect of such gains is not the key criterion by which substitution occurs. Instead, organizational managers are self-seeking. In meeting proximate productivity and profit goals, they irresponsibly shift troubles and opportunity costs to clients, users, and applicants without regard to *their* preferences and efficiencies. While the advantages may be loudly proclaimed and also enjoyed by users and investors, the downside is largely invisible and hence irrelevant to those inside.

As per usual, some categories of people find almost any machine-led interaction a challenge. The distribution of digital acumen is uneven in any population. The digital divide exists not just in access to technology but also the capacity to cope with day-to-day encounters with it. For those left behind, the fallback of human contact recedes as a possibility. It gets harder to reach a proper person who is actually on the job. Those managers and officials who remain may no longer have the titles that could indicate what they actually can do for the "outsider." Their offices and titles have switched to be more relevant for intra-agency dealings and linkages with other businesses and organizations. Ordinary clients can be presumed "taken care of" through phone and website. To the degree they exist, the remedial personnel are typically not in geographic locations that are easy to reach, installed instead on a hinterland campus or in a country offshore where there is a different "native knowledge" in play. Call centers have procedures but empathy is more problematic.

Digital troubles make for the most boring stories that there are. This is still another cost. Part of the benefit of an experience, including the bad times of interruption and non-normative slow down, is the anticipation of telling others. Even during the involvements themselves, maybe especially during the involvements, our experiences come alive with our reflections of the telling. Adding insult to injury, there is little prospect of constructing a narrative of one's bad time in the thickets of technology delay. So this is time doubly dead. Nobody wants the blow-by-blow account and the experiences are hard to reconstruct even for oneself. There are no big moments, no build-up to emotional pinnacles, and no souvenirs, electronic or otherwise. Our blood may boil, we may let out expletives, but they are into the digital wilderness. If nobody hears our "oh fuck" (usually a dependable performative), has there been one? We are, like Jack Katz's drivers who are "pissed off in LA" (Katz 1999), alone in our fester. It was no good in real time, no good in retrospect, and no good in the telling.[4]

The makers and inventors race toward ever-new apps and gizmos, more powerful and speedy than the ones before, also sometimes striving for better simulations of real interaction. Some consumers race to adapt, keep up, and adopt. But as new imperfections and unanticipated glitches arise, all users must face them. There are also non-bug advances that just require new ways of engagement that only the technical cognoscenti can easily absorb. Sometimes the limits are so great that the product flunks, or at least is much delayed. We have the grand examples from the champions of user-friendly design, Apple Corporation. Its Newton was way too ahead of its time, its "Yosemite"

---

[4] Thanks to John Urry for raising the issue of "daydreams" and also for complaining about "three strikes."

operating system was judged "pesky."[5] Apple Maps remain a failure. That's Apple, not the many fly-by-night operations that tempt our in-box. Solutions do often get worked out, although not always—Jobs' NEXT could not be made to work.

Often, of course—albeit at varying rates and degrees—users achieve competence. Even when still with bugs, early adopters make a new technology plausible for eventual widespread acceptance. Especially for the early and adept, life-speed increases. As Wajcman notes (2015: 171), a rapid technology shift "requires an ongoing investment in skill acquisition" and this involves unpaid user time. Those who don't or can't make the investment may be slowed down. Because of sunk costs in a prior system or due to age or other circumstance, some individuals and types of organizations go backward. In effect, advance in the technology translates into obsolescence for certain humans. Those digitally challenged may be forced out of the game altogether. They may be the last ones who have to actually walk into the store to pay for a product or go into a bank to get money. An otherwise sophisticated colleague of mine would not switch to Microsoft Word for years because he did not want to disrupt a decade of writing and storing text through WordStar. Eventually he was so out of step, so beyond the tipping point of Word, that he had to join the MSW pact. Individuals, agencies, and businesses in poor countries, including those frozen out by political embargo, may not be able to upgrade the software they originally acquired. Without the upgrades, their existing apparatus de-grades. Their equipment can't do what it once could do; new bugs appear because systems can't be updated.

## Speed Thrills

For dealing with machines of any kind, high-tech or low—including the human body—there are people who are especially given to push against the barriers: cognitive, material, and biological. Ironically, while the impediments make their appearance as troubles, it is their presence that provides the conditions for triumph. Exceeding the usual pace of dealing with them brings satisfaction, potentially even *thrill*. As the high-wire performer Karl Wallenda is quoted as saying, "To be on the wire is life; the rest is waiting."[6] For Wallenda on the wire, those mundane constraints melt away. The opportunity of beating the norms is a recurrent source of challenge and reward. People do not live merely to enhance ease. When needed, they even create artificial

[5] <http://www.networkworld.com/article/2927497/software/apple-finally-fixes-pesky-os-x-yosemite-wifi-bug.html> (accessed June 2016).
[6] Quote is from Erving Goffman 1969.

impediments. Those with access to cars and planes take up mountain climbing. Some who could otherwise be assured warmth and relaxation bundle up to ski down hillsides, black diamond or otherwise. Such thrill-seeking involves rejecting some technologies—e.g. central heating or cars—it means embracing others. Players search for racket strings that are tenser, balls that bounce higher, boxing gloves that crush harder. What is acceptable or not is specific to a given activity or sport but technology and material manipulation is always part of the match.

It is, once again, not just clock-time but the experience and its display that also figures in. A tennis volley has it as potential; we don't know what will actually come our way; we don't know exactly from where the ball will come across the net, at what speed, or with what kind of bounce. Unbelievably and, if possible, with real elegance—and not a whisk of wasted motion—one returns a serve that comes with force of remarkable power. Physical impediments "melt away"—the famous phrase from Marshall Berman (1982). The outside stimuli come so fast they can't be cognitively handled but they somehow are. They are somehow enfolded into the material–human matrix.

When not ourselves involved in reaching for the high, we may be vicarious spectators to others' accomplishments. In his effort to develop an "anthropology of art," Alfred Gell (1988, 1998) proposes that art is experience of the *uncanny*. We have no sense of just how this thing—this painting, this carved prow of a boat, this volley (back to my example) could have come into being just as it did—with its force, elegance, and exceptionality. It is so masterful that it is mystery; the mundane is gone—or at least put under challenge. We are lost in time and have no experience of its moment-by-moment passage. The opposite of being on hold or queuing at airport security, it is friction-free. "Time stands still"; the experience is so full, it seems empty. The paradox compounds. The faster it goes, the less there is of it. Let's call it a "radical presentism."[7]

Again, convention sets in and what may have been breakthrough can become routine. But it is the technology component that is given to decay. What was once a racecar or just a speedy conventional automobile (my Mother's hot "rocket engine" Oldsmobile 88)—becomes banal. The car, once a source of general thrills regardless of make or model, becomes mere linkage "with a system of necessity" (Tomlinson 2007: 52). That ends the mystique. Ballet, Shakespeare, and running the mile do not degrade—if at all—in the same way. So in the making of life, the making of meanings, and the purpose of it all, technology can never properly hold sway. However exciting they appear on first entry, the Macs, the Ubers, and the microchips will crumble. Only the social is here to stay.

---

[7] I Googled this term and found it as a concept in science fiction; my use is different.

# 9

# Speed Traps and the Temporal

## Of Taxis, Truck Stops, and TaskRabbits

*Sarah Sharma*

I begin with a story about the temporal; a story about time and social difference.

A friend and I were waiting for a southbound train during a weekday morning commute at St. Clair station in Toronto when the announcer informed riders that the line was experiencing a twenty-minute delay. People expressed their frustration with eye-rolls and exasperated groans. But just as quickly as the disrupted service was announced a series of plan Bs went into effect across the subway platform. Some were going to wait it out and took to leaning against the walls. A few people hurried out of the exits informing others "I guess I'm going to walk." Mothers with strollers headed toward the elevators.

As I contemplated my own plan B, my girlfriend had already jumped into action. She had done a quick scan of the crowd and honed in on a young man in a pressed dark suit walking quite fast while staring down at his phone. He did so with such practiced agility that she knew exactly where he was headed: to the financial district. She also knew he was "Ubering" rather than calling a cab because of the way he was typing and holding his phone up to look at the screen under the dim light of the subway station. My friend was in a rush herself and didn't have the twenty minutes to wait for a train. Waiting at the hospital for her was her new baby born twelve weeks premature. He was in need of the expressed breast milk she had in her transportable cooler bag hanging from her right shoulder. She sped up beside the smartly dressed young man and started to walk in step, "You getting an Uber? Going south, past Wellesley? I'm going to the hospital. Can I come with you?" He happily agreed but he also never lost his pacing, never stopped walking or typing until the brief moment that they stood together at the corner of St. Clair and Yonge when their Uber pulled up.

My dear friend was in survival mode trying to keep her early baby alive and well. Her already acute awareness of what she needed to do in a given moment was even more heightened. She was activating the necessary survival skills that come along with becoming responsible for the life of another. But what is most remarkable about this scene is that she knew exactly where this young man was headed and how he was going to get there. He had all the signifiers of the iconic and privileged protagonist of fast living in a culture that is dominated by the discourse that the world is speeding up. He had on a suit, a quick step, and was tapping madly away into his smartphone. He was plugged in and on the go, using network time to navigate the space of flows so he could bypass the public transportation system that had ground to a temporary halt. He could maintain control over his time by ordering up a driver with his Uber app and get to work without losing a minute. He was in charge of his mobility and his time but also the time and mobility of others.

Enter the driver: the Uber driver's labor is oriented entirely around navigating the rhythm of the streets while maintaining the time demands of their fares. They speed up, slow down, and are made to wait depending on the needs of whoever gets into the back seat. Relationships of synchronization permeate the entire social fabric. There is an expectation that certain bodies recalibrate to the time of others as a significant condition of their labor. As a result, specific temporal regimes and strategic dispositions are cultivated in order simply to survive within the normalizing temporal ordering of everyday life. Cab drivers limit fluid intake so they don't have to stop for bathroom breaks. Nighttime security guards sleep during the day. Back-strained desk workers do yoga stretches at their desk (Sharma 2014). While my girlfriend was also employing strategies to maintain control over her time she bore none of the recognizable accouterments of time management in this so-called culture of speed. No sense of her current relationship to time could be accurately gleaned or conceived of by an outside observer. When she hitched a ride on this young man's vector she was immensely fatigued with tired eyes and a still protruding but empty belly. Her arms were full of bags stocked with time-sensitive materials for the reproduction of the social order. These three figures, or what I refer to as temporalities, at the corner of Yonge and St. Clair are an example of the interdependent and relational nature of time. They exist together on a grid of temporal power relations. It is in this way that time is culturally collective.

The term "temporal" does not imply a transcendent sense of time or the time of history. I mean for the temporal to denote *lived* time. The temporal is not a general sense of time particular to an epoch of history but a specific experience of time that is structured in specific political and economic contexts. The temporal operates as a form of social power and a type of social difference. Temporalities do not experience a uniform time tied to a particular technology but rather a time particular to the labor and other forms of social difference that produce them. Individual experiences of time depend upon where people are positioned within a larger economy of temporal worth. The temporal subject's day includes technologies of the self that are cultivated through synchronizing to the time of others and also having others synchronize to them. In this way the meaning of one's time is in large part structured and controlled by both the institutional arrangements inhabited and the time of others—other temporalities. Not all such temporal entanglements are this fleeting, as my story indicates. Moreover, I would suggest it is only on the surface that temporal entanglements appear as such. Instead, these temporal crossings are endemic of deeper, more enduring forms of structural difference experienced at the level of time. But this view into the temporal I want to forefront is too often obscured by a more dominant cultural conversation about time; the now common one about speed.

That the world is speeding up is as much a popular cultural concern as it is a matter of contemporary theoretical importance. It is an observation about the contemporary moment shared by Marxists and marketers alike. The critique of speedup is not so much an accurate description of the contemporary world as it is a limiting discourse that actually perpetuates structural inequalities at the level of time (Sharma 2014). What most populations encounter is not the fast pace of life but the structural demand that they must *recalibrate* in order to fit into the temporal expectations demanded by various institutions, social relationships, and labor arrangements. To recalibrate is to learn how to deal with time, be on top of one's time, to learn when to be fast and when to be slow. Recalibration accounts for the multiple ways in which individuals and social groups synchronize their body clocks, their sense of the future or the present, to an exterior relation; be it another person, pace, technology, chronometer, institution, or ideology. Invitations and expectations to recalibrate permeate the social fabric differently for different populations. What is shared, however, is the looming expectation that everyone must become an entrepreneur of time-control.

When discussing the politics of temporal difference in a range of settings that has included academics but also designers, activists, marketers, and even occupational therapists, the conversation quickly digresses into guesses about what is faster, what is slower, and what takes more time or less. I get asked to comment on Fitbits and other productivity apps and what the emergence of such programs for living means for the politics of time-management. I am consistently asked publicly during Q and A for my own tips and secrets for managing the time pressures of academia with having two children. This departure into narratives of productivity and new technology, as well as personal time-management advice, suggests to me that temporal difference is even more political than I first imagined. The critique of speedup parades as

133

a time politics while it ignores larger structural political issues related to labor and social difference. To discuss gender, institutional time, and the potential of a politics of refusal is one thing, but to ask how one can "do it all" re-entrenches the gendered institutional control of time. To point to new technologies as altering temporal experiences is a fine observation but it says nothing of the politics of time without understanding that time is itself technological. Time is not a technological measurement of what is real; it is not a phenomenon caused by technological measurement—rather it is a structuring relation of power. It is an intoxicating concern: how to have a better relationship to time and technology. But this cultural fixation on time control and one's ability to modulate time, to manage it better, slow it down and speed it up, is antithetical to the collective sense of time necessary for a political understanding of time. Moreover, ascribing new temporal milieus and environments to new technologies without also considering the differential politics of time that is altered in the advent of this or that technology misses the opportunity to engage with the social experience of time.

How can individual time-management anxieties be set aside so that the relational and collective social experience of time might be acknowledged? I argue that the cultural understanding of time-control needs to be complicated and denormalized, delinked from new technology. Taking a cue from Judy Wajcman in her book *Pressed For Time: The Acceleration of Life in Digital Capitalism* (2015), what is most pressing is not resisting speedup or creating new technologies to better control time, but instead cultivating new social realities related to time. In this chapter I extend my work on temporal difference to account for the broader range of media technologies people orchestrate as part of the struggle to stay in time. The accouterments of time control are too often conceived of as consisting of Fitbits, productivity apps, VIP airport lounge passes, standing desks, and the privilege of being able to command and depend upon the labor of others. But recourse to these normalizing instruments of time control is not a universal experience. In fact most of the ways in which individuals attempt to exert the control and management of time barely registers under the rubric of time-management in this so-called culture of speed. As Wajcman argues: "We live our lives surrounded by things but we seem to think of only some of them as being technologies" (2015: 29). I am guided by the notion that we must continue to broaden our conception of technology as it relates to time management, a theory of media that has its roots in the medium theory of Harold Adams Innis (1951) and Marshall McLuhan (1964), but also recognize that the time-management strategies of so much of the population recedes from view because of the overmediatized and limiting notion of time that circulates culturally. Before complicating the category of time control, the first step is to shift the register from speedup to the temporal.

## Speedup and All of Its Trappings

At the turn of the twenty-first century, a set of questions that focused on the impact of technologies built for acceleration and faster-moving capital on the democratic fate of a sped-up globe emerged across the disciplines. I refer to this line of critical inquiry as "speed theory." Paul Virilio was one of the first to write of speed in this vein, in 1970s France, and he remains its most prominent figure. But the critiques of the culture of speed continue to accelerate (1986). Speed culture goes by many epitaphs: "the 24/7 world" (Hassan 2003b; Crary 2013) "liquid times" (Bauman 2000), "hypermodern times" (Lipovetsky 2005), "the culture of acceleration" (Tomlinson 2007), "the coming of immediacy" (Tomlinson 2007), "dromocratic society" (Armitage 2000), "the new temporalities of biopolitical production" (Hardt and Negri 2000), "the chronoscopic society" (Hassan 2003b), and "chronodystopia" (Armitage and Roberts 2003). Of course, the advent of the new millennium isn't the first time speed has been the object of critical inquiry. Such work fits within an important trajectory of thought that includes histories of capital as it became coterminous with different technologies and their temporal and spatial effects. Such critical histories describe clocks, trains, telegraphs, and other global metronomes with their attendant temporal dictates of ticks, tocks, nanoseconds, and light years (Marx 1867/2002; Thompson 1967; Kern 1983; Schivelbusch 1987; Carey 1989; Postone 1993; Abram 1997; Griffiths 1999; Galison 2003; Glennie and Thrift 2009).

While critical theorists of speed examine different elements of speed culture, there is a shared sentiment: new technologies and faster moving capital herald grave political and social consequences. "Speed" is the commanding by-product of a mutually reinforcing complex that includes global capital, real-time communication technologies, military technologies, and scientific research on human bodies. Democratic deliberation gives over to instant communication, or what Virilio refers to as "live contemplation." Political interaction is replaced by monetary transaction. Space, the apparent *real* ground of politics, is subsumed by speed. "Real-time is not very different from classical tyranny, because it tends to destroy the reflection of the citizen in favor of a reflex action" (1986: 87). Speed theorists argue that geopolitics (a politics based in space) is supplanted by chronopolitics (a politics based in time). The yielding of space to time not only dissolves the grounding of politics but it gives rise to a way of being in time that is antithetical to the political public sphere.

Speed theory is without a doubt indebted to Marx's formulation of the clock's quantification of work and the production of value and socially necessary time. Part of this analysis includes attention to the new social formations that arise because of accelerated capital and technologies including the changing quantity of labor time versus leisure time. They align with Marx's

135

formulation of socially necessary time (1867/2002). Speed theory is also largely sympathetic to E. P. Thompson's thesis in "Time, Work, Discipline and Industrial Capitalism" (1967) concerned with how the new chronometers imposed by governmental, military, and capitalist interests have replaced earlier, collective perceptions of time that he believed flowed from the collective wisdom of human societies. Marx and Thompson are both necessary to thinking about how capital robs the worker of time, whether by diminishing personal time, controlling the bounds of a working day, stalling clocks, or establishing the age limits of child labor. Yet the protagonist in the theoretical critiques of speed is no longer the worker or any specific subjugated population for that matter. Instead, it is a generalized individual who feels suddenly out of time. The subject of value and the subject of most attention in the critique of speed is the same subject who confirms speedup most readily as *the* new reality—whether the jetsetter, the financial worker, public man, or the theorist. While pointing out the indentured conditions of contemporary labor and living brought on by ubiquitous technologies is an important analysis of contemporary life, it does not deal with the uneven cultural politics of time. The theory of social difference that emerges out of speed theory revolves around a simplistic binary. Zygmunt Bauman, in *Globalization: The Human Consequences*, maintains that "the inhabitants of the first world live in a perpetual present, going through a succession of episodes hygienically insulated from their past as well as future. These people are constantly busy and perpetually short of time, since each moment in time is non-extensive" (1998: 88). He goes on to say, as for the slow class:

> People marooned in the opposite world are crushed under the burden of the abundant, redundant and useless time they have nothing to fill with. In their time nothing ever happens. They do not "control time"—but neither are they controlled by it, unlike the clocking in, clocking out ancestors subject to the faceless rhythm of factory time. (1998: 88)

In the end there are only two temporal poles of chronopolitical life that are dealt with: fast classes and slow classes (Virilio 1986), tourists and vagabonds (Bauman 1998), inhabitants of chronotopia and chronodystopia (Armitage and Roberts 2003), and the time rich and the time poor (Rifkin 1987). These two temporal classes are imagined to be much like ships that never pass. And, neither seems to meet the temporal requirement of civic life; where one should be contemplative and deliberative as a form of political temporal composure.

Theories of liberal democracy assume a way of being in time, but the assumption itself is not a time politics; it is one single, and albeit very powerful, discursive mobilization of time.[1] What continues to animate public sphere

---

[1] See for example Scheuerman 2004.

theorizing is an expectation that political civic life is only political insofar as it *takes place in a space and time separate from state and market*. The right practice of time, a democratic one, must be free of institutional restraints, whether economic or cultural. It is a time that must be unfettered in order to be contemplative. While I do not have the space to elaborate here, in terms of theorizing publics, at every level from the local to the global, oppositional to the bourgeois public sphere, temporality is an invisible and unremarked relation of power. "Publics" figure almost exclusively within the theoretical imaginary as spatial constructs. Delineations are made between ideal publics and the "other" space: the public sphere and the private sphere (Habermas 1999), public space and oppositional space (Fraser 1992), the agora and the *oikos*, anthropological public space and non-place (Augé 1995), and public space and speed-spaces (Virilio 1986). The spatial logic of liberal democracy is also evident in the constant questioning of "where" publics might be—are they local, global, subaltern, national, or regional. Are they here or are they there? Is the television talk show a new public space (Livingstone and Lunt 1994) and what about the Internet today (Poster 2006)? The newest technologies looming on the horizon are often met with questions of how they might change social space and they ways individuals interact with each other in space. The *agora*, for example, the venerated space of antiquity that continues to animate contemporary theorizing of the public sphere, was not merely a space. If the temporal is acknowledged, then the public sphere is also a time. It was a space of free time for political thinking for the minority of free citizens. It was an experience of time and social space produced by the *time* of women and slaves who worked in the *oikos*. Speed theory espouses a conception of the public conditioned upon a politics of time that is about the *pace* of one's time rather than how its citizens or denizens are *constituted in* time. The democratic expectation, to be free and have time, is a liberal bourgeois demand that lends itself better to arguments for lifestyle choices like "how do you do it all" rather than recognition of the politics of time.

The theoretical calls to *slow down* function in a very similar vein.[2] Within this slow-living imaginary, time is treated as something to which we all have equal access (Sharma 2014). Slowness is not outside of the normalizing temporal order. It encompasses its own particular ideological time claims and beholds its own exclusive temporal practices. There is a dominating sensibility within this discourse on slowness that being a "good" political citizen requires transcendence. Transcendence pervades in both taking the necessary time out and abstracting oneself from the energy and traffic of everyday life. But this traffic conditions the very possibility for some to transcend. Slowness, as a

---

[2] See Parkins and Craig 2006.

form of managing or resisting speed, is in and of itself not a time politics. Slowing down does not necessarily change (and certainly does not ameliorate) the ways in which individuals and social groups are tangled together in time.

Focusing on the issue of fast or slow "pace" without a nuanced and complex conception of the temporal does an injustice to the multitude of time-based experiences and strategies of survival specific to different populations that live, labor, and sleep under the auspices of global capital. The social fabric is composed of individuals' and social groups' sense of time, and possibility is shaped by a differential economy, limited or expanded by the ways and means they find themselves in and out of time. Thus what characterizes life are the differential and inequitable ways in which time is made to matter and is experienced. What matters is how time is worked upon and experienced at the intersections of inequity, and how, in any particular technological moment, there are multiple temporalities to be considered.

Speedup as a descriptor of the moment is hard to shake. I suggest it is compelling for a few mutually reinforcing reasons: it justifies a culture of overwork and overconsumption and the unnecessary exhaustion that comes with it. Speedup justifies the need for the labor of others to help maintain and reproduce the conditions and quality of one's own life, including one's exhaustion. But speedup might be less an accurate description of the world than it is a universalizing polemic promulgated by those threatened for the first time by the possibility of not being in control of time. One doesn't have to venture far to offer up the observation that theories of the world speeding up and out of control are written almost solely by men in the Western academy. But this is hardly an adequate intellectual conclusion on my part: to suggest that time is far more multiple and differential than this masculinist discourse of speedup has assumed and leave it at that. I offer a cautionary tale regarding the discourse of speed and its circulatory power; it is not speed per se but the explanatory power of speed that is responsible for perpetuating inequalities at the level of time. The temporal is a corrective to the discourse of speedup. I suggest the temporal complicates the narratives of speedup that permeate culture and theory, but also that a temporal perspective into speed is necessary in order to account for how time is actually lived across the social.

## Enter the Temporal

The fixation on speed and the problem of tempo leaves individuals and social groups more vulnerable to biopolitical control. When better time management is imagined to be the solution to speed, what is occurring is greater institutional control over the time of one's life; not just one's lifetime but the immediate minutes, how the days pass, and what time is supposed to mean for the modern subject. Foucault uses the term *biopower* to describe how the various institutions and disciplines arising in the eighteenth century monitored, intervened, and controlled the productive capacities of individuals and populations at large. Through different techniques and practices these institutions of the state, as well as other institutions of modern power such as the army, family, police, schools, and medical professions, would administer life through the optimization and intensification of the life force. When Foucault argues that biopower is the power to "live or let it die," the temporal is explicit (1977). Life is not taken. It is "let to live" through investment or "let to die" through disinvestment, slowly. One of the core features of neoliberalism is widespread disinvestment; the rolling back of the state's regulation of health, welfare, and other public services. But all bodies do not experience such disinvestment in the same way. One of the central paradoxes of neoliberalism is that while the state has disinvested in most bodies, some are reinvested in by more exclusive means through the market. The bodies that are invested in are the ones most vital to contemporary capitalism, precisely because they don't need to work in order to survive. One of the growing sights of investment I would argue is cultivating meaningful experiences of time, working upon one's time-sense. It depends upon belief in the speed of life to gain entry into subjects' lives in the first place.

Across the landscape of everyday life, interventions into time are presented as invitations to experience a novel temporal experience—to slow down, take a breather, nap, meditate, and rest at work on-site and on demand. We are witnessing the emergence of infrastructure of temporal care built around maintaining the time needs of particular subjects. By "time needs" I mean the discursive construction of one's lifetime and time of life being of particular importance to the contemporary moment. Temporal architectures are composed of built environments, commodities and services, and technologies directed to the management and enhancement of a certain kind of subject's time—a privileged temporality. For someone like the contemporary business traveler an immersive environment oriented around their time maintenance combines technologies and human labor that allow them to recalibrate and get resituated within the particular time demands of global capital. The airport's temporal infrastructure attends to accidents and risks within a biopolitical economy of time. It does the reproductive work to enhance, activate, and effectively transform the body's capacity to produce as well as alter the subject's experience of time to the rhythm of a capitalist work ethic. This temporal infrastructure maintains highly structured temporal experiences and normalizes a set of mutually reinforcing conceptions of time. While capital develops at the expense of bodies, it makes clear which bodies will be taken care of. Take for instance Minute Suites, appearing across American airports (see Figure 9.1). These WIFI-powered napping suites replete with desks, beds,

**Figure 9.1.** Minute Suites Traveler's Retreats offer in-transit travelers a place to "nap, relax, work" in private

workstations, and a on-site service staff offer the paying airport guest the chance to recharge and work or nap in private.

The rise of a temporal architecture elevates the cultural significance of waiting from the dead time of doing nothing to a time of self-improvement and a privileged moment of reprieve. Everyone manages time in one way or the other, for better or for worse. But for most populations, the management of time is more or less private and invisible—hidden from the view of others. And even for subjects of value at the airport, for example, waiting has not always taken on such a public character. It was done in exclusive lounges with other temporally compatible subjects. Today, the emerging architecture of time maintenance designed for the business traveler offers a public display of busy-ness where they can retreat privately in public view. People exercising good time management are visible everywhere and culturally applauded for doing it so well. There they are managing their time like pros and making good use of the architecture of time maintenance erected for their labors. These technologies of time maintenance reinforce the idea that subjects of value cannot be easily replaced, but the secondary labor they depend upon can.

The speed theorist also reinforces this value when they focus solely on new technologies and a singular experience of time. If this business traveler and their Minute Suites and all the gadgets and productivity apps that adorn them were generalizable across the social fabric then perhaps the argument could be

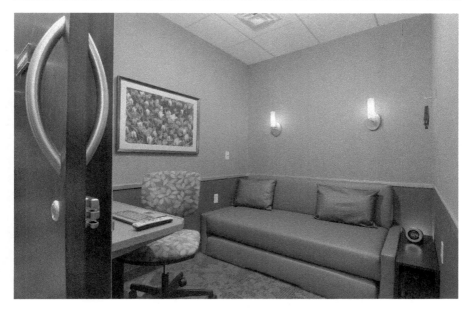

**Figure 9.2.** Interior view of a Minute Suite

made that this is a culture of speed and the politics of time needs to be directed toward dismantling this tempo. But the continued focus on this population and this tempo, in theory and in the consumer market, obscures attention away from the other temporalities that labor in order to maintain this time. One need not even have to look past the Minute Suite concierge to see the differential temporalities that compose the architecture of time maintenance. Thinking politically about time requires attention to these temporal entanglements and how time is experienced as a form of social difference.

## Architectures of Time Maintenance Beyond the Jet-Set

Late summer 2015 I am at a truck stop in Sarnia, a town between Ontario and Michigan before the border crossing between the US and Canada, the restrooms for gas station patrons are out of order and women are redirected to the truck stop facilities (see Figures 9.3 to 9.6). The sparkling condition of the facilities for women reveals not just excellent maintenance staff but the fact that female truckers are far and few between. The truckers' lounge has TV screens, an on-site hairdresser, and showers for the truck drivers. There are also coin-automated massage chairs, a free magazine collection, and unlimited

**Figure 9.3.** A slow day at the lounge at the Sarnia Truck stop. The space is designed to allow drivers to sit and watch TV while waiting for their number to be electronically displayed letting them know when a shower is free

**Figure 9.4.** The "Relax and Enjoy" toilet/shower at the Sarnia Truck Stop. The Denny's ad to the right promises fast food as fuel for the body

brewing coffee. Showers are controlled by an electronic waiting system displayed on the television screen—numbers are called when the facilities become free. There are pamphlets and posters that advertise a website directing would-be truckers to lifeasatrucker.com. The website promises that the biggest advantage of a career in driving is the solitary time it provides to

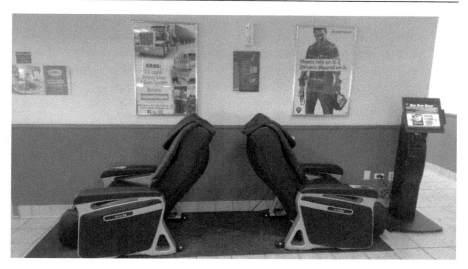

**Figure 9.5.** Coin and credit card automated massage chairs at the Sarnia Truck Stop. Before sitting down one can also place a food order at the adjacent Denny's via the electronic kiosk. Ads overhead refer to job opportunities in trucking and mechanics

**Figure 9.6.** A hair salon for driver's grooming needs while waiting for truck maintenance and repair

contemplate and reflect on one's life. The available services are not so much about enhancing the truck driver's quality of time or level of productivity but instead making their stop enjoyable while meeting the most basic of needs. The truck driver's meaning of time, their temporal outlook or sense of the moment, is not highly invested in. There are no signs indicating how tired,

143

busy, or high-tech their lives are in this apparent world of speed. Instead their architecture of time maintenance is about hygiene, grooming, and sustenance, in a timely and orderly fashion. They are there to refuel the body and the tank while not wasting too much time. Oil changes and haircuts take about the same amount of time. The food options are fast.

## The Desk of a University Department Manager

The office manager of my outgoing department at the University of North Carolina at Chapel Hill is the frontline of a department that is comprised of thirty faculty members, forty active graduate students, and 800 undergraduates. She has her desk set up in a very deliberate way (see Figure 9.7). If you look closely enough you can see that is ordered in such a way to help her maintain an oasis of calm in an environment that she has little control over. At any given moment one of these 875 people might need something via email or in person. UPS comes flying in and out, the mail person appears twice a day, there are jammed photocopiers and printing problems, disgruntled students and people lost in the hallways. None of these are actually part of her main job description. I get a brief sense of what her day is like a few times a week when my own office on the second floor loses its Internet connection and my defunct computer is

**Figure 9.7.** The desk of an office manager at a university reveals an invisible system of time control/management. Her post-it note attached to her screen reminds her to breathe and for how long

144

not going to be replaced. It is my last semester at the university before I move to the University of Toronto in January and my own temporal architecture is slowly being dismantled. I start using the desk behind her, the one usually reserved for the work-study students. Succulents and aloe plants, motivating mantras from American feminists, and inspirational posters pepper her desk. Most striking is the yellow post-it note stuck to her computer screen with the reminder: "Inhale 5, Hold 2, Exhale 6." I ask her how often she uses her post-it note message and she smiles coyly and says, "Whenever it catches my eye when I'm feeling stressed out. No one knows what I'm looking at. I just have all this stuff coming at me all the time, you never know what it will be." She stretches at her desk and makes sure she stands up and walks around every hour. In discussing the possibility of a standing desk for her she responds, "they aren't for staff I don't think."

## Taxi Cab Interiors

The front seat of a taxicab offers a rare glimpse into the taxi driver's relationship to time (see Figure 9.8(a) and (b)). The taxi driver in most major metropolitan cities in North America is almost always newly immigrated and waiting for accreditation papers. Many are seeking asylum. The taxi driver straddles multiple temporalities, both personally (the offset clocks of time zones that dictate phone calls home, the slow progress of work visa applications, the movement of their children through the US school system) and professionally (the tempos of those they must transport, the slow traffic, night and day, the ticking of the clock, and the running meter). The front seat is a private space for the taxi driver. Rarely are fares invited to sit in the front when there is room in the back. It is where drivers keep their personal belongings that help them get through the day. There are coffee mugs, packages of quat, cigarettes, pillows, eye masks, blankets, cellphone consoles, water, hand sanitizer, and half-eaten meals. Overhead on the visor, there are pictures of family members, CDs, business cards, and picture postcards of elsewhere. Hailing a cab with a large group of people, when everyone won't fit in the back seat, often results in frenetic scurrying. Drivers quickly push their belongings on to the floor, stuff things into glove compartments and the sides of the doors, or collect it all in a pile to dump in the trunk.

But these scattered front-seat objects are hardly just things. Together, they compose the taxi driver's daily rituals of time management. As the expendable bodies of a labor force that can easily be replenished, there is no need for the structures of capital to endow the taxi driver's time with importance. Much like the desks of office managers, the cab interiors reflect rituals of

Figure 9.8(a).

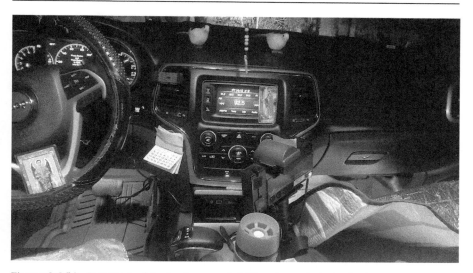

**Figure 9.8(b).** Interiors of taxi-cabs reveal deliberate and strategic time management rituals that fall under the radar of how time control is culturally conceived: thermoses, extra cups, visors, paper calendars, religious iconography, worry beads, toys of sleeping offspring at home. Many of these objects serve as reminders of the passing of time and why the drivers drive

time-maintenance devised strategically and creatively—in relation to the other temporalities that the driver must navigate around and between.

In one of the cab interiors (Figure 9.9), the visor, the coffee, a post-it-note calendar is clearly visible. What is harder to make out but perhaps most interesting is the range of religious iconography, including a rosary and the photos of Jesus that are on his driving wheel and on the meter. He also has family memorabilia assembled in the front seat. When discussing his cab interior and his choices, his answers all reflect the temporal. The birds remind him of the two types of people in the world and help balance him so he can stay calm and keep his business mindset and keep going. There is a figuring of Minnie-mouse that is his 5-year-old daughter's; it reminds him why he works late at night. The religious pieces are reminders of the temporality of life and death, the passing of time, and a greater power over his minute, day, life, and afterlife.

All of these rituals to stay in time at the truck stop, the department office and the taxicab, are also technologies of the self by those whose labor is oriented to the maintenance of life/reproduction of time for others. These are also forms of labor who fall outside of the common picture of fast urban life in the discursive world of speed. The taxi driver, truck driver, and office assistant are the human infrastructure for more privileged tempos. This is a quality of labor central to gigs, wage labor, and other forms of devalued care labor required to reproduce the productive requirements of others. And in all of these spaces there are even more layers of temporal interdependence that could be detangled with more layers of complexity. There are even more service staff securing, cleaning, and maintaining the university office, the places the taxi drivers stop and rest at, and the truck lounge. And each of these subjects will also devise and strategically attempt to control their own time without recourse to an elaborate architecture of time maintenance created to keep them in time.

One's relationship to the temporal order of things, the value of their time, can be rendered visible by how time is strategically managed and controlled. This is where the politics of time intersects with time control. The control of time is never individual; it is always collective. To achieve time control, to work toward it constantly, could be an empty political goal. The ultimate desire to control one's time is not a sufficient endpoint or starting point for politicizing time.

## "I control my own time, I control my own time, I control my own time"

Mohammed is a London Uber driver. He provides bottled water, crisps, and biscuits in the back of his Uber. He has a mini-vacuum he keeps in the front seat so he can quickly clean up the crumbs. It is Saturday in Central London around midnight. The pub patrons are home already and the clubbers still clubbing. Midnight is quiet in this part of London. The next rush is hours away. Mohammed tells me he had started a career in computer engineering but after a year of uninspiring days working at a desk under a strict management team he felt like he was wasting time. Becoming an Uber driver felt like the "ultimate freedom." He tells me that he really enjoys the work because it lets him be in control of his time. He makes this proclamation right after relaying he has spent the last thirty minutes quite bored and waiting in his car for a fare. Mohammed doesn't really take entire days off either. He sometimes decides in the moment if he is going to drive or not. If he's out and feeling bored or not having fun or just sitting around at home and feels guilty about not working he turns his phone on. This sentiment echoes other workers in the gig economy made up of menial outsourced labor.

TaskRabbit is an online outsourcing company that helps busy people "live smarter" by connecting them to people within the vicinity who can take care of a range of domestic errands like furniture assembly, grocery shopping, and cleaning. Their tagline reads: "We'll do what you don't want to do, so you can do what you love." The *New York Times* recently ran an exposé on workers in the sharing economy at Fiverr, TaskRabbit, Uber, and Lyft (August 2014). One of the taskers profiled was a single mother who had spent almost sixteen hours doing menial work for others that included assembling Ikea furniture, gardening, and taking someone to the airport before the crack of dawn. At the end of the day she has worked well beyond an acceptable workday. She also has a backache and a tension headache to show for it, along with 200 dollars. She recognizes that it was a good day in terms of cash but not a sustainable livelihood. She expresses that the ultimate pay-off for this type of precarious work is that at least she can control her own time.

The invoking of time control in these two examples is set against another temporal condition of generalized precarity—the unguaranteed future. In fact, the mention of the control of time actually refers to a tiny slice of time: control over one's immediate working conditions, sometimes the hour, in the absence of security. Even if the boss is decentralized and diffuse, incarnate in every transaction, the relationship is fleeting and more palatable than other types of workplace domination and exploitation. Likewise, those who need task rabbits suggest that the technology "greases an otherwise awkward exchange" (Singer 2014). Taskers and Uber drivers plug in and plug out when they want to. They determine the length of their working day as well as their own geography. As a type of labor that is downloaded on demand, they might not know the exact contours of their day or even what they will be doing the next hour but their labor gets to feel like a choice even if there is so clearly no choice but to work. Having control over one's time in the absence of security and with the promise of laboring under temporal parameters of the day one chooses seems like an acceptable trade-off.

But it is not just that time control here operates like an ideological precept, a Zen meditation one can repeat as a justification for tenuous and precarious working conditions that is concerning. Instead, it is because the mantra "I control my own time" is said while entirely recalibrating to the time of others and while doing tasks others have devalued as useless pursuits of their own time. "I control my own time" is also a statement espoused by those controlling the time of others by outsourcing all of their tasks. Both promulgate time control as an unquestioned good. What is entirely obscured is the fact that one's productive life and sense of time well spent runs on the energy of other more expendable bodies—other temporalities.

## Conclusion

Time-management is signified by a world of clocks, spreadsheets, smart-phones, Fitbits, stations for charging electronic devices and questions like, "how does she do it all." Increasingly it looks like Minute Suites and on-site massages, yoga at the desktop, and the ability to outsource life to a rabbit. All of these techniques for staying in time actually foster a deeper cultural fixation on the management of time—leaving one in a state of constant marginal dissatisfaction. Time cannot actually be entirely managed and controlled on one's own, after all. But time management also comes by way of breast pumps and post-it notes with reminders to breathe, by way of a coffee pot at a truck stop and a picture of Jesus next to a figurine of Minnie mouse on the dash-board of a taxicab. These techniques reveal the differential social experience of time; one entirely ignored in the discursive construction of speed as the universal experience of time today.

I have had a tendency to leave the critical questions of new technology aside out of principle to show that having a political approach to time does not necessarily hinge upon the digital or digital speeds. But there are increasingly good reasons to sharpen up here and address the digital in relation to my suggestion of a temporal approach to speed and time. To return to the senti-ment from Judy Wajcman that I began with, it is not a question of new technologies but of constructing new temporal social realities that can be harnessed and cultivated by and through technology. I wonder if the multiple temporalities that compose the social fabric, and their various uneven entanglements could be rendered more visible by new technological means. Is there a way to provoke or capture the collective rationality of time via new technological means? And by this I do not mean the global village or the beauty of connectedness but rather to conceive of apps freed from productiv-ity and individual time control, ones that provoke recognition of the rhythm of material interdependencies. For example, how could technologies actively promote work/life imbalance in order to reveal the problem of this dominat-ing construct in the first place. Perhaps there are programs that could reveal one's temporal privilege and will tally up the performance of busyness versus the interdependent labor involved in one's performance of busyness. I pose this playfully in closing in part to change the conversation that occurs between theorizing time and technology from the all-too-common digression of determining if something is faster or slower, if there is a good way to save or make more time, or how one manages to balance it all. The change I am envisioning is one toward provoking recognition of temporal privilege, one that might forefront who has time to even think about time (says the academic obsessed with the cultural politics of time). Surely there are deeper, more structural problems to attend to with regard to the politics of time than determining if privileged individuals have enough of it. A temporal perspective might relieve us from the trappings of speed and speed theory and push those interested in time politics to begin from the points of time's collective entanglement.

# 10

# Bending Time to a New End

## Investigating the Idea of Temporal Entrepreneurship

*Ingrid Erickson and Melissa Mazmanian*

For the growing hordes of knowledge workers who populate the offices, co-working spaces, and coffee shops of the twenty-first century, the speed of the world feels fast, yet time is scarce (Tomlinson 2007; Wajcman 2008; Golden 2009; Wajcman 2015). For this group of individuals—those professionals who trade in information and whose jobs are often characterized by flexible hours, mobile work, and a high degree of identification between individual and profession (Alvesson 2001; Robertson et al. 2003; Alvesson 2004)—individual autonomy is expected, yet control over everyday life feels increasingly impossible (Schulte 2015). Whereas the rhetoric of technological progressivism would have us believe that our advanced state is one of optimal efficiency, seamless connectivity, and satisfying sociality, the everyday experiences of workers suggest something different: a constant struggle between time, autonomy, and obligations that force people, often inequitably, into ongoing (and often exhausted) situations of negotiation and compromise (Prasopoulou et al. 2006; Gregg 2011; Sharma 2014).

According to many scholars and pundits, such working (and living) conditions are enabled and perpetuated by capacities embedded in ever more ubiquitous, wearable, networked, and multifunctional information and communication technologies (ICTs) (Hörning et al. 1999; Hassan 2003a; Lee and Sawyer 2010; Agger 2011; Starwarz et al. 2013). The desktop computer of yore is now an exponentially more powerful machine in our pocket; the respites from networked connection on flights and faraway places are falling away as infrastructures reach higher and further. This group of workers were some of the earliest adopters of mobile technologies and also some of the first to feel their sociotechnical effects (Davis 2002). Early research on BlackBerry use, for instance, showed that when mobile technologies are highly embedded in a professional context, they not only enable new technological possibilities, but also engender new social expectations that qualitatively shift what it is to "be" and experience oneself as a competent professional (Mazmanian et al. 2013). In one study, after the introduction of the BlackBerry into the legal team in a manufacturing company, new expectations of competency took hold swiftly. Despite the legal team's adamancy that mobile devices would not affect their working habits or relationships, the cultural shift was fast and definitive—no longer was it enough to do your job knowledgeably, but now the expectation was to do it in a mobile-timely (i.e. nearly instantaneous) fashion as well (Mazmanian 2013). Today, nearly a decade after this initial research, we rarely question the connection between professionalism and timely communication (Mazmanian and Erickson 2014). We expect that people will have a device in their hand (or nearby) at all times and that they will be actively using it.

With these professional expectations firmly in place, knowledge workers have their work cut out for them. Despite, or perhaps because of, their assumed agency they generally strive to be prompt, responsive, and ever-present in their communications and expect their colleagues be similarly engaged (Towers et al. 2006; Mazmanian et al. 2013). Situated within a universe of smartphones, tablets, and an array of applications for every potential task or need, many willfully take on the burden of managing their time in ways seen to promote ideals of efficiency and effectiveness. Such individuals are ever-looking to squeeze in opportunities for multitasking, distributed collaboration, or other perceived forms of modern professional competency (Keisler and Hinds 2002; Reinsch et al. 2008). We do not question the state of this reality. The hundreds of knowledge workers that we have interviewed over the years have fleshed out its contours in great detail, confirming both the truth of the tight coupling between timeliness and contemporary work as well as its effects. Instead, in this chapter we reassert how much this reality is a product of shifting social values and sociotechnical expectations. We then go one step further to suggest that, just as this reality has been architected by the interweaving of technology and society, any attempts to move away from current expectations, taken-for-granted ways of working, and the bludgeon of constant availability lie in this same arena.

Employing a critical perspective informed by institutional theory (Scott 2014), we begin by asserting that that the temporal experience described here is informed by a collectively shared, and often unquestioned, orientation to time that is rigidly institutionalized in Western cultures (Nowotny 1996; Snyder 2013). This orientation begets a dominant temporal logic,[1] which

---

[1] We adapt this concept from institutional theory and its theorization of "institutional logics." As defined by Scott (2014), an institutional logic comprises "the belief systems and related practices that predominate in an organizational field." By *temporal logic* we mean the socially legitimated,

we designate as *circumscribed time*. Like an institutional logic, this dominant temporal logic informs and animates the values and norms that comprise modern forms of work (as well as the broader engagements of social life as a whole); it manifests itself in the most micro and implicit time-related practices, moral judgments, and rhetorical discourses. More than just setting the stage, however, circumscribed time has also pervaded how people experience and engage with ICTs. It is embedded in the designs of technologies and applications.[2] Open the app store on any mobile device and one can find hundreds of productivity applications built according to the logic of efficiency and the idealized practices of time management.[3] Less directly, circumscribed time also pervades the design assumptions of collaborative, point-of-sale, and financial technologies, imbuing much of modern technology with its value-laden core.

We assert that this dominant temporal logic has too often been overlooked (largely due to its institutionalized normalcy) when trying to understand the prevailing modes of temporal paucity, undermined autonomy, and constant connectivity that characterize the lives of today's many knowledge workers. In the remainder of this chapter we first delineate what we mean by *circumscribed time*, we then draw out the notion of *temporal entrepreneurship*—the set of activities that individuals and groups engage in that (intentional or otherwise) lead to questioning, manipulating, reworking, and occasionally shifting the dominant temporal logic. This is distinct from practices we call *temporal rebellion*, or acts of resistance that are a reaction to circumscribed time, and, at least at first glance, appear to undermine dominant logics. Rather, we argue that because such forms of resistance essentially uphold a strict bifurcation between use/non-use (i.e. engaging with time via ICTs or "detoxing" from these engagements) they paradoxically serve to reaffirm the power of dominant temporal logics. Such rebellion is thus paradoxical because "temporal rebels" do little to question the underlying expectations around how people can and should orient to time via their communication patterns, physical locations of work, and work practices. By contrast, *temporal entrepreneurs*, as we hope to show, are reorienting to time in a way that better fits their individual

shared assumptions about time that are embedded in institutional and societal norms, discourses, material and technological processes, and shared ideologies. A temporal logic defines what is rational, normal, and expected, and imbues a society with a definition of *what time is* that directs individuals in *how they should operate in and through time*. It provides an understanding of time that becomes so embedded that it seems to define reality.

[2] In a related publication with co-author Ellie Harmon (Mazmanian et al. 2015b), we detail how the software application Microsoft Outlook incorporates the logic of efficient time use in an advertisement focused on an imaginary female user continuously adjusting her schedule to find time for her yoga practice.

[3] For a history of productivity norms and time management in the workplace, see Chapter 7 by Melissa Gregg in this volume.

and collective needs and experiences. In proffering a set of new ideas about time and coupling them with mechanisms for larger social dissemination, such individuals are moving from resistance or idealism to entrepreneurial action. This new set of temporal norms begins to outline a refashioned, collective orientation to time that showcases its unexplored facets.

## Studying Knowledge Workers

Before unfolding this argument any further, we want to make note of the data upon which our ideas rest. Collectively, we draw on a decade of inductive research on the use and experience of communication technologies by professionals in the United States. Combined, our data comprise upwards of 250 interviews from five separate research projects that over the course of several years investigated: investment bankers; venture capitalists; corporate lawyers; in-house counsel; footwear sales representatives; management consultants; hotel managers; hotel sales representatives; architects; designers; and freelancers. In addition to interviewing—which was our primary method of choice— we also engaged in other qualitative ethnographic methods to document the experiences of our subjects, including direct observation, shadowing, and the use of diary studies. The focus of each research project was to understand daily work practices, use of communication technologies, and social norms that surrounded each of these occupations and their respective organizational cultures. All data were analyzed through methods aligned with grounded theory, including multiple rounds of inductive coding and iterative cycles between coding and theorizing (Strauss and Corbin 1998; Charmaz 2006). Details about data collection and analysis can be found in prior publications (Mazmanian et al. 2013; Mazmanian 2013; Mazmanian et al. 2015a). As we argue elsewhere, looking across and within a set of distinct qualitative studies can engender rich forms of theorizing. We find that such "empirical reassembling" is a productive way to engage reflectively with qualitative data across studies and across time (Mazmanian and Erickson 2016).

## The Logic of Circumscribed Time

Moving from data to discussion we begin with some additional words on the dominant temporal logic we've named *circumscribed time*. The way that we in Western, developed contexts view the nature of time today is based on a set of embedded assumptions. Through our experiences, our technologies, and our norms we iteratively articulate a common idea that time is *chunkable, single-purpose, linear,* and *ownable* (Mazmanian et al. 2015b). In other words, we

155

orient to time by breaking it apart into units—days, weeks, hours, minutes. In contemporary society, we tend to imbue those units with a single purpose: "I am going to work on this book chapter for the next 25 minutes"; "I am going to do yoga for a half an hour"; "I will be gone from work for the day," etc. We understand these units to be in a linear relation to one another—they progress forward inexorably into the future, one piece followed by the next and so on. Additionally, we typically claim time to be our own—even at work. This statement, of course, suggests that we are commissioned with responsibilities for which we have to figure out the best and most efficient method of execution. Time is our resource in this sense, but such a fragile one that we shoulder the onus to invest well. These ideas are echoed in the words of Egger and Wagner, who suggest that "time is homogeneous, objective, measurable, and infinitely divisible" (1992: 249). Finally, and for our argument most importantly, these conceptions of time's reality engender a set of values about how time is best used, best designed for, or best expressed. When taken together, these values articulate a logic about what is good or ideal, which, in turn, generates a set of norms and common practices. Next, we explicate this logic.

### Time is Chunkable

The expectation that time is chunkable is conditioned by an understanding that time exists in units (a second, a minute, a year) and that temporal units are equal. Understanding time as chunkable is the basis for what has been referred to elsewhere as "gridded" or "clock" time. This temporal orientation emerged in the seventeent–nineteenth centuries alongside the adoption of clocks, watches, and railroads (Thompson 1967; Zerubavel 1982, 1980). We see this expectation embedded in current calendaring systems that default to thirty- or sixty-minute chunks that can be dragged across various slots with ease. The "dragging" of activities across time implicitly suggests that temporal chunks are "equal" in the sense that an activity performed in one chunk of time is equivalent to that same activity performed in another chunk of time. By rendering time into apparently equal measurable units, such systems encourage an assumption that activities form according to the shape of temporal units rather than vice versa. In addition, such applications suggest that chunks of time are malleable, responsive, and exist in relative isolation; a single swipe of a finger can transform a 2.00 p.m. appointment to a 3.00 p.m. appointment with no regard for the possible domino effect of such a move. Time chunks thus set the stage for future-oriented temporal manipulation and valuation; they assume that we are able to know, in advance, the duration of tasks and experiences and slot them into our gridded schedules accordingly, and without heed for unanticipated activities, delay, or miscommunication.

## Time is Allocated for a Single Purpose

Aligned with chunkable time is the assumption that each chunk is allocated to a single purpose. The common rhetoric of "family time," "work time," and "me time" suggests that certain activities are appropriate only in certain social spheres. Even "dead time" denotes a very specific relationship between time and "productive" activity (or lack thereof). The assumed purity of the relationship between time and activity becomes all the more noticeable in a culture both fascinated and fearful of the promise of multi-tasking (Gonzalez and Mark 2004). While the possibilities of doing multiple things at once are seductive, many norms and organizational policies continue to reinforce a "single purpose" understanding of time, often one that occurs in a fixed place. Thus, even as we herald the possibilities of technology-enabled interaction layering, people maintain a taken-for-granted correspondence between certain "types" of time and the tasks, ways of being, and social roles that (rationally and normatively) inhabit certain temporal and spatial spaces. Dinner tables at 6.00 p.m. are for "parents" not "professionals" while boardrooms in the middle of the day are clearly the stronghold of "professionals" rather than "parents."

## Time is Linear

The dominant temporal logic also conceptualizes time as linear. In other words, one chunk of time leads to another in a straight progression. While chunks of time can be manipulated and reordered in the course of a day (or week, or month), each chunk of time has a limited duration and each activity has a beginning and an end. An hour is an hour is an hour. In the course of a day (or a lifetime) hours stack up like a vector, moving one forward in a straightforward progression. The various ways in which we account for historical evolution in terms of timelines or display visions of the future as straight trajectories perpetuate a notion of linear progress. Timelines, calendars, course syllabi, ten-day forecasts, etc., all underscore the temporal logic that time moves forward at a standard rate.

## Time is Owned (Ownable) by the Individual

Finally, time is understood as a resource that is owned by an individual. Individual ownership of time is often conceived of as integral to personal autonomy and professional freedom (Zerubavel 1979). Paradoxically, the assumption that time is owned by the individual invites others to ask for temporal commitments—the host of which must be effectively processed without hesitation or guilt. In today's society it is up to the individual to manage his or her time effectively, and with the injunction to manage one's time well comes an abdication of responsibility for how others manage their time. If time is owned by the individual then it is up to the individual to manage competing demands—others need not worry about making claims on that time.

In short, the logic articulated by a notion of circumscribed time infers that time should be harnessed into "productive" capacity by approaching it as something that can be chunked, allocated to a single use, experienced linearly, and owned. In turn, the norms of society place the burden on individuals to manage and "balance" time as a steward, optimizing this precious resource by way of strategic control and management. Time is a resource that can, and should, be mastered. As related to knowledge work, circumscribed time has become the taken-for-granted context upon which workplace tasks and relationships play out.

## Opting Out as Temporal Rebellion

There are several ways to address the phenomenon of circumscribed time. As stated in the previous section, many attempt to master its norms and follow its edicts. It is, after all, the logic upon which much of modern capitalism is based (Mazmanian and Erickson 2014; Mazmanian and Erickson 2016). There are others, in contrast, that rebel against the strictures of circumscribed time by denying its hold. Throughout our fieldwork and lately in societal discourse at large—particularly in the United States—people speak often about "reclaiming their time," of "opting out," and other forms of what we term *temporal rebellion*. An example of temporal rebellion might be limiting the time in which you are available to others via digital networking, such as not reading or replying to emails on the weekends or in the evenings. Another example might be choosing to reinforce certain spatial locales for certain types of interactions, such as not doing anything work-related when you are at home, or vice versa. These small acts of defiance are finding root in wider social venues as the recent weeklong project called "Bored and Brilliant"[4] sponsored by the local public radio station in New York City, WNYC. This social experiment was dubbed as "a week of challenges to help you detach from your phone and spend more time thinking creatively." To participate, people signed up for daily challenges that were meant to force them to disengage from their devices, supposedly engendering awareness and possibly reform of their own practices with regard to technology.

[4] <http://www.wnyc.org/series/bored-and-brilliant/> (accessed June 2016).

The ethos of this and the many similar directives[5] like it are that one must develop social, temporal, and cognitive muscles in order to resist (or withstand) the inevitable and all-consuming draw of technology (and the people, expectations, obligations, and activities that said technology mediates). Those that are able to do so, who can muster the agency to step out of the commonly perceived temporal norms of modern life, are donned as heroes in the same way that a tightly toned athlete or a saintly ascetic might be—as one whose abilities reflect their exceptionalism. Able to resist the tantalizing technical baubles that tempt at every turn, temporal rebels revel in the reward of a slowed-down existence where time is no longer something that humbles, but is something that one need not attend to at all—if only for a brief while.

Unlike those individuals and organizations that celebrate the controlled management of time, temporal rebels seek to step out of time (as it is socially or professionally contrived) and act according to their own inner tempo. This naturalistic orientation to time belies the primary rhetoric that surrounds many of the new applications and services that support temporal rebellion, namely that time as it is socially enacted today impedes individual autonomy and creative possibility. Stepping away from these social mandates allows one to get in touch with personal rhythms, often linked closely to one's biology (instead of one's society). Recently, a number of mobile applications have been developed to support this urge for temporal rebellion. One popular application is called Moment,[6] whose tagline reads: "Put down your phone and get back to life." (Its logo, not coincidentally, is a flower, which seemingly attempts to evoke its technologically contrived relationship to time as "natural.") Reinforcing the determinist feeling that the speed and temporal norms of modern society are exemplified—and indeed controlled—by the mobile phone, this application has just announced a new addition to accompany its first, Moment Family, which takes a slightly more dictatorial approach to temporal rebellion by forcing users (various members of a family) off their respective devices when a certain temporal set point is reached.

Alternately, applications like OFFTIME[7] promise a solution for temporal rebels that "enable[s] people to customize their connectivity and create bespoke bubbles of space and time, where they can be at ease and in control.... [OFFTIME] isn't just downtime. It's is a gift to yourself and the people you care about. It might just be the most valuable gift there is: your time and attention." There is the connotation with these applications that people can be "off the temporal grid" or leave the social expectations of availability or

---

[5] This is only one example, but there are many others including Camp Grounded, Digital Detox, and articles such as this: <http://www.fastcompany.com/3012521/unplug/baratunde-thurston-leaves-the-internet> (accessed June 2016).

[6] <https://inthemoment.io/> (accessed June 2016).

[7] <http://offtime.co/bigpicture> (accessed June 2016).

rapid response behind simply by flicking a switch. Indeed, it is ironic that each of these applications call on technology to control time spent with technology—though none admit the incongruousness of this claim. Similarly, both are aptly named as tools that refocus their users on what are assumed to be valued (but non-normative) temporal states—being off the clock and in the moment. In this way they reflect an older tool in this arsenal developed by graduate student Fred Stutzman when he was trying to write his dissertation. The tool that he created allows a user to define a block of time in which they will be irrevocably disconnected from the Internet. Notably it is named "Freedom."[8]

While temporal rebellion feels agentic, especially for Americans who tend toward individualistic problem-solving to address social ills, this form of activity does nothing to destabilize or redress the predominating temporal logic that we describe as circumscribed time. In many ways, it implicitly reifies the current social construction even more by suggesting that there is little to be done other than opt out (if only for an hour or a weekend). And, of course, it does little to question *who* can opt out and the position of relative power that such moves imply (Sharma 2014). Unlike other socially contested topics of the day that highlight the power of social construction, such as the politics of gender or the manifestation of civil society, time, even by temporal rebels, appears to be a naturally contrived reality, something to be accepted, adjusted to, or rebelled against, rather than reconsidered or amended.

## Bending Time as a Temporal Entrepreneur

Yet, there is another set of individuals in our dataset that interact with time's perceived restraints differently. We call these people *temporal entrepreneurs* in order to highlight that they are, intentionally or otherwise, introducing new actions and orientations into the predominate temporal discourse. They are innovating in a way that can shift the current understanding of time, both at an individual and collective level. Our concept of temporal entrepreneurship is inspired by the theory of institutional entrepreneurship (Garud et al. 2002; Prasad et al. 2014; Quattrone 2015). In this framework of organizational and field-level change, institutional entrepreneurs employ their social skills and agency (Fligstein 1997; Fligstein 2013; Fligstein and McAdam 2012) successfully to insert an alternate conception of reality into the extant social framework of an organization and/or organizational field. Institutional entrepreneurs of this ilk often exploit a fissure in the way(s) that reality is perpetually re-enacted in

---

[8] <https://freedom.to> (accessed June 2016).

an everyday social system (Giddens 1984; Lounsbury et al. 2003), revealing areas where the extant institutional logic is weak. As a result, existing norms can be called into question, opening up an opportunity for reflection that can lead to larger social change. Often institutional entrepreneurs are considered at the macro level only, as they tend to be agents of change who primarily help to induce new fields or industries at the sector level. However, more recent work by Battilana, Boxenbaum, and colleagues (Battilana et al. 2009) and Kellogg (2009) highlights how institutions can also change from the bottom up. It is in the spirit of this strand of institutional theory that we graft on our notion of time.

Institutional entrepreneurship requires not only the introduction of new ideas. Just as critical is the reception of said ideas. Tactics, strategies, and new temporal engagements need to become recognized and legitimated slowly by a larger collective. This mixture of both creative actions and spreading adoption is included in our development of the notion of temporal entrepreneurship. As such, we seek to showcase specific examples that illustrate inklings of new, risky engagements with time that we have seen in our data, as well as some of the ways we see our respondents beginning to gain traction to support these ideas.[9] As in classic stories of innovation, our temporal entrepreneurs and their entrepreneurial ideas are primarily on the periphery of most social activity; we are not unveiling anything herein that we expect to see reshaping society anytime soon. Rather, our emphasis is, first, on developing the notion of temporal entrepreneurship in contrast to temporal rebellion, and to begin a conversation in which new conceptions of time might be understood in relationship to shifting logics rather than as something entirely anti-social. In the quotidian practices of certain individuals, collaborative teams, or small communities, we see actors fashioning prototypes for new temporal possibilities that are more compatible with lived experience than alignment with the norms of circumscribed time (O'Carroll 2008). These new temporal possibilities are the small acts of entrepreneurial change we detail in this section.

### Entrepreneurial Notions of Time

The defining characteristic of an entrepreneur is that he or she dabbles in "risky ideas," seeking to get them adopted by customers (or members of society) as welcome improvements or new additions. In temporal entrepreneurship the same is true. In particular, we observe three ways in which participants in our

---

[9] In much of our fieldwork to date, these actors—coincidentally or not—are women. This point bears much further analysis than we can undertake here, but suffice to say that this not only raises the question of whether or not our standard understanding of time is gendered, it also prompts further inquiry regarding why women may be in this position in the first place.

study engage with time in new, entrepreneurial ways. To put these ideas in their proper context, it is important to be mindful of the fact that proffering temporal alternatives is not necessarily a neutral proposition in many professional circles. Suggesting that there is a better way of understanding time—particularly in business contexts, but beyond this as well—reveals that there is a misalignment with the predominant practices of time management. Calling this out as an individual risks appearing weak or lacking, like a modern-day worker unable to keep up with the demands of the job or an individual who lacks contemporary multitasking or planning skills. Thus, while the three alternate notions of time we identify in our data were not practiced or articulated as forms of protest, they hint at a potential undermining of dominant temporal norms, and in so doing create risk for those who engage with time differently.

## Spectral Time

Our data reveal that not every temporal experience is easily articulated, planned for, measurable, or able to be rendered into a schedule. We call this "spectral time" (Mazmanian et al. 2015b). This term references moments that do not lend themselves to scheduling (i.e. chunking), either because the act seems too mundane to justify articulation (i.e. getting dressed), because it is difficult to assess (i.e. travel time), or simply because it cannot be anticipated (i.e. creative phases). In alignment with Reddy and Dourish's concept of temporal trajectory (Reddy and Dourish 2002), spectral time suggests that temporal experience is more than a grid of accountable blocks; multiple temporalities create flows that often defy both logical rendering and seamless manipulation.

In our data we saw spectral time exemplified in the case of Morgan, a trained architect who now runs her own design firm. A new business owner, Morgan regularly needs to traverse New York City, and occasionally places further afield, to develop business for her small firm, make presentations, collect data at client sites, or attend professional functions that reinforce her strong ties to the city's architectural community. She has two permanent employees, a set of close collaborators, and a plethora of other contacts at any one time that she's trying to impress and satisfy—similar to many of the knowledge workers we spoke to across our studies. Morgan's method for achieving temporal equanimity leverages the fact that a majority of her clients and colleagues depend on less-than-dependable infrastructures like trains and subways throughout their day; as such, it is rare for time to stay within its grid here, even in the best of circumstances. Taking advantage of this common experience of temporal imprecision, Morgan has developed a hybrid system in which she uses her mobile device to microcoordinate (Ling and Yttri 2002) each meeting or event, emailing ahead at each juncture to acknowledge her physical presence and her expected arrival. Morgan uses technology to loosen rather than tighten time, and her skill in so doing is helping to legitimate a new professional definition of timeliness that is relative, not absolute.

## Cohabited Time

Our subjects also express the view that, while it may be on their calendar and in their minds as something that must be managed, time is never wholly owned, but rather shared or interlinked. These synchronous linkages to multiple social worlds—professional, personal, family, etc.—are often experienced as stressors in people's lives; individuals seek to delineate the social roles that they are engaging at any one moment as each role ties them to a hierarchical web of personal and professional expectations. Yet stories from our data suggest that for certain workers, those from younger generations in particular, the need to attend to multiple fronts and (potentially) appease conflicting demands is less problematic, if not less present in their lives at all. This lack of stress seems to suggest a shift in the way that we attend to one another. Instead of drawing on the norms of co-present interaction, which tend to reinforce a point of singular, shared attention, there appears to be a new norm emerging that expects that any one moment in time may be subject to multiple interactions. We call this "cohabited time." Take the case of Adam, a marketing manager at a food and beverage company. He understands that he sits at the center of a social ecosystem, which is a very important asset to him professionally. To take advantage of this position, he must move adroitly among these varying personas at a moment's notice. When he is present on location at a remote event, for example, he communicates with distant colleagues, calls his absent girlfriend, and is physically present for his onsite team. This strategic engagement is not so much multitasking as it is a form sociotechnical code switching, where one can (or must) fashion a rudimentary coexistence with multiple faces and voices as close to synchronously as possible. Adam shares his time the way that we share our presence on the planet— it is used individually but always with the recognition that it is cohabited by multiple others at the same time. And, perhaps most significantly, his peers and colleagues now expect this.

## Porous Time

These two alternative notions of time forecast the third and perhaps most destabilizing conception of time articulated by our interviewees. This is the notion that time now encompasses multiple contexts simultaneously. Before the intrusion of technology, the rhythms or tempo of a specific moment were related to the situated location in which it took place. Now, these anchoring mechanisms no longer apply. Further, when multiple locations are involved all at once a different kind of moment emerges—one that sits above the particularities of any one place with the exception of occasional intrusions such as the sound of a police car's siren passing by or a crying child in another room, or jarring reminders of a temporal/physical coupling when the power goes out or the network goes down. To say that these moments are porous means that they let through (both in and out) various pieces of all the contexts assembled via technology in that moment.

In previous work (Mazmanian et al. 2015b), we speak of this type of time as a mosaic. In reiterating this allusion here, we stress two important aspects of thinking: first, that the dimensions of many mediated encounters today are akin to a tapestry that has been woven from partial fragments into a recognizable whole. This amalgamated nature of time showcases how it is actively constructed, not simply path-dependent in an ever-unfolding line. Moreover, naming time to be a mosaic highlights the invisible work (Star and Strauss 1999) that is required to fashion it into something that has social coherence—that is meaningful, comprehensible, and actionable—or as something that has currency to others as well as oneself. As workers are increasingly small pieces in ever larger, globalized enterprises, they must put in more and more effort to make whole what would otherwise be seen as independent parts.

Porous time acknowledges the merging of multiple social spheres into a layered or fitted set of simultaneous interactions. Sometimes this is fine-meshed porosity—screen-like, as it were (i.e. stand close and you see one apparent reality, step back and you see another)—where tasks, worlds, and identities seem tightly integrated. One of our subjects, Chad, appears to merge worlds and identities rather holistically, moving in and out of his role as father of two and the demands of being a corporate executive with apparent ease. We saw this in action when one of his daughters suggested playing the board game *Clue* on a Sunday afternoon. We all (mother, father, older daughter, younger daughter, and ethnographer) gathered around the board, moving our pawns, bantering, and deducting the details of the murder. Between each round of the game, when others were clearing the pieces and rearranging the cards, Chad typed on his iPhone until it became clear that it was time to begin the next game. Chad was able to keep track of the progress of the game and merge his work into this scene harmoniously. No one around him appeared to be frustrated and Chad was actively engaged with his family. When asked later what he was doing, Chad listed various substantive emails that he wrote during this time. In his words, it was "real work."

What these three alternate pictures of time bring to mind is not the struggle of temporal rebellion already described. No one has stepped away from their obligations nor taken a temporal time out. Neither, however, do these vignettes showcase actors bent on optimal time management and efficiency.

Rather, these actors all showcase, some more than others, an acceptance of time as something more than the ownable, linear, gridded reality we typically understand it to be. These individuals are, in their own ways, rejecting the prevailing norms for a set of new proto-practices that acknowledge that time also has spectral, obligated, and porous aspects. In so doing, we suggest, as external researchers, that they are beginning to act as temporal entrepreneurs.[10]

### Finding Temporal Traction

Earlier we noted the need for entrepreneurs not only to adhere to their risky, unproven ideas, but also to find engagement in ways that enable them to bring these ideas to a wider audience. The interviewees mentioned earlier are each introducing and slowly normalizing a new aspect of time into their social lives—some more intentionally than others. Chad, the board game-playing executive, for instance, might be seen by some as an example of technological utopianism or cultural demise, but our point in showcasing him here is that he has figured out how to incorporate and even embrace several new dimensions of time into his life with equanimity. Notably, the rhythm of his interaction(s) is not dictated by a pre-ordered grid, but instead rather sloppily flows across shared contexts, both immediate and distant. He seeks not to manage any of this, as would a commander, but rather to be in an attuned and ready position to ride time's wave, as would a surfer. Moreover, he succeeds in maintaining a connection to all parties involved (i.e. family, clients) and does not falter in meeting their respective needs. The strength of this image has nothing to do with Chad's technology use, but rather his ability to accept time as something fluid and dynamically contextual that he must embrace with agility and internal direction rather than rigidity and extreme foresight. Importantly, he successfully enacts this fluid idea of time with all of his interlocutors and, in so doing, begins to legitimate it as a new type of temporal normalcy.

Yet, even entrepreneurs like Steve Jobs need a means to publicize their great ideas. In closing out this chapter we note two ways that we see temporal entrepreneurs extending their new ideas outward for larger circulation beyond their own personal preferences or ecosystems.

Recall the way that Morgan, the architect, acknowledges spectral time in her daily rhythms. She is not trying to achieve temporal mastery to better stay within the gridded lines of her calendar—this is in no way her prerogative.

---

[10] Again, we remind the reader that these actors did not call themselves temporal entrepreneurs; this is our analytical moniker to highlight certain practices as having potential to shift institutional logics. Indeed, not all subjects in our set of studies have the same agency to introduce these alternatives into their practices for a variety of reasons.

Rather, she has ingeniously figured out how to exploit the vagaries of a local infrastructure (and which infrastructures do not have eccentricities?) to fold spectral, obligated, and porous time together by purposely extending the social space of interaction beyond its physical boundaries. This is a highly strategic act on her part, which allows her to maintain both professional face and her own situated temporal rhythm with apparent seamlessness.

More importantly for her rendering as a temporal entrepreneur, Morgan has also successfully established this communication norm within her firm and her larger set of collaborators. She is not perceived as late or lazy, but as highly competent. Primarily exploiting several features of existing technologies, but also upholding all of the semiotic references to professionalism in their field, Morgan is slowly institutionalizing a sociotechnical practice of hybridized professional encounters that embrace a version of "networked spectrality." This is slowly leading to incidents of isomorphism, as Morgan is a very public face within New York's architectural community. Morgan is innovatively rewriting the temporal script, which, in its own small, revolutionary way, is shifting the temporal expectations of her field.

The last example of entrepreneurial traction we showcase involves an organizational change effort aimed at providing elite consultants predictable time in which they were disconnected from work. Perlow and colleagues outline how a collective strategy of managing temporal work conditions can enable teams to maintain the client expectation of 24/7 availability while carving out individual time off for each individual (Perlow and Porter 2009; Mazmanian 2012; Perlow et al. 2015). Conducting "predictable time off" (PTO) experiments, Perlow shows how collective strategies that enabled each team member to take one night "off" a week unintentionally inspired teams to reorient to time as a collective, rather than individual, resource. In tracing the effects of a work intervention premised on the collective goal of enabling team members to take modest amounts of predictable time off, Perlow's work suggests how explicit activities designed to change communication and work practices can challenge core beliefs about competence and commitment, specifically in terms of how "successful" consultants should orient to time. Notably, such a goal may not be seen as collective in many environments, but in high-intensity team-based work individuals cannot simply plan for a predictable night off without collective engagement from the group. The concept of collective temporal resources illustrates how shared beliefs around the nature of time can have profound effects on the way time is structured and negotiated in collectives.

The organization of this company's time as a collective asset first and foremost highlights an adoption of the idea that time is a shared entity—in this case a resource that can be divvied up among teammates and managed to support the needs of all. This flies in the face of conventional wisdom that tends to address issues of work addiction, and the individual and social costs of temporal intensity suggest that it us up to individuals to take charge and manage increasing temporal demands (Fassel 1990; Porter and Kakabadse 2006; McMillan and O'Driscoll 2008). Moreover, neither is it a clear case of obligated time until you look at things quite closely. This company has created a new internal system that at its core acknowledges that shared time belongs to no one individual to control, manage, or squander. Like the reference to the climate made earlier, time here is a resource that is understood to be individually consumed, but never without regard or consequences for others. Time management then is about social coherence and the sustainability of professional relations when not everyone is present at all times. In setting this new norm for modern professionalism, this company is providing a platform that gives peripheral ideas like obligated and spectral time important entrepreneurial traction and ballast. More importantly, it is well poised to shift temporal norms away from those dictated by circumscribed time through its interactions with collaborating partners at both the individual and organizational level.

## Conclusion

There is little argument that technology is helping to shape modern forms of work. What there should be argument about, however, as we aver in this chapter, is how those sociotechnical forms of work are shaped by time. As a society, we tend to pose few questions about the nature of time or its associated norms; rather, it seems natural to strive toward efficiency by adjusting schedules, attempting to multitask, and putting pressure on ourselves to manage our time expertly. We have lost sight of the fact that this is but one version of time, socially constructed just as any alternate could be. By naming this predominant version—*circumscribed time*—and identifying how it sets up social expectations, values, and norms in the way that any other social institution would do, we take a first step toward temporal entrepreneurship.

The second, and hopefully more sustaining, contribution of this chapter is our idea of temporal entrepreneurship, born of the many conversations with knowledge workers over the years from various fields. While many of these workers express feelings of stress and pressure brought on by the dominant temporal logic in society today, we see in their responses and related actions the seeds of a new way of conceiving time. These ideas are at a germinal state, to be sure, but importantly they are not conceptions of time that attempt to stop or freeze it, as would be the path of the temporal rebel, or ideations of efficiency that subscribe to a traditional path of time management. In lighting out for new territory, these unwitting temporal entrepreneurs are incubating small, alternative temporal moves and slowing normalizing them in their immediate interactions. We celebrate these moves not only for their innovative natures, but also for the new ideas of professionalism they are simultaneously gestating. Like these innovative individuals, we suggest that instead of opting for the path of temporal rebellion, the more sustainable path forward may be in bending time to include a more encompassing reality—one that includes spectral, obligated, and porous temporal elements both in professional environments as well as society at large.

# 11

# Speed, Time, Infrastructure

## Temporalities of Breakdown, Maintenance, and Repair

*Steven J. Jackson*

> Life is in the transitions as much as in the terms connected.
>
> William James, "A World of Pure Experience," 1904

This chapter concerns the importance of *breakdown, maintenance and repair* to human and material stability and change—and whether new ways of thinking about such phenomena might also help us to rethink relationships between technology and time. While Part II of this volume has examined other dimensions of the material shaping of technology, I want to call particular attention to processes of failure and restoration as core and widely neglected dimensions of infrastructure, even—perhaps especially—within the core transport, communication, and computing infrastructures commonly held responsible for contemporary experiences of speed and acceleration. As I'll argue, such processes are complex, omnipresent, deeply skilled, and rooted in our relationships to and with material things—and for all of these reasons widely neglected in our theorizing. They are also sites from which a different temporal sensibility in and around technology might begin to emerge.

The chapter that follows opens by questioning a classic line on the relationship between emerging technologies and the social experience of time. It then turns to alternatives to this line, and argues that reimagining modern infrastructures from the standpoint of breakdown, maintenance, and repair (rather than design, invention, or adoption) may lead us toward different outcomes in our thinking around time and technology. It takes up a small but growing body of work in infrastructure and repair studies that has begun to rebalance the story of technology by restoring attention to the myriad acts and moments, large and small, mundane and creative, conservative and transformational—by which systems and infrastructures are fixed, maintained, and extended. And it concludes with speculation on the temporal and ethical possibilities that emerge when breakdown, maintenance, and repair—the "slow underbelly" of modernist stories of speed and technology—are taken more centrally into account.

## Speed, Time, and Infrastructure: The Classic Line

Earlier contributors to this volume have explored the deep and intimate relationship between technology and time that has occupied and challenged work in the social sciences since their inception. From "the annihilation of space and time" (Marx 1973) and the accelerated forms of "exposure" reworking urban life (Simmel 1950), to contemporary experiences of "chronopolitics" (Virilio 1986) and "time-space compression" (Harvey 1989), technologies of transport, communication, and computing have long been central to arguments for the growing speed and acceleration of contemporary life. Such theoretical contributions find their counterpart in the less nuanced stories around time and technology offered in popular writing around technology, media reports, and the self-accounts of the technology industries themselves. In their simplest *Wired* magazine form, these stories posit a simple causal arrow: technology accelerates, and life adjusts.

But as attested to by a growing body of theoretical and empirical work (including many of the contributions to this volume), the relationship between technology and time is more varied, complex, and uncertain than all that. My own entrée into these questions is through the varied forms of time and timeliness organized and structured through *infrastructure*: and conversely, the myriad forms of maintenance and repair required to sustain it. Growing from work in the history of technology and pragmatist, interactionist, and feminist traditions in sociology, science studies, and information science, recent work in infrastructure and repair studies offers numerous resources for reimagining the story of technology and speed. Against global pretensions of acceleration, for example, historian of technology David Edgerton (2011) has argued for the long, slow, and highly partial integration of what we usually celebrate as "cutting edge" technologies into social life, in contrast to the slow and enduring impact of older and frequently mundane technologies as these are taken up and creatively repurposed through ordinary use around the world; or as Paul Edwards (2004) has observed, "the most salient characteristic of technology in the modern (industrial and post-industrial) world is the degree to which most technology is *not* salient for most people, most of the time" (2004: 185). This work has emphasized the role of infrastructure in shaping human experiences of time (including our notions of temporal scale and "modernity" itself) but also the role of time and temporal passage (e.g. through moments of growth, stabilization failure, or decline) in shaping the physical forms and dynamics inherent to infrastructure. This situates infrastructure firmly *in* and *of* time, rather than as an agent or force impinging on it from the outside.

A second resource for reimagining relationships between time and technology may be found in an influential notion of infrastructure first advanced by Star and Ruhleder (1996). In their account, infrastructure provides the framework or scaffolding for social and technical activities of all sorts, and exemplifies a number of key features or properties: its embedding in other structures; its frequent transparency (or invisibility) in use; its reach or scope beyond single sites of practice; its connections to norms and conventions grounded in wider communities of practice; its embodiment in standards; its dependence on an installed base of practices and material objects; and its tendency to "reappear" (or return to conscious reflection) under conditions of failure or breakdown. If this definition calls out the relational quality of infrastructure—exemplified elsewhere in the dictum, "one person's infrastructure is another person's barrier" (Star 1999)—it also underscores its timeliness: its positioning, sometimes delicate, within wider flows and relations through which its meaning and viability *qua* infrastructure (as opposed to disparate and unmoored grouping of objects) is assigned. This exposes infrastructure to the vagaries of time and change in the world, and makes questions of "*when* is an infrastructure?" (Star 1999) no less central than questions of what, where, or for whom.

From this starting point, other propositions around the relationship between time, speed, and infrastructure become possible: for example, that our stories of time and infrastructure are always stories of *multiple* times, and the challenging and power-laden processes by which these are brought into workable and temporary alignment; that the cast of actors involved in these stories may be larger and more varied than technology-centered accounts may suggest; and that infrastructure itself is subject to all the same processes and pressures: a *creature*, and not just agent, of time. Such insights underscore the need to set the story of speed against other temporalities which must also be accounted for in any balanced discussion of technology, time, and social life: temporalities of breakdown, ruin, and decay for example; and of maintenance and repair. The sections that follow explore each of these in turn.

## Temporalities of Breakdown, Ruin, and Decay

A small but growing body of recent work across the social sciences has (re)turned to problems of breakdown, ruin, and decay, both as ever-present realities in the social life of things and people, and as sites of generativity from which the new is being perpetually (re)produced. DeSilvey (2006) for example has explored the residual material culture of a derelict homestead in Montana to argue for the live and fertile processes unleashed through ruination, showing how the "disarticulation" of objects—for example, a book box slowly giving way to mice and rot—may complicate both assumptions around the "timeless" nature of objects and a series of ontological distinctions (e.g. artifact vs. environment, nature vs. culture) that have long framed and limited the imagination of social scientists. Edensor (2011) has shown the complex and multiple temporalities that shape and sustain heritage buildings (here, St. Ann's Church in central Manchester) as dynamic and ongoing *assemblages*, subject to processes of transformation over time through their interactions with weather, pollution, salts, living agents ranging from bats, birds, and rodents to moss, bacteria, and people. Scholars of architecture, urban planning, and information science have begun to question their fields' predominant emphases on design, reimagining buildings, devices, and other material artifacts instead as unruly *events* unfolding across time and space, and upheld by ongoing acts of ordering and stabilization, in the absence of which "buildings must die" (Cairns and Jacobs 2014). In some instances, renewed attention to breakdown has become a tool for unsettling received academic and political categories: for example, the turn to notions of "ruin" and "debris" in recent postcolonial scholarship (Stoler 2008); or growing attention to processes of "abjection" and other forms of infrastructural violence in anthropology (Anand 2012; Ferguson 2012). In others, attending to waste and ruination has given rise to whole new genres and subfields of work: for example, the emerging fields of waste or discard studies (Lepawsky 2014; Liboiron 2014) and the associated project of "garbology" (Humes 2013).

But if these principles hold for building and empires, they are no less true of other kinds of infrastructures, including those commonly credited with producing the experiences of speed and compression at the heart of accelerationist narratives. In many parts of the world, railways are in physical decline, as lines fall into disuse, rail beds erode, and plant life (previously held at bay through aggressive programs of spraying and weed control) creeps in. Decay shows up in the cracks that mark and degrade American highways, in a collective state of physical decline since their heyday of national expansion in the 1950s. Normally shy of publicity, infrastructure is most likely to make the news in the West these days in the form of spectacular bridge collapses, as chronically underfunded infrastructure—the victim of tax resentments and funding cuts that follow in turn from a kind of political decay—breaks and fails. Histories of telecommunications development around the world are replete with ruin, as undersea cables break, computing stock (for example, as introduced by international donor investments ranging from rural telecenters to One Laptop Per Child) fails and degrades, and wires are stripped and resold for copper (Rosner and Ames 2014; Chan 2014). The presumed weightlessness of "the digital" itself may be subject to complex processes of decay, as storage erodes, firmware fails, files corrupt, and the voltages marking binaries of 1 and 0 grow fuzzy and indistinct (Cantwell-Smith 1998; Blanchette 2011).

What can broken objects and the processes that produce them give to the sociology of speed? To begin, such instances remind us that key instrumentalities of speed—the core and "cutting edge" infrastructures from which contemporary experiences of speed and acceleration are held to flow—are for all that no less subject to the processes of reversal, ruin, and decline that characterize other forms of social and material existence in the world. For all their vaunted power and reach, transport, communication, and other infrastructures central to the acceleration of temporal experience from Marx's time to our own remain in many ways light and fragile creatures, prone to the constant threat of failure and decay. Attending to breakdown points us toward the active and ontologically productive nature of ruin, and the irreducible presence of embedded materialities with rhythms and propensities all their own, which can only ever be sometimes, and for a while, slowed, arrested, and aligned. These possibilities are contained and made invisible by any number of categorical distinctions (artifact vs. waste, order vs. dirt (Douglas 1978), etc.) and too often by presumptions of agency and value in the stories we tell about the material world around us. But when allowed to "speak," breakdown and ruin can complicate these settled categories, calling to light new forms of order and ordering and (re)directing attention to the innumerable transformations always already underway in the object worlds around us. Through such mechanisms,

> processes of decay and the obscure agencies of intrusive humans and non-humans transform the familiar material world, changing the form and texture of objects, eroding their assigned functions and meanings, and blurring the boundaries between things. (Edensor 2005: 318)

If such processes give rise to new things, they also give rise to new lines and principles of order: contrary to frequent assumption, sites of ruin and decay may be marked less by the absence of form than by its multiplication and diversification: a profusion, rather than attenuation, of order.

In sum, temporalities of breakdown upend linear and teleological histories by reminding us that time flows at many different paces and in many different directions at once, not all of them fast or—as conventionally understood—

forward. They remind us of the enduring materiality of time, and of the fact that things remain live and active, even (perhaps especially!) after their moments of design, general use, and cultural glory have passed. They challenge easy stories of origin and end point, showing instead the endless processes of emergence and transformation from and ultimately to which objects arise and eventually go. Such processes themselves may be generative and productive, giving rise to processes of learning, invention, and discovery that are graced under other circumstances with the name "innovation." This may help us to extend and broaden the forms and scales against which human-centered understandings of time operate, from the quantum (Barad 2007) to the geological (Parikka 2015). The much-celebrated instrumentalities of speed are no less subject to these forces, showing all the same variances, multiplicities, and fragilities. The evidence for decline and decay is all around us. In the words of the great Nigerian novelist Chinua Achebe (1958), "things fall apart."

## Temporalities of Maintenance and Repair

Except that, much of the time, they *don't*. If the world is replete with instances of breakdown, ruin, and decay and certain groups encounter breakdown more frequently and forcefully than others, the more common experience is that the systems and infrastructures around us *mostly* work, for *most* people, *most* of the time. Because of this, we have tended to regard enduring function as a natural and more or less permanent feature of systems, rather than as the ongoing, frequently artful, and often fraught accomplishment that it is. Indeed, if we are to think to the longevity of systems at all (which we generally don't) we are most likely to attribute it backwards to moments of origin and the virtues of good design.

Such perceptions neglect, however, the centrality of maintenance and repair to working infrastructures of all kinds—and the complex and some-times ambivalent temporalities built and expressed through such action. Support for this position can be found once again through recent work in architecture. Following from their argument for the necessary mortality of buildings, Cairns and Jacobs (2014) attach enormous importance to the role of maintenance and building staff as ongoing shapers and transformers of buildings' living identities. As this work attests, notions of static form and imaginations of timeless design that have long preoccupied the field are both inaccurate and a disservice to the real-world processes and labors by which buildings are sustained and made to evolve or "learn" (Brand 1995) through time. Strebel's (2011) study of concierge workers in a Glasgow housing estate documents the routine inspections, maintenance activities, and minor repairs by which the "momentum" of the building—its unique temporal trajectory and unfolding into the future—is sustained. Neither purely backward-looking nor restorative in nature, and lost under the field's normal fixation on architectural form and intention, such activities shape and reshape buildings as dynamic entities through time, ensuring their status as live and timely objects.

More recent work by Graham and Thrift (2007) has extended this line to consider the various forms of maintenance and repair through which such futures are forestalled. Drawing on the classic Heideggerian distinction between things "ready-to-hand" vs. "present-at-hand," along with recent work in infrastructure and urban studies, they trace the myriad forms of maintenance and repair by which modern cities are constituted and sustained (as opposed to the broken, chaotic, and impossible places they would quickly become if maintenance and repair work were withdrawn). Cities are in many ways no more (and no less!) than a complex assemblage of infrastructural systems, held in partial states of function and connection through large (and largely neglected) collections of maintenance and repair work. Under ordinary circumstances, such work remains "invisible," subsumed within the flow and function of urban life; it is only when massive and catastrophic failure threatens that maintenance and repair is restored to widespread attention (giving our public discourses around infrastructure a flair for the dramatic). This fact, and the general failure to extend urban theory by accounting for conditions in cities of the "global South" (where experiences and responses of failure and repair may be simply too prominent to ignore), helps to:

> sustain widespread assumptions that urban "infrastructure" is somehow a material and utterly fixed assemblage of hard technologies embedded stably in place, which is characterized by perfect order, completeness, immanence and internal homogeneity rather than leaky, partial and heterogeneous entities. (Graham and Thrift 2007: 10)

The error of this assumption is made clear in any even-handed consideration of electricity, computing, and automobility: key infrastructures in shaping and defining life in contemporary cities. As Graham and Thrift enumerate, such infrastructures are both prone to widespread vulnerability and breakdown (ranging from or brown-outs and security glitches, to potholes, vehicle failure, and congestion) and sustained only at the cost of enormous private and public investments in maintenance and repair—investments increasingly undermined by neoliberal policies that further marginalize repair work and workers and heighten the vulnerability of core urban infrastructures. (for more on this point, see also Graham 2001).

The centrality of maintenance and repair work to urban infrastructure and experience has been further elaborated in a striking series of studies by Denis and Pontille (2014, 2015) around maintenance and repair work among sign crews in the Paris subway. As the authors show, such work is central to the "material ordering" by which the subway's wayfaring systems and urban flow more generally are sustained. They trace first the stabilization of representation through an ambitious program of standardization launched in the 1990s that sought to unify and prescribe (to a remarkable level of detail) all activities pertaining to the design, production, and placement of signs across all components of the greater Paris transport network. But this work, they argue, provides an as-yet insufficient account of the objects in question, for it fails to track the numerous threats and vulnerabilities that threaten the continued existence and intelligibility of the signage system. From mold to graffiti, discoloration to vandalism and theft, the crews charged with maintaining the integrity of the system work to uphold vulnerable and fragile objects against a heterogeneous and sometimes hostile environment. In contrast to the initial design work, maintenance is necessarily vigilant, reactive, and improvisational, attentive to emerging conditions that threaten the ongoing viability of signs across time and context. These two projects—standardization and design and maintenance and repair work as separate but aligned responses that together uphold the effective and timely performance of signs as objects.

My own work with colleagues and students has explored the work of computing and mobile phone repair across a range of sites, from mobile phone repair operations in Namibia and Bangladesh to amateur fixing movements in the global North. Such projects have underscored both the constant (if neglected) processes of breakdown and decay that characterize the real-world existence of computational infrastructures, and the varying regimes of maintenance and repair that nevertheless sustain them as working (under most circumstances, for most people, most of the time). This has included work on the widespread neglect of maintenance and repair in formal development programs (for example, computing for education programs in rural Namibia, see Jackson et al. 2011, 2012), and the role that this neglect plays in undermining various "information and communication technology for development" (ICTD) initiatives. It has also begun to explore the varied "repair worlds" by which Southern computational infrastructures are sustained, arguing for these as sites of difference, innovation, and power which, if properly considered, can begin to correct the extreme geographic tilt in global understandings of innovation (whereby computational skill and innovation is held to be the property of a narrow caste of designers and engineers in rarefied locales like Silicon Valley, rather than the diverse, widely distributed, and heterogeneous phenomenon that it in fact is (Jackson et al. 2011, 2012)).

This work has documented how repair work is organized and sustained in such settings, including at the nexus of local social and professional networks and global flows of objects and knowledge, including vast and complex material circulations in everything from parts and tools to the detritus ("waste") flowing in and out of repair shops (Jackson et al. 2011; Ahmed et al. 2015; see also Houston 2014). It has also documented the particular forms of skill, learning, and innovation embedded in repair work, as expressed across a range of common and not-so-common operations (e.g. "flashing," "servicing," "jumpering," "reballing") and shared through extended and complex networks of apprenticeship and collaboration (Ahmed et al. 2015) (see Figure 11.1). Our more recent work has explored the nature and problem of "values in repair," arguing for the importance of maintenance and repair as sites for the extension and reworking of values and valuation in and around technology, and a necessary counterpart to the better-studied problem of "values in design" (Houston et al. 2016).

Taken collectively, these and other examples from the emerging field of repair studies help to cast light on both the ubiquity and diversity of repair work, and its role within wider systems of material and social order. Here two additional observations may be in order. First, while often routine and mundane in character, maintenance and repair work may also embed crucial elements of skill, innovation, and creativity. A beautiful instance of this can be found in Klemp et al.'s (2008) analysis of the repair of a single wrong note struck during a solo by jazz pianist Thelonious Monk during a 1953 performance of jazz standard "In Walked Bud." Working with recordings and session notes from this and two other performances, the authors show how Monk's initial error is "saved" through the complex reworking of subsequent phrases that weave the erroneous note into a new musical fabric distinct from the original. The repair is performed in real time, and worked out in collaboration with the other members of Monk's group, who hear Monk's "error" and join him in constructing a path through which the initial dissonance of the mistake is gathered, extended, and recouped giving the performance its own novel identity and coherence. This underscores the emergent and relational quality of repair, and its location within ongoing streams of action that are themselves temporally and situationally organized. As Klemp et al. (2008) note:

> when we listen to music, we hear neither plans, nor mistakes, but *takes* in which expectations and difficulties get worked on in the medium of notes, tones and rhythms. Notes live in connection with each other. They make demands on each other, and, if one note sticks out, the logic of their connections demands that they be reset and realigned.

**Figure 11.1.** Repair worker in Gulistan underground market, Dhaka, Bangladesh; photo courtesy of Syed Ishtiaque Ahmed

While not all instances of repair will achieve this lofty level of achievement (nor is every repair worker Thelonious Monk!), improvisation remains central to the work of maintenance and repair writ large. This point is made clear in groundbreaking early work by Orr (1996) and Henke (2000), whose photo-copier repair technicians and building mechanics work with available tools, resources, knowledges, and collectively held experience (stored in the form of "war stories") to restore function and order in the wake of local and context-ually framed breakdowns. Variety in the nature of these breakdowns however—in complex sociotechnical systems, no two failures are alike—demands the adaptive and creative rather than rote application of repair skill and knowledge. This makes repair work resistant to the codifying tendencies that structure work under more controlled and settled environments, including sites of industrial design and production. This situated and improvisational quality has led scholars to language and metaphors that will at first blush seem at odds with the often mundane and ordinary nature of maintenance and repair work: Graham and Thrift (2007) have talked about it as a form of ingenuity, for example; Denis and Pontille (2015) have described it as a kind of dance.

Second, while in some instances the temporal identity of repair as restora-tive or transformative will be clear, in others the line will be fuzzy at best. Take the example of "looping" or "jumpering," widely practiced by mobile phone repair technicians in the informal markets of Dhaka and Kampala (and discussed in greater detail in Houston 2014; and Ahmed et al. 2015). Under this technique, faulty subcomponents (sound cards, accelerometers, etc.) are neither fixed nor replaced but bypassed, as repair technicians solder new pathways on to faulty motherboards, rerouting connections so that compromised components are removed from the general flow, thus preserving and restoring overall device integrity. This work is deeply knowledgeable and skillful, demanding both practical understanding of motherboard geographies (which vary significantly by model and manufacturer), and fine-grained motor skills capable of laying thin lines of solder that establish the desired connections but not others. But while this work restores global function, it does not reproduce an original per se: the phone that emerges at the end is demonstrably *not* the same device, nor is it a copy or return to an earlier form At the level of function, the phone now works differently, containing some but not all of its earlier possibilities. Internally and externally, it bears the marks of its labor as well as the breakdown that occasioned it (broken circuits, scratched casings, etc.). The phone has become in effect a different object: new but not radically new, separated from and connected to its past by the forms of breakdown, maintenance, and repair through which it has passed.

Understood as mechanisms of ordering and modes of temporal practice, maintenance and repair offer distinct and valuable contributions to ongoing debates in the sociology of speed. At the broadest level, such instances suggest a different kind of temporal sensibility, one grounded not in linear or teleological faith, but in honest recognition of the fragility of things, and a respect (even wonder!) for the ongoing work by which stability and order (such as they are) are sustained: what I've elsewhere described as a form of "broken world thinking" (Jackson 2014). Temporalities of maintenance and repair, as deployed in the expansive sense here, gather and blend the unruly timelines of things. In their absence, objects are left to go their own ways, becoming in turn homes for *other* things: rust, mice, and plants for example; or in the case of a growing number of subways and train stations around the world, overflow housing for poor and marginalized groups displaced, in part, by speed. Such instances point to sites, moments, and experiences too often obscured by global stories of speed and acceleration. They also suggest other forms and kinds of timeliness—some of them mundane and slow—by which the effect of speed and acceleration is produced and sustained.

Our frequent blindness to such facts has any number of intellectual and practical consequences. In the venture capital and scientific funding worlds, it is much easier to attract support for new and "transformative" programs of work than the maintenance and continuation of old ones (even where the worth of such programs has been established beyond dispute). In worlds of technology, the neglect of maintenance and repair (and the primacy of design it produces) helps to maintain a narrow and provincial geography of innovation in which the people and processes that matter are constrained to a few square miles of northern California (and a small handful of analogue sites around the world). A similar provincialism may characterize the geography of speed, which may turn out on closer inspection to apply most dramatically to what turns out to be a rather narrow and rarefied class of places, actors, and moments. Taking maintenance and repair seriously invites us to broaden these stories, and to rethink our timelines. To neglect such moments is to collude in the forms of invisibility that such stories help to produce: both around the nature and status of repair work and workers themselves, and the vast range of efforts which in fact characterize and produce temporal experience today.

## Discussion: Repair, Time, and Ethics

Taken collectively, these varied observations around breakdown, maintenance, and repair offer a different possible starting point for our discussions around technology and social life, including the questions of speed explored in this volume. I have argued elsewhere for the contributions such thinking might make to other areas of concern. Some of these tie to immediate and highly practical issues: for example, the design of devices and infrastructures that might better enable and support (rather than frustrate and lock out) possibilities of repair; or the construction of more repair-friendly policies (for example, the reform of intellectual property and liability law to embed rights to repair as concomitant rights of ownership and use). Others are more speculative, and speak to alternative ways of knowing and engaging the social and material worlds that take seriously the notion of breakdown, maintenance, and repair as facts, rather than exceptions, to ordinary life.

As a contribution to the sociology of speed, three additional observations may be in order. The first concerns the distributional consequences of breakdown and repair—both as experience unevenly distributed in the world, and as form of necessary work that nevertheless goes routinely overlooked and undercompensated: a type of blindness that costless or teleological accounts of technology and speed help to exacerbate. Like other global accounts, undifferentiated discussions of speed and acceleration risk missing the vast differences that mark and separate the temporal experiences of variously placed social actors. If "fast" is an affordance of our new technically mediated orders, it is not one available to all. If some revel and reel in the heady experience of speed, others see their lives slowed down (or engage in slow and patient work to produce it). Where some are made to move faster, others are forced to wait. While such distributional consequences have periodically attracted the attention of scholars of speed (see Chapters 9 and 10 in this volume) the core of the point remains perhaps best expressed in classic work by Doreen Massey written in response to an earlier round of debates around the nature of global acceleration and "time-space compression." As Massey insists:

> different social groups and different individuals are placed in very distinct ways in relation to these flows and interconnections. This point concerns not merely the issue of who moves and who doesn't, although that is an important element of it; it is also about power in relation to the flows and the movement. Different social groups have different relationships to this anyway-differentiated mobility: some are more in charge of it than others; some initiate flows and movement, others don't; some are more on the receiving end of it than others; some are effectively imprisoned by it. (1994: 61)

Attending to breakdown, maintenance, and repair may help deepen and extend the distributional analysis of speed, suggesting once again categories of temporal experience neglected under prevailing accounts of acceleration, as well as key forms of labor (themselves neither mobile nor speedy) by which *others'* experiences of speed are supported and maintained. It may also help counter the myths of unity and self-efficacy that emerge when systems and infrastructures are presented with their fragilities and labors stripped away.

The second point concerns the rich and suggestive relations between break-down, maintenance, and repair, and the ethical and political possibilities suggested under a growing body of work around fragility, precariousness, and care. This work has emphasized shared experiences of fragility as both description of the contemporary moment and starting point for a common ethics and politics in the wake of the various "posts" and "neos" we inhabit: "-colonialism," "-modernism," "-liberalism," etc. Andrew Sayer (2011), for example, has argued for shared vulnerability to suffering as grounds for a more robust consideration of ethics within the social sciences, restoring questions of value and values to the center of the field. William Connolly (2013) has pointed to the "fragility" of our geological, biological, and climate systems, along with growing instabilities in economie unmoored by neoliberal reform, as necessary starting points for new and pluralistic democratic projects. In the absence of these, the consequences of fragility are passed "down" to those least equipped to bear them, following a circuit first described by Simmel:

> Every new pressure and imposition moves along the line of least resistance which, though not in its first stage, usually and eventually runs in a descending direction. This is the tragedy of whomever is lowest . . . He not only has to suffer from the deprivations, efforts, and discriminations, which, taken together, characterize his

position; in addition every new pressure on any point whatever in the superordinate layers is, if technically possible at all, transmitted downward and stops only at him. (Simmel 1950: 236–7, cited in Connolly 2013: 23)

Writing in the wake of 9/11 and the devastations of the Iraq War, Judith Butler pursues the consequences of what she terms "a primary vulnerability to others" (2006: xiv), a recognition "that there are others out there on whom my life depends, people I do not know and may never know" (2006: xii). The shared nature of such vulnerabilities are exposed through violence, but also marked and honored through mourning: an act that affirms and upholds relations of mutual vulnerability, a way of staying with others through grief that acknowledges our shared exposure to the vicissitudes of pain, loss, and destruction.

The most direct and suggestive link of all, however, may be to a growing body of work in feminist ethics and technoscience underscoring the presence and centrality of *care*: as affective state, as ethical relation, and as mundane form of practical work. As developed by scholars from Tronto (1993) and Star (1991) to Mol (2008) and de la Bellacasa (2012), care provides an alternate entry point to many contemporary concerns, including but not limited to the problems of time, speed, and repair foregrounded here. In an influential definition offered by Tronto, care includes:

everything that we do to maintain, continue and repair "our world" so that we can live in it as well as possible. That world includes our bodies, our selves, and our environment, all of which we seek to interweave in a complex, life sustaining web. (1993: 103)

Care builds from and expresses a commitment to interdependence and (mutual) vulnerability, a recognition that human endurance and flourishing in the world are never autonomous and self-sustaining accomplishments, but rather arise at the intersection of innumerable relationships, webs of dependencies in which life and experience is suspended and sustained. This entails (deep!) ethical commitments and attachments: those with whom we find ourselves immediately entangled, but also more distant others whose existence is subject to the same vulnerabilities and dependencies as our own. But if care speaks to the ethical and the affective, it also speaks to and is expressed in *action*: "vital ethico-affective everyday doings that engage with the inescapable troubles of interdependent existences" (de la Bellacasa 2012: 199).

Such work has made many and important contributions in extending and reshaping work in science and technology studies and the broader social sciences. Here I wish to emphasize the *material* implications of care, and the deep and suggestive connections between care and the processes of breakdown, maintenance, and repair described earlier—a connection that scholars have only begun to unfold (see, inter alia, Jackson 2014; Denis and Pontille 2015; de la Bellacasa 2015; Houston and Jackson 2016). As core feminist scholarship asserts, care in its inter-human dimension extends beyond affective disposition or "structure of feeling" to encompass the rich and ongoing forms of work, labor, and interaction by which the status and well-being of others is acknowledged and upheld. This can include work both physical and bodily in nature: for example the sense of care intended when we speak of caring for a sick child, a hospital patient, or an aging parent. But the same kind of attending to physical need and frailty may characterize our interactions with the non-human worlds around us, perhaps especially when such actions begin to express and take on affective and normative weight. Like forms of care directed toward humans, maintenance and repair work starts from a basic recognition of vulnerability and decline, a feel for "the fleshiness and fragility of life" (Mol 2008: 11). Like human-directed care, it involves forms of work and labor designed to forestall such outcomes, upholding and sustaining objects in viable or working order. Like human care, maintenance and repair builds on and extends commitments to connection and interdependency, sustaining individual entities within wider networks of value and relationality. And like human care, maintenance and repair involve acts of perceptual and affective attention, a "listening forth" organized around a fundamental openness to the state and status of others. If this implies a normative relation, it also specifies a *temporal* one: from soil, to subway signs, to mobile phones, the care of things may involve a *staying with* in time and place, a subjecting and reorienting of one's own time to other temporal flows and processes, including the temporalities of breakdown and decay (long and slow, sudden and protracted) that must be accommodated and adjusted to in the ongoing doing of repair work. To engage in repair-as-care is therefore to open and tie oneself to the rhythms, flows, and timeliness of another. Such rhythms of care (what de la Bellacasa 2015 calls "care time") may stand at odds with efforts at mastery and control. Uncertainties in the irruption of breakdown are one reason, for example, why maintenance and repair work, even more than production, is difficult to anticipate and account for under modern regimes of planning and management. For all these reasons, care—for people as for things—remains an inescapably timely, and relational act.

Taken together, temporalities of breakdown on one hand, and repair and care on the other, can help to correct holes and imbalances in current understandings of the relationship between technology, time, and social life. Temporalities of breakdown help to remind us that "speed," where it is to be found, is a hard-won and by no means automatic accomplishment. They point us toward sites and moments that challenge and contest the

orientations toward the simple linear narratives that characterize and mar
many accounts of speed, both academic and popular. They point to the
deep and multiple presences of *other* temporalities, including those grounded
in the materiality of objects and things, which may support, undermine, or
remain indifferent to more human-centered understandings and experiences
of time (what is fast to a rock?). And they remind us that time, as a property of
interactions, may flow in every which way at once, only sometimes summing
to a unified pace and direction.

Temporalities of repair and care complete this picture, suggesting the real work
by which order is held in place, and things made to persist in the conditions we
have found them in (or *given* them, through processes of construction and
design). They point to the real-world actions and relations, both effective and
affective, by which we operate on time and the timeliness of human and non-
human others, coaxing and inviting certain processes of change while forestall-
ing or working against others. They underscore the deeply material character of
this work, and the practical processes by which time, as a property of situated
interactions, is made to take on shape and weight in the world.

Collectively, such perspectives help us to relocate understandings of time
itself: from external backdrop or yardstick, to something emerging at the
center of human and material experience in the world, reminding us that
time happens in interactions, and not the other way around. This sense is
central to a long line of pragmatist work, and is perhaps best expressed in the
James quote that led this chapter, given here in its full context:

> Life is in the transitions as much as in the terms connected; often, indeed, it seems
> to be there more emphatically, as if our spurts and sallies forward were the real
> firing-line of the battle, were like the thin line of flame advancing across the dry
> autumnal field which the farmer proceeds to burn. It is "of" the past, inasmuch as
> it comes expressly as the past's continuation; is if "of" the future in so far as the
> future, when it comes, will have continued it. (1904: 212–13)

Appropriately pursued, this mode of thought moves time and transition to the
very center of human and material trajectories through the world:

> a metaphysics of transiency, in which human life is seen as a wandering, a
> traveling, a bemusement which rocks side to side, comedy and tragedy, break-
> through and setback—yet, in all, a purposive, even progressive, trip. (McDermott
> 2007: 157, cited in Klemp et al. 2008: 5)

## Conclusion

Breakdown, maintenance, and repair are central to the accomplishment of
"speedy" infrastructures (as indeed all things with standing and duration in

the world). The material worlds around us embed rich and varied temporalities of their own, many of which run counter to general and undifferentiated stories of speed. The actual rhythms that shape and define human experience in the world are multiple and diverse, and while under the right circumstances they may "sum" to speed, they are never wholly constituted or defined as such. An important subset of these rhythms is grounded in the ongoing work of maintenance and repair by which the durability of such systems, together with their distinct processes of change and unfolding into the future, are produced, sustained, and transformed.

How might the sociology of speed change by taking such features into account? It would become more diverse and less confident, opening itself to a greater range of temporal experience, including slownesses, departures, and reversals obscured or neglected under more linear and teleological accounts. It would be more resolutely sociomaterial, cognizant of rhythms and tempos emerging from spheres of existence beyond the human—the temporality of objects, the timeliness of things. At the same time, it would pay wider heed to human work and labor, including the myriad forms of maintenance and repair through which experiences of speed are produced, sustained, and accommodated under the circumstances of individual and collective lives, making each of us in small and varied ways agents, and not just "dopes," of speed. And it would be more attentive to speed's distributional character and consequence, including for actors whose work and experiences are rendered invisible under present accounts. Abstract and undifferentiated stories of time, speed, and technology may be inclined to write such experiences off as marginal, limited, or residual—echoes or sidelines, perhaps regrettable ones, in the global story of speed. I believe they are constitutive, and will determine how true such stories turn out to be.

# References

Abbott, A. 2001. *Time Matters*. Chicago: University of Chicago Press.

Abram, D. 1997. *Spell of the Sensuous: Perception and Language in a More-than-Human World*. New York: Vintage.

Achebe, C. 1998. *Things Fall Apart*. London: Anchor.

Adam, B. 1990. *Time and Social Theory*. Cambridge: Polity.

Adam, B. 1995. *Timewatch: The Social Analysis of Time*. Cambridge: Polity.

Adam, B. and Groves, C. 2007. *Future Matters: Action, Knowledge, Ethics*. Leiden: Brill.

Agger, B. 2011. "iTime: Labor and Life in a Smartphone Era." *Time and Society* 20: 119–36.

Ahmed, S. I. and Jackson, S. J. 2015. "Learning to Fix: Knowledge, Collaboration, and Mobile Phone Repair in Dhaka, Bangladesh," in *Proceedings of the 2015 Information and Communication Technologies for Development (ICTD) Conference*. Singapore, May 2015.

Aiken, L. H., Clarke, S. P., and Sloane, D. M. 2002. "Hospital Staffing, Organization, and Quality of Care: Cross National Findings." *International Journal for Quality in Health Care* 14 (2002): 5–13.

Akrich, M. "The De-Scription of Technical Objects," in W. Bijker and J. Law (eds.), *Shaping Technology/Building Society: Studies in Sociotechnical Change*. MIT Press: 1992, pp. 205–24.

Allen, P. 2011. "The Singularity Isn't Near." *MIT Technology Review*. <http://www.technologyreview.com/view/425733/paul-allen-the-singularity-isnt-near> accessed June 2016.

Alvesson, M. 2001. "Knowledge Work: Ambiguity, Image and Identity." *Human Relations* 54: 863–86.

Alvesson, M. 2004. *Knowledge Work and Knowledge-Intensive Firms*. New York: Oxford University Press.

Anand, N. 2012. "Pressure: The PoliTechnics of Water Supply in Mumbai." *Cultural Anthropology* 26(4): 542–64.

Anderson, J. and Rainie, L. 2014. "Digital Life in 2025." Pew Research Group. <http://www.pewinternet.org/2014/03/11/digital-life-in-2025> accessed June 2016.

Antin, D. 1984. *Tuning*. New York: New Directions.

Aragon, C. R., Poon, S. S., Monroy-Hernández, A., and Aragon, D. 2009. *A Tale of Two Online Communities: Fostering Collaboration and Creativity in Scientists and Children*. New York: ACM.

# References

Armitage, J. 2000. *Paul Virilio: From Modernism to Hypermodernism and Beyond*. London: Sage.

Armitage, J. and Roberts, J. 2003. *Living with Cyberspace: Technology and Society in the 21st Century*. New York: Continuum.

Arthur, B. 2013. *Complexity Economics: A Different Framework for Economic Thought*. Santa Fe: Sante Fe Institute Working Paper.

Atkinson, M. 1984. *Our Masters' Voices: The Language and Body Language of Politics*, London and New York: Routledge.

Augé, M. 1995. *Non-Places: Introduction to an Anthropology of Supermodernity*. London: Verso.

Auyero, J. 2012. *Patience of the State*. Durham, NC: Duke University Press.

Autor, D. H., Katz, L. F., and Krueger, A. B. 1998. "Computing Inequality: Have Computers Changed the Labor Market?" *Quarterly Journal of Economics* 113(4): 1169–213.

Bailyn, L., Drago, R. W., and Kochan, T. A. 2001. *Integrating Work and Family Life: A Holistic Approach*. Cambridge, MA: Massachusetts Institute of Technology. <http://web.mit.edu/workplacecenter/docs/WorkFamily.pdf> accessed June 2016.

Barad, Karen. 2007. *Meeting the Universe Halfway: Quantum Physics and the Entanglement of Matter and Meaning*. Durham, NC: Duke University Press.

Baratz, M. 2015. "The Communication of the Future Is So Real You Can Touch It." Fast Company, Co.Design. <http://www.fastcodesign.com/3040689/the-touchable-future-of-communication-4> accessed June 2016.

Barnard, C. 1938/1968. *The Functions of the Executive*. Cambridge, MA: Harvard University Press.

Bartlett, A. 2007. "The City and the Self: The Emergence of New Political Subjects in London," in S. Sassen (ed.), *Deciphering the Global: Its Spaces, Scales and Subjects*. New York and London: Routledge, pp. 221–42.

Battilana, J., Leca, B., and Boxenbaum, E. 2009. "How Actors Change Institutions: Towards a Theory of Institutional Entrepreneurship." *The Academy of Management Annals* 3: 65–107.

Bauer, J. M., and Latzer, M. (eds.). 2015. *Handbook on the Economics of the Internet*. Cheltenham: Edward Elgar.

Bauman, Z. 1976. *Socialism: The Active Utopia*. London: George Allen and Unwin.

Bauman, Z. 1998. *Globalization: The Human Consequences*. New York: Columbia University Press.

Bauman, Z. 2000. *Liquid Modernity*. London: Blackwell.

Beck, U. 2002. "The Cosmopolitan Society and Its Enemies." *Theory, Culture and Society* 19(1/2): 17–44.

Becker, H. S. and Faulkner, R. R. 2009. *"Do You Know . . . ?" The Jazz Repertoire in Action*. Chicago: University of Chicago Press.

Beinhocker, E. 2006. *The Origin of Wealth*. Cambridge, MA: Harvard Business Press.

Benjamin, W. 1996. "Capitalism as Religion," in M. Bullock and M. W. Jennings (eds.), *Selected Writings*, Vol. I. Cambridge, MA, and London: The Belknap Press of Harvard University Press, pp. 288–91.

Benjamin, W. 1999a. "On the Image of Proust," in *Selected Writings*, Vol. II. Cambridge, MA: Belknap Press of Harvard University Press (orig. pub. 1929), pp. 237–47.

Benjamin, W. 1999b. *The Arcades Project*, trans. Harward Eiland and Kevin McLaughlin. Cambridge, MA: The Belknap Press of Harvard University Press.

Benjamin, W. 1999c. "Goethe." In *Selected Writings*, Vol. II. Cambridge, MA: Belknap Press of Harvard University Press, 161–93 (orig. pub. 1928).

Benjamin, W. 2003a. "Central Park," in *Selected Writings*, Vol. IV. Cambridge, MA: Belknap Press of Harvard University Press (orig. pub. 1939), pp. 161–99.

Benjamin, W. 2003b. "On Some Motifs in Baudelaire," in *Selected Writings*, Vol. IV. Cambridge, MA: Belknap Press of Harvard University Press (orig. pub. 1940), pp. 313–55.

Benjamin, W. 2003c. "On the Concept of History," in *Selected Writings*, Vol. IV. Cambridge, MA: Belknap Press of Harvard University Press (orig. pub. 1940), pp. 389–400.

Benjamin, W. 2003d. "Paralipomena to 'On the Concept of History'," in *Selected Writings*, Vol. IV. Cambridge, MA: Belknap Press of Harvard University Press (orig. pub. 1940), pp. 401–11.

Benjamin, W. 2003e. "The Paris of the Second Empire in Baudelaire," in *Selected Writings*, Vol. IV. Cambridge, MA: Belknap Press of Harvard University Press (orig. pub. 1938), pp. 3–92.

Benjamin, W. 2003f. "Blanqui," in *Selected Writings*, Vol. IV. Cambridge, MA: Belknap Press of Harvard University Press (orig. pub. 1938), pp. 93–5.

Benjamin, W. 2003g. "The Study Begins with Some Reflections on the Influence of Les Fleurs du mal." In *Selected Writings*, Vol. IV. Cambridge, MA: Belknap Press of Harvard University Press (orig. pub. 1938), pp. 96–8.

Berners-Lee, M. and Clark, D. 2013. *The Burning Question*. London: Profile.

Betts, R. K. 2007. *Enemies of Intelligence*. New York: Columbia University Press.

Blanchette, J.-F. 2011. "A Material History of Bits." *Journal of the American Society for Information Science and Technology* 62(6): 1042–57.

Boden, D. 1983. "Talk International: An Analysis of Conversational Turn Taking and Related Phenomena in Seven Indo-European Languages," in *Annual Meetings of the American Sociological Association, Detroit*.

Boden, D. and Molotch, H. 1994. "The Compulsion of Proximity," in D. Boden and R. Friedland (eds.), *NowHere: Space, Time, and Modernity*. Berkeley: University of California Press.

Boden, D. and Zimmerman, D. (eds.). 1993. *Talk and Social Structure: Studies in Ethno-methodology and Conversation Analysis*. New York: Wiley.

Boltanski, L. and Chiapello, E. 2007. *The New Spirit of Capitalism*, trans. Gregory Elliot. London: Verso.

Brand, S. 1995. *How Buildings Learn: What Happens After They're Built*. New York: Penguin.

Brandt, M. W., Kavajecz, K. A., and Underwood, S. E. 2007. "Price Discovery in the Treasury Futures Market." *Journal of Futures Markets* 27(1): 1021–51.

Brown, W. 1965a. "Informal Organization?" in W. Brown and E. Jaques (eds.), *Glacier Project Papers*. London: Heineman Educational Books 144–62.

Brown, W. 1965b. *Exploration in Management*. Harmondsworth: Penguin Books.

Brown, W. 1971. *Organization*. London: Heinemann Educational Books.

# References

Brown, W. 1976. "A Critique of Some Current Ideas About Organization," in J. Gray (ed.), *The Glacier Project: Concepts and Critique*. New York: Crane Russak.

Brundtland Report. 1987. *Our Common Future*. New York: World Commission on Environment and Development.

Bschor, T. et al. 2004. "Time Experience and Time Judgment in Major Depression, Mania and Healthy Subjects." *Acta Psychiatrica Scandinavia* 109: 222–9.

Budish, E., Cramton, P., and Shim, J. 2013. "The High-Frequency Trading Arms Race: Frequent Batch Auctions as a Market Design Response." *The Quarterly Journal of Economics* 130(4). <http://faculty.chicagobooth.edu/eric.budish/research/HFT-FrequentBatchAuctions.pdf> accessed June 2016.

Butler, J. 2006. *Precarious Life: The Powers of Mourning and Violence*. London: Verso.

Cairns, S. and Jacobs, J. 2014. *Buildings Must Die: A Perverse View of Architecture*. Cambridge MA: MIT Press.

Callon, M. 1986. "Some Elements of a Sociology of Translation: Domestication of the Scallops and the Fishermen of St Brieuc Bay," in J. Law (ed.), *Power, Action and Belief: A New Sociology of Knowledge?* London: Routledge and Kegan Paul, pp. 196–233.

Callon, M. (ed.). 1998. *The Laws of the Markets*. Oxford: Blackwell.

Campos-Castillo, C. and Hitlin, S. 2013. "Copresence: Revisiting a Building Block for Social Interaction Theories." *Sociological Theory* 31(2): 168–92.

Cantwell-Smith, B. 1998. *On the Origin of Objects*. New York: Bradford Books.

Caplan, J. 1988. *Government Without Administration: State and Civil Service in Weimar and Nazi Germany*. Oxford: Clarendon Press.

Carey, J. W. 1989. *Communication as Culture: Essays on Media and Society*. New York: Routledge.

Carey, P. 2015. "Silicon Valley Marks 50 years of Moore's Law." *San Jose Mercury News*, April 20. <http://www.mercurynews.com/business/ci_27934824/silicon-valley-marks-50-years-moores-law> accessed June 2016.

Carter, I. 2001. *Railways and Culture in Britain*. Manchester: Manchester University Press.

Castells, M. 1996. *The Rise of the Network Society*. Oxford: Blackwell.

Champy, J. 1995. *Re-Engineering Management*. London: Harper Collins.

Chan, A. 2014. *Networking Peripheries: Technological Futures and the Myth of Digital Universalism*. Cambridge, MA: MIT Press.

Chang, L. 2008. *Factory Girls: From Village to City in a Changing China*. New York: Random House.

Charmaz, K. 2006. *Constructing Grounded Theory: A Practical Guide Through Qualitative Analysis*. London: Sage.

Chen, X. and de'Medici, T. 2010. "Research Note—the 'Instant City' Coming of Age: Production of Spaces in China's Shenzhen Special Economic Zone." *Urban Geography* 31: 1141–7.

Christensen, C. 2013. *The Innovator's Dilemma: When New Technologies Cause Great Firms to Fail*. Cambridge, MA: Harvard Business Review Press.

Cicourel, A. 1964. *Method and Measurement in Sociology*. Glencoe, IL: Free Press.

Clark, N. 2010. "Violent Worlds, Vulnerable Bodies: Confronting Abrupt Climate Change." *Theory, Culture and Society* 27: 31–53.

Condren, C. 2006. *Argument and Authority in Early Modern England: The Presuppositions of Oaths and Offices*. Cambridge: Cambridge University Press.

Connolly, W. 2013. *The Fragility of Things: Self-Organizing Processes, Neoliberal Fantasies, and Democratic Activism*. Durham, NC: Duke University Press.

Conway, B. 2011. "Wall Streets Need For Trading Speed: The Nanosecond Age." *The Wall Street Journal*, June 14. <http://blogs.wsj.com/marketbeat/2011/06/14/wall-streets-need-for-trading-speed-the-nanosecond-age/> accessed June 2016.

Crary, J. 2013. *24/7: Late Capitalism and the Ends of Sleep*. London: Verso.

Crouch, C. 2004. *Post-Democracy*. Cambridge: Polity Press.

Curtis, S. 2009. "Images of Efficiency: The Films of Frank B. Gilbreth," in V. Hediger and P. Vonderau (eds.), *Films that Work: The Productivity of Media*. Amsterdam: Amsterdam University Press, pp. 85–99.

Czarniawska, B. 2013. "Is Speed Good?" *Scandinavian Journal of Management* 29: 7–12.

Daniels, J. 2009. *Cyber Racism: White Supremacy Online and the New Attack on Civil Rights*. Lanham, MD: Rowman and Littlefield Publishers.

Davis, G. B. 2002. "Anytime/Anyplace Computing and the Future of Knowledge Work." *Communications of the ACM* 45: 67–73.

Dayrell, C. and Urry, J. 2015. "Mediating Climate Politics: The Surprising Case of Brazil." *European Journal of Social Theory* 18: 257–73.

De la Bellacasa, M. P. 2012. "Nothing Comes Without Its World": Thinking with Care." *The Sociological Review* 60(2): 197–216.

De la Bellacasa, M. P. 2015. "Making Time for Soil: Technoscientific Futurity and the Pace of Care." *Social Studies of Science* 45(5): 691–716.

Denis, J. and Pontille, D. 2014. "Maintenance Work and the Performativity of Urban Inscriptions: The Case of Paris Subway Signs." *Environment and Planning D: Society and Space* 32: 1–13.

Denis, J. and Pontille, D. 2015. "Material Ordering and the Care of Things." *Science, Technology, and Human Values* 40(3): 338–67.

DeSilvey, C. 2006. "Observed Decay: Telling Stories with Mutable Things." *Journal of Material Culture* 11(3): 318–38.

Dodd, N. 2008. "Goethe in Palermo: Urphanomen and Analogical Reasoning in Simmel and Benjamin." *Journal of Classical Sociology* 8: 411–45.

Dodd, N. 2014. *The Social Life of Money*. Princeton, NJ: Princeton University Press.

Douglas, M. 1978. *Purity and Danger: An Analysis of the Concepts of Pollution and Taboo*. New York: Routledge.

Du Gay, P. 2000. *In Praise of Bureaucracy: Weber/Organization/Ethics*. London: Sage.

Du Gay, P. 2006. "Machinery of Government and Standards in Public Service: Teaching New Dogs Old Tricks." *Economy and Society* 35(1): 148–67.

Edensor, T. 2005. *Industrial Ruins: Space, Aesthetics, and Materiality*. London: Bloomsbury Academic.

Edensor, T. 2011. "Entangled Agencies, Material Networks and Repair in a Building Assemblage: The Mutable Stone of St. Ann's Church, Manchester." *Transactions of the Institute of British Geographers* 36: 238–52.

Edgerton, D. 2006. *The Shock of the Old: Technology and Global History Since 1900*. London: Profile.

# References

Edgerton, D. 2011. *The Shock of the Old: Technology and Global History Since 1900*. Reprint edition. Oxford: Oxford University Press.

Edwards, P. 2004. "Infrastructure and Modernity: Force, Time, and Social Organization in the History of Sociotechnical Systems," in T. Misa and P. Brey (eds.), *Modernity and Technology*. Cambridge, MA: MIT Press.

Egger, E. and Wagner, I. 1992. "Time-Management: A Case for CSCW," in *Proceedings of the ACM Conference on Computer-Supported Cooperative Work*, pp. 249–56.

Ehrenberg, A. 2010. *The Weariness of the Self*. Montreal: McGill-Queen's University Press.

Eisenstadt, S. N. (ed.). 2002. *Multiple Modernities*. Piscataway, NJ: Transaction Publishers.

Elinder, M. and Erixson, O. 2012. "Gender, Social Norms, and Survival in Maritime Disasters." *PNAS* 109(33): 13220–4.

Ellison, N. B. 2004. *Telework and Social Change: How Technology is Reshaping the Boundaries between Home and Work*. Westport, CT: Praeger.

Fassel, D. 1990. *Working Ourselves to Death: The High Cost of Workaholicism and the Rewards of Recovery*. New York: HarperCollins.

Ferguson, J. 2012. "Structures of Responsibility." *Cultural Anthropology* 26(4): 558–62.

Fernando, V. 2010. "Think Tank Warns that Hong Kong's Dangerous Dependence on Finance Could Result in Catastrophe." *Business Insider*. <http://www.businessinsider.com/hong-kong-financial-sector-too-big-2010-6> accessed June 2016.

Fischer, C. 1994. *America Calling: A Social History of the Telephone to 1940*. Berkeley: University of California Press.

Fisher, M. 2006. "Wall Street Women: Navigating Gendered Networks in the New Economy," in M. Fisher and G. Downey (eds.), *Frontiers of Capital: Ethnographic Reflections on the New Economy*. Durham, NC: Duke University Press, pp. 209–36.

Fligstein, N. 1997. "Social Skill and Institutional Theory." *The American Behavioral Scientist* 40(4): 397–405.

Fligstein, N. 2013. "Understanding Stability and Change in Fields." *Research in Organizational Behavior* 33: 39–51.

Fligstein, N. and McAdam, D. 2012. *A Theory of Fields*. Oxford: Oxford University Press.

Foucault, M. 1977. *Discipline and Punish*. New York: Vintage.

Fountain, C. 2005. "Finding a Job in the Internet Age." *Social Forces* 83(3): 1235–62.

Fraser, N. 1992. "Rethinking the Public Sphere: A Contribution to the Critique of Actually Existing Democracy," in C. Calhoun (ed.), *Habermas and the Public Sphere*. Cambridge, MA: MIT Press, pp. 108–42.

Freeman, R. B. 2002. "The Labour Market in the New Information Economy." *Oxford Review of Economic Policy* 18(3): 288–305.

Friedman, E. J. 2005. "The Reality of Virtual Reality: The Internet and Gender Equality Advocacy in Latin America." *Latin American Politics and Society* 47: 1–34.

Frisby, D. 2002. *Georg Simmel*. London: Routledge.

Galison, P. 2003. *Einstein's Clocks, Poincare's Maps: Empires of Time*. New York: W. W. Norton and Company.

Garud, R., Jain, S., and Kumaraswamy, A. 2002. "Institutional Entrepreneurship in the Sponsorship of Common Technological Standards: The Case of Sun Microsystems and Java." *Academy of Management Journal* 45: 196–214.

Gell, A. 1988. "Technology and Magic." *Anthropology Today* 4(2): 6–9.

Gell, A. 1998. *Art and Agency*. Oxford: Clarendon Press.

Gergen, K. 2000. *The Saturated Self: Dilemmas of Identity in Contemporary Life*. New York: Basic Books.

Giddens, A. 1984. *The Constitution of Society: Outline of the Theory of Structure*. Berkeley, University of California Press.

Giddens, A. 2002. *Runaway World*. London: Profile Books.

Gilbreth, L. M. 1914. *The Psychology of Management: The Function of the Mind in Determining, Teaching and Installing Methods of Least Waste*. New York: Sturgis and Walton.

Gillespie, R. 1991. *Manufacturing Knowledge: A History of the Hawthorne Experiments*. Cambridge: Cambridge University Press.

Glennie, P. and Thrift, N. 2009. *Shaping the Day: A History of Timekeeping in England and Wales 1300–1800*. Oxford: Oxford University Press.

Goffman, E. 1969. *Where the Action Is*. London: Allen Lane.

Golden, L. 2009. "A Brief History of Long Work Time and the Contemporary Sources of Overwork." *Journal of Business Ethics* 84: 217–27.

Gonzalez, V. M. and Mark, G. 2004. *Constant, Constant, Multi-tasking Craziness: Managing Multiple Working Spheres*. SIGCHI Conference on Human Factors in Computing Systems, 2004 Vienna, Austria. New York, 113–20.

Gore, A. 2013. *The Future*. London: W. H. Allen.

Graham, M. 2014. "Internet Geographies: Data Shadows and Digital Divisions of Labour," in M. Graham and W. H. Dutton (eds.), *Society and the Internet: How Networks of Information and Communication are Changing Our Lives*. Oxford: Oxford University Press, pp. 99–116.

Graham, S. 2001. *Splintering Urbanism: Networked Infrastructures, Technological Mobilities, and the Urban Condition*. New York: Routledge.

Graham, S. and Thrift, N. 2007. "Out of Order: Understanding Repair and Maintenance." *Theory, Culture and Society* 24(3): 1–25.

Grant, M. G. 2013. "The Red Light and the Cloud: A History of the Future of Sex Work." *The Medium*. <https://medium.com/@melissagira/the-red-light-and-the-cloud-9a936daaddb8> accessed June 2016.

Gregg, M. 2011. *Work's Intimacy*. Malden, MA: Polity.

Gregg, M. 2015. "Getting Things Done: Productivity, Self-Management and the Order of Things," in K. Hillis, S. Paasonen, and M. Petit (eds.), *Networked Affect*. Cambridge, MA: MIT Press.

Gregg, M. (Forthcoming) *Counterproductive: A Brief History of Time Management*. Durham, NC: Duke University Press.

Grey, C. 2009. "Speed," in P. Hancock and A. Spicer (eds.), *Understanding Corporate Life*. London: Sage, pp. 27–45.

Griffiths, J. 1999. *A Sideways Look at Time*. New York: Putnam.

Groys, B. 2013. *Art Power*. Cambridge, MA: MIT Press.

Habermas, J. 1999. *Structural Transformations of the Public Sphere*. Cambridge, MA: MIT Press.

Hansen, J. 2011. *Storms of My Grandchildren: The Truth about the Coming Climate Catastrophe and Our Last Chance to Save Humanity*. London: Bloomsbury.

Hardt M. and Negri, N. 2000. *Empire*. Cambridge, MA: Harvard University Press.

Harvey, D. 1989. *The Condition of Postmodernity: An Enquiry into the Origins of Cultural Change*. Oxford: Blackwell.

Harvey, D. 1990. *The Condition of Postmodernity: An Enquiry into the Origins of Cultural Change*. Cambridge, MA and Oxford: Blackwell.

Harvey, R. 2007. "The Sub-National Constitution of Global Markets," in S. Sassen(ed.), *Deciphering the Global: Its Spaces, Scales and Subjects*. New York and London: Routledge, pp. 199–216.

Hassan, R. 2003a. "Network Time and the New Knowledge Epoch." *Time and Society* 12: 225–41.

Hassan, R. 2003b. *The Chronoscopic Society: Globalization, Time, and Knowledge in the Network Economy*. New York: Peter Lang.

Hassan. R. 2009. *Empires of Speed: Time and the Acceleration of Politics and Society*. Leiden: Brill Academic Publishers.

Haythornthwaite, C. and Weldman, B. (eds.). 2002. *The Internet in Everyday Life*. Malden, MA: Wiley-Blackwell.

Henke, C. R. 2000. "The Mechanics of Workplace Order: Toward a Sociology of Repair." *Berkeley Journal of Sociology* 43: 55–81.

Hennessy, P. 2004. "The Lightning Flash on the Road to Baghdad: Issues of Evidence," in W. G. Runciman (ed.), *Hutton and Butler: Lifting the Lid on the Workings of Power*. Oxford: Oxford University Press and British Academy, pp. 61–81.

Hislop, D. 2015. *Mobility and Technology in the Workplace*. London: Routledge.

Holmes, S. 2009. "In Case of Emergency: Misunderstanding Tradeoffs in the War on Terror." *California Law Review* 97(2): 301–55.

Hörning, K. H., Ahrens, D., and Gerhard, A. 1999. "Do Technologies Have Time? New Practices of Time and the Transformation of Communication Technologies." *Time and Society* 8: 293–308.

Hossfeld, K. J. 2001. "'Their Logic Against Them': Contradictions in Sex, Race and Class in Silicon Valley," in K. Ward (ed.), *Women Workers and Global Restructuring*. Ithaca, NY: Cornell University Press, pp. 149–78.

Houlne, T. and Maxwell, T. 2013. *The New World of Work: From the Cube to the Cloud*. Irving, TX: Inspire on Purpose.

Houston, L. 2014. "Inventive Infrastructure: An Exploration of Mobile Phone Repair in Kampala, Uganda." Unpublished PhD dissertation, Lancaster University, Department of Sociology.

Houston, L. and Jackson, S. J. 2016. "Caring for the 'Next Billion' Mobile Handsets: Opening Proprietary Closures through the Work of Repair." *Proceedings of the 2016 Information and Communication Technologies for Development (ICTD) Conference*. Ann Arbor, May 2016.

Houston, L., Jackson, S. J., Rosner, D., Ahmed, S. I., Young, M., and Kang, L. 2016. "Values in Repair," in *Proceedings of the 2016 SIGCHI Conference on Human Factors in Computing*. Association for Computing Machinery, San Jose, May 7–12, 2016.

Humes, E. 2013. *Garbology: Our Dirty Love Affair With Trash*. New York: Avery Books.

Hutchins, E. 1995. *Cognition in the Wild*. Cambridge, MA: MIT Press.

Illouz, E. 2007. *Cold Intimacies: The Making of Emotional Capitalism*. London: Polity.

Imbert, P. (ed.). 2008. *Theories of Inclusion and Exclusion in Knowledge-Based Societies.* Ottawa: University of Ottawa Press.

Innis, H. 1951. *The Bias of Communication.* Toronto: Toronto University Press.

Ishil, H. and Xiao, X. 2014. "MirrorFugue." MIT Media Lab. <http://www.media.mit.edu/research/groups/1453/mirrorfugue> accessed June 2016.

Jackson, S. J. 2014. "Rethinking Repair," in T. Gillespie, P. Boczkowski, and K. Foot (eds.), *Media Technologies: Essays on Communication, Materiality, and Society.* Cambridge, MA: MIT Press.

Jackson, S. J., Pompe, A., and Krieshok, G. 2011. "Things Fall Apart: Maintenance and Repair in ICT for Education Initiatives in Rural Namibia," in *Proceedings of the 2011 iConference.* Association for Computing Machinery, Seattle, February 8–11.

Jackson, S. J., Pompe, A. and Krieshok, G. 2012. "Repair Worlds: Maintenance, Repair, and ICT for Development in Rural Namibia," in *Proceedings of the 2012 Computer-Supported Cooperative Work (CSCW) Conference.* Association for Computing Machinery, Seattle, February 11–15, 2012.

Jacobs, J. 1961. *The Death and Life of Great American Cities.* New York: Random House.

James, W. 1904. "A World of Pure Experience." *Journal of Philosophy, Psychology, and Scientific Methods* 1(20): 533–43.

Jefferson, G. 1991. "List Construction as a Task and Resource," in G. Psathas (ed.), *Interactional Competence.* New York: Irvington, pp. 63–92.

Jefferson, G. 1996. "On the Poetics of Ordinary Talk." *Text and Performance Quarterly* 16(1): 1–61.

Kafka, F. 2015. *Franz Kafka: The Office Writings.* New York: Princeton University Press.

Kanter, R. M. 1989. *When Giants Learn to Dance.* London: Unwin Hyman.

Katz, J. 1999. *How Emotions Work.* Chicago: University of Chicago Press.

Katz, K. L., Larson, B. M., and Larson, R. C. 1991. "Prescription for the Waiting-in-line Blues: Entertain, Enlighten, and Engage." *Sloan Management Review* 32(Winter): 44–53.

Keisler, S. and Hinds, P. 2002. *Distributed Work.* Cambridge, MA: MIT Press.

Keller, S. and Price, C. 2011. *Beyond Performance: How Great Organizations Build Ultimate Competitive Advantage.* London: John Wiley and Sons.

Kellogg, K. C. 2009. "Operating Room: Relational Spaces and Microinstitutional Change in Surgery." *The American Journal of Sociology* 115: 657–711.

Kennedy Address. 1963. *Public Papers of the Presidents: John F. Kennedy.* Assembly Hall, Paulskirche, Frankfurt, June 25.

Kern, S. 1983. *The Culture of Time and Space 1880–1918.* Cambridge, MA: Harvard University Press.

Khagram, S., Riker, J. V., and Sikkink, K. (eds.). 2002. *Restructuring World Politics: Trans-national Social Movements, Networks, and Norms.* Minneapolis: University of Minnesota Press.

Khurana, R. 2010. *From Higher Aims to Hired Hands: The Social Transformation of American Business Schools and the Unfulfilled Promise of Management as a Profession.* Princeton, NJ: Princeton University Press.

Kittler, F. A. 1999. *Gramophone, Film, Typewriter,* trans. G. Winthrop Young and M. Wutz. Stanford: Stanford University Press.

# References

Klemp, N., McDermott, R., Raley, J., Thibeault, M., Powell, K., and Levitin, D. J. 2008. "Plans, Takes, and Mis-takes." *Critical Social Studies* 1: 4–21.

Knorr Cetina, K. and Preda, A. (eds.). 2004. *The Sociology of Financial Markets*. Oxford: Oxford University Press.

Kolbert, E. 2015. *The Sixth Extinction: An Unnatural History*. London: Bloomsbury.

Koopman, C. 2009. *Pragmatism as Transition: Historicity and Hope in James, Dewey, and Rorty*. New York: Columbia University Press.

Kovac, P. 2014. *Flash Boys: Not So Fast: An Insider's Perspective on High-Frequency Trading*. Directissima Press.

Krippner, G. R. 2001. "The Elusive Market: Embeddedness and the Paradigm of Economic Sociology." *Theory and Society* 30(6): 775–810.

Kronman, A. 1993. *The Lost Lawyer*. Cambridge, MA: Harvard University Press.

Kurzweil, R. 2006. *The Singularity is Near*. London: Gerard Duckworth.

Kvochko, E. 2014. "The Online, Freelance, Globalizing World of Work." *Techonomy*. <http://techonomy.com/2014/03/online-freelance-globalizing-world-work/> accessed June 2016.

Lancaster, J. 2004. *Making Time: Lillian Moller Gilbreth, A Life Beyond "Cheaper by the Dozen."* Boston: Northeastern University Press.

Lanier, J. 2013. *Who Owns the Future?* New York: Simon and Schuster.

Larmore, C. 1987. *Patterns of Moral Complexity*. Cambridge: Cambridge University Press.

Latham, R. and Sassen, S. (eds.). 2005. *Digital Formations: IT and New Architectures in the Global Realm*. Princeton, NJ: Princeton University Press.

Latour, B. 1987. *Science in Action*. Cambridge, MA: Harvard University Press.

Latour, B. 2005. *Reassembling the Social: An Introduction to Actor-Network Theory*. Oxford: Oxford University Press.

Laughlin, G., Aquirre, A., and Grundfest, J. 2012. "Information Transmission between Financial Markets in Chicago and New York." Social Science Research Network. <http://ssrn.com/abstract=2227519> accessed June 2015.

Law, J. and Urry, J. 2004. "Enacting the Social." *Economy and Society* 33: 390–410.

Lee, H. and Sawyer, S. 2010. "Conceptualizing Time, Space and Computing for Work and Organizing." *Time and Society* 19: 293–317.

Lepawsky, J. 2014. "The Changing Geography of Global Trade in Electronic Discards: Time to Rethink the E-Waste Problem." *The Geographical Journal* 181(2): 147–59.

Lepore, J. 2014. "The Disruption Machine." *The New Yorker*, June 16.

Lewis, M. 2014. *Flash Boys: Cracking the Money Code*. London: Penguin.

Liboiron, M. 2014. "Why Discard Studies?" *Discard Studies*. <http://discardstudies.com/2014/05/07/why-discard-studies/> accessed June 2016.

Linden, E. 2007. *Winds of Change: Climate, Weather and the Destruction of Civilizations*. New York: Simon and Schuster.

Ling, R. and Yttri, B. 2002. "Hyper-coordination via Mobile Phones in Norway," in J. E. Katz and M. Aakhus (eds.), *Perpetual Contact: Mobile Communication, Private Talk, Public Performance*. Cambridge: Cambridge University Press, pp. 139–69.

Linkner, J. 2014. *The Road to Reinvention*. London: Jossey Bass.

Lipovetsky, G. 2005. *Hypermodern Times*, trans. Andrew Brown. Malden, MA: Polity.

Livingstone, S. and Lunt, P. 1994. *Talk on Television: Audience Participation and Public Debate*. London: Routledge.

Lounsbury, M., Ventresca, M., and Hirsch, P. M. 2003. "Social Movements, Field Frames and Industry Emergence: A Cultural-Political Perspective on U.S. Recycling." *Socio-Economic Review* 1: 71–104.

Lovink, G. 2008. *Zero Comments: Blogging and Critical Internet Culture*. London: Routledge.

Lovink, G. and Dean, J. 2010. *Blog Theory: Feedback and Capture in the Circuits of Drive*. Cambridge: Polity.

Löwy, M. 2006. *Fire Alarm: Reading Walter Benjamin's "On the Concept of History."* London: Verso.

Lucent Technologies. 1998. "True Wave ® RS Nonzero-Dispersion Optical Fiber." <http://www.worldonecom.com/fibercable/truewave.pdf> accessed June 2016.

Luhmann, N. 1981. *Politische Theorie im Wohlfahrtsstaat*, München/Wien: Olzog.

Lyons, G. 2015. "The Road Investment Strategy is a Victory for 'Predict and Provide' over Transport Planning." *Local Transport Today* 663: 18.

MacDonald, I., Burke, C., and Stewart, K. 2006. *Systems Leadership*. Aldershot: Gower.

MacKenzie, D. 2009. *Material Markets: How Economic Agents are Constructed*. Oxford: Clarendon.

MacKenzie, D. and Millo, Y. 2003. "Constructing a Market, Performing Theory: The Historical Sociology of a Financial Derivatives Exchange." *American Journal of Sociology* 109(1): 107–45.

MacKenzie, D., and Pardo-Guerra, J. P. 2014. "Insurgent Capitalism: Island, Bricolage and the Re-Making of Finance." *Economy and Society* 432: 153–82.

MacKenzie, D., and Wajcman, J. 1985. *The Social Shaping of Technology*. Milton Keynes: Oxford University Press.

MacKenzie, D. 2014. "Be Grateful for Drizzle." *London Review of Books* 36: 27–30.

MacKenzie, D. 2015. "Mechanizing the Merc: The Chicago Mercantile Exchange and the Rise of High-Frequency Trading." *Technology and Culture* 56(3): 646–75.

MacKenzie, D. Forthcoming. "Shaping Algorithms: A Historical Sociology of High-Frequency Trading." Working paper.

MacKenzie, D., Muniesa, F., and Siu, L. (eds.). 2007. *Do Economists Make Markets? On the Performativity of Economics*. Princeton, NJ: Princeton University Press.

MacKenzie, D., Beunza, D., Millo, Y., and Pardo-Guerra, J. P. 2012. "Drilling Through the Allegheny Mountains: Liquidity, Materiality and High-Frequency Trading." *Journal of Cultural Economy* 5(3): 279–95.

Marsden, E. (ed.). 2011. "Control and Accountability in Highly Automated Systems." *Les cahiers de la sécurité industrielle*. <http://www.icsi-eu.org/docsi/documents/csi1109-network2011-accountability-1.pdf> accessed June 2016.

Marshall, B. 1982. *All That Is Solid Melts Into Air: The Experience of Modernity*. New York: Penguin.

Marx, K. 1867/2002. *Capital, Volume 1*. London: Penguin.

Marx, K. 1973. *Surveys from Exile*. Harmondsworth: Penguin.

Massey, D. 1994. "Power-Geometry and a Progressive Sense of Place," in J. Bird, B. Curtis, T. Putnma, G. Robertson, and L. Tickner (eds.), *Mapping the Futures: Local Cultures, Global Change*. New York: Routledge.

Mayo, E. 1933. *Human Problems of an Industrial Civilization*. New York: MacMillan.

Mazmanian, M. 2012. "Predictable Time Off?: Leveraging Personal Needs to Change the Micro Dynamics of Teamwork." *U.C. Davis Qualitative Research Conference, Best Paper*. Davis, CA.

Mazmanian, M. 2013. "Avoiding the Trap of Constant Connectivity: When Congruent Frames Allow for Heterogeneous Practices." *Academy of Management Journal* 56: 1225–50.

Mazmanian, M. and Erickson, I. 2014. "The Product of Availability: Understanding the Economic Underpinnings of Constant Connectivity." *ACM Conference on Computer Human Interaction (CHI)*. Toronto: ACM.

Mazmanian, M., Orlikowski, W. J., and Yates, J. 2013. "The Autonomy Paradox: The Implications of Mobile Email Devices for Knowledge Professionals." *Organization Science* 24: 1337–57.

Mazmanian, M., Beckman, C., and Harmon, E. 2015a. "Ethnography Across the Work Boundary: Benefits and Considerations for Organizational Studies," in K. Elsbach and R. Kramer (eds.), *Handbook of Innovative Qualitative Research Methods: Pathways to Cool Ideas and Interesting Papers*. London: Taylor and Francis.

Mazmanian, M. and Erickson, I. 2016. Markets of Availability and Commodification of Time in 21st Century Work: Inducing Macro-Level Insights From Micro-Level Data," in B. Bechky and K. Elsbach (eds.), *Qualitative Organizational Research: Best Papers from the Davis Conference on Organizational Research,* Volume III (pp. 199–224). Charlotte, NC: Information Age Publishing. Charlotte, NC: Information Age Publishing Inc.

Mazmanian, M., Erickson, I., and Harmon, E. 2015b. "Circumscribed Time and Porous Time: Logics as a Way of Studying Temporality." *CSCW: Computer Supported Cooperative Work*, March 14–18, Vancouver, British Columbia. ACM, 1453–64.

McChrystal, S. 2014. *My Share of the Task*. London: Penguin.

McDermott, J. 2007. *The Drama of Possibility*. New York: Fordham University Press.

McLuhan, M. 1964. *Understanding Media*. New York: McGraw Hill.

McMillan, L. H. W. and O'Driscoll, M. P. 2008. "The Wellsprings of Workaholism: A Comparative Analysis of the Explanatory Theories," in R. J. Burke C. L.and Cooper (eds.), *The Long Work Hours Culture: Causes, Consequences and Choices*. Bingley: Emerald Group.

Menand, L. 2005. "Fat Man: Herman Kahn and the Nuclear Age." *The New Yorker*, June 27. <http://www.newyorker.com/magazine/2005/06/27/fat-man> accessed June 2016.

Messenger, R. 2014. "Last Days of Speed Typing Glory." *OzTypewriter: The Wonderful World of Typewriters*, November 15. <http://oztypewriter.blogspot.com/2014/11/last-days-of-speed-typing-glory.html> accessed June 2016.

Mitchell, T. 2011. *Carbon Democracy*. London: Verso.

Moe, R. 1994. " 'The Re-Inventing Government ' Exercise: Misinterpreting the Problem, Misjudging the Consequences." *Public Administration Review* 542: 111–22.

Mol, A. 2008. *The Logic of Care: Health and the Problem of Patient Choice*. New York: Routledge.

Molotch, H. 1988. "The Rest Room and Equal Opportunity." *Sociological Forum* 3(1): 128–32.

Molotch, H. 2012. *Against Security: How We Go Wrong at Airports, Subways and Other Sites of Ambiguous Danger*. Princeton, NJ: Princeton University Press.

Moorhouse, F. 1993. *Grand Days*. London: Vintage.

Morris, I. 2010. *Why the West Rules—For Now*. London: Profile.

Morris, R. 2014. "Thesis Defense: Crowd Sourcing Mental Health and Emotional Well-Being." *MIT Media Lab*. <http://www.media.mit.edu/video/view/morris-2014-09-08> accessed June 2016.

Motesharrei, S., Rivas, J., and Kalnay, E. 2014. "Human and Nature Dynamics (HANDY): Modelling Inequality and Use of Resources in the Collapse or Sustainability of Societies." *Ecological Economics* 101: 90–102.

Mulvey, L. 1975. "Visual Pleasure and Narrative Cinema." *Screen* 16(3): 6–18.

Nil, R., Jacobshagen, N., Schächinger, H., Baumann, P., Höck, P., Hättenschwiler, J., Ramseier, F., Seifritz, E., and Holsboer-Trachsler, E. 2010. "Burnout: eine Standortbestimmung." *Schweizer Archiv für Neurologie und Psychiatrie* 161: 72–7.

Noren, L. 2014. "Creative Collaboration: Technology, Teams, and the Tastemakers' Dilemma." Dissertation, New York University, ProQuest Dissertations Publishing. AAT 3665190.

Nowotny, H. 1996. *Time: The Modern and Postmodern Experience*, Cambridge: Polity.

O'Carroll, A. 2008. "Fuzzy Holes and Intangible Time: Time in a Knowledge Industry." *Time and Society* 17: 179–93.

Osborne, D. and Gaebler, T. 1992. *Re-Inventing Government*. Reading, MA: Addison-Wesley.

Orr, J. 1996. *Talking About Machines*. Ithaca, NY: Cornell University Press.

Pagallo, U. 2013. "What Robots Want: Autonomous Machines, Codes, and New Frontiers of Legal Responsibility," in M. Hildebrandt and J. Gaakeer (eds.), *Human Law and Computer Law: Comparative Perspectives*. Dordrecht: Springer.

Parikka, J. 2015. *A Geology of Media*. Minneapolis: University of Minnesota Press.

Parkins, W. and Craig, G. 2006. *Slow Living*. Sydney: University of New South Wales University Press.

Parks, T. 2014. *Italian Ways: On and Off the Rails from Milan to Palermo*. New York: Norton.

Pearce, F. 2007. *With Speed and Violence: Why Scientists Fear Tipping Points in Climate Change*. Boston: Beacon Press.

Perlow, L. A. and Porter, J. L. 2009. "Making Time Off Predictable—and Required." *Harvard Business Review* (October): 102–9.

Perlow, L. A., Mazmanian, M., and Hansen, E. 2015. "Shifting Towards a Collective Temporal Orientation: Enabling a Sustainable Performance Culture." Academy of Management Conference, Vancouver, BC.

Perrow, C. 1979. *Complex Organizations: A Critical Essay*. Glenview: Scott, Foresman and Company.

Peters, T. 1987. *Thriving on Chaos*. Basingstoke: Macmillan.

Peters, T. 1992. *Liberation Management*. Basingstoke: Macmillan.

Pfeiffer, D. 2006. *Eating Fossil Fuels: Oil, Food and the Coming Crisis in Agriculture*. Gabriola Island, BC: New Society Publishers.

Porter, G. and Kakabadse, N. K. 2006. "HRM Perspectives on Addiction to Technology and Work." *Journal of Management Development* 25: 535–60.

Poster, M. 2006. *Information Please: Culture and Politics in the Age of Digital Machines.* Durham, NC: Duke University Press.

Postone, M. 1993. *Time, Labor, and Social Domination: A Reinterpretation of Marx's Critical Theory.* New York: Cambridge University Press.

Prasad, P., Prasad, A., and Baker, K. 2014. "Smoke and Mirrors: Institutional Entrepreneurship and Gender Identities in the US Tobacco Industry, 1920–1945." *Organization*: 1–23.

Prasopoulou, E., Pouloud, A., and Panteli, N. 2006. "Enacting New Temporal Boundaries: The Role of Mobile Phones." *European Journal of Information Systems* 15: 277–84.

Prigogine, I. 1997. *The End of Certainty.* New York: Free Press.

Pryke, M. and Allen, J. 2000. "Monetized Time-Space: Derivatives—Money's 'New Imaginary'?" *Economy and Society* 29(2): 329–44.

Qiu, J. L. 2009. *Working-Class Network Society: Communication Technology and the Information Have-Less in Urban China.* Cambridge, MA: MIT Press.

Quattrone, P. 2015. "Governing Social Orders, Unfolding Rationality, and Jesuit Accounting Practices: A Procedural Approach to Institutional Logics." *Administrative Science Quarterly* 60: 411–45.

Quinlan, M. 2004. "Lessons for Governmental Process," in W. G. Runciman (ed.), *Hutton and Butler: Lifting the Lid on the Workings of Power.* Oxford: Oxford University Press and British Academy, pp. 115–30.

Rapoza, K. 2013. "One in Five Americans Work from Home: Numbers Seen Rising." *Forbes.* <http://www.forbes.com/sites/kenrapoza/2013/02/18/one-in-five-americans-work-from-home-numbers-seen-rising-over-60/#3217b4114768> accessed June 2016.

Reddy, M. and Dourish, P. 2002. "A Finger on the Pulse: Temporal Rhythms and Information Seeking in Medical Work." ACM Conference on Computer Supported Cooperative Work, CSCW. ACM, 344–53.

Reheis, F. 1996. *Kreativität der Langsamkeit. Neuer Wohlstand durch Entschleunigung.* Darmstadt: Wissenschaftliche Buchgesellschaft.

Reinsch, N. L. J., Turner, J. W., and Tinsley, C. H. 2008. "Multicommunicating: A Practice Whose Time Has Come?" *Academy of Management Review* 33: 391–403.

Rifkin, J. 1987. *Time Wars: The Primary Conflict in Human History.* New York: Simon and Schuster.

Rifkin, J. 2009. *The Empathic Civilization: The Race to Global Consciousness in a World in Crisis.* Cambridge: Polity.

Rittel, H. and Webber, M. 1973. "Dilemmas in a General Theory of Planning." *Policy Sciences* 4: 155–69.

Robertson, M., Scarbrough, H., and Swan, J. 2003. "Knowledge Creation in Professional Service Firms: Institutional Effects." *Organization Studies* 24: 831–57.

Robinson, J. and Godbey, G. 1999: *Time for Life. The Surprising Ways Americans Use Their Time*, 2nd edition. University Park: Pennsylvania State University Press.

Roethlisberger, F. J. and Dickson, W. J. 1939. *Management and the Worker: An Account of a Research Program Conducted by the Western Electric Company, Hawthorne Works, Chicago.* Cambridge, MA: Harvard University Press.

Rohr, J. 1998. *Public Service, Ethics and Constitutional Practice*. Lawrence: University of Kansas Press).

Rosa, H. 2010. *Alienation and Acceleration. Towards a Critical Theory of Late-Modern Temporality*. Malmö/Arhus: NSU Press.

Rosa, H. 2013. *Social Acceleration: A New Theory of Modernity*. New York: Columbia University Press.

Rosa, H. 2014. "Remember that Time is Knowledge, Health and Happiness: On the Mysterious Disappearance of Leisure," in M. Fludernik and M. Nandi (eds.), *Idleness, Indolence and Leisure in English Literature*. Houndmills, Basingstoke, and New York: Palgrave Macmillan, pp. 293–7.

Rosenau, J. N. and Singh, J. P. (eds.). 2002. *Information Technologies and Global Politics: The Changing Scope of Power and Governance*. Albany: State University of New York Press.

Rosner, D. K. and Ames, M. G. 2014. "Designing for Repair? Infrastructures and Materialities of Breakdown." Proceedings of the 2014 Computer Supported Cooperative Work Conference, San Antonio, April 2014.

Sacchetto, D. and Andrijasevic, R. 2015. "Beyond China: Foxconn's Assembly Plants in Europe." *South Atlantic Quarterly* 114(1): 215–24.

Sacks, H., Schegloff, E., and Jefferson, G. 1974. "A Simplest Systematics for the Organization of Turn-Taking for Conversation." *Language* 50: 696–735.

Sassen, S. 1991/2001. *The Global City*. Princeton, NJ: Princeton University Press.

Sassen. S. 2005. "Introduction. Digital Formations: Constructing an Object of Study," in R. Latham and S. Sassen (eds.), *Digital Formations: IT and New Architectures in the Global Realm*. Princeton, NJ: Princeton University Press, pp. 1–34.

Sassen, S. 2008. *Territory, Authority, Rights: From Medieval to Global Assemblages*. Princeton, NJ: Princeton University Press.

Sassen, S. 2012. "Interactions of the Technical and the Social: Digital Formations of the Powerful and the Powerless." *Information, Communication and Society* 15(4): 455–78.

Sassen, S. 2013. "Global Finance and its Institutional Spaces," in K. Knorr Cetina and A. Preda (eds.), *The Oxford Handbook of the Sociology of Finance*. Oxford University Press.

Sassen, S. 2014. *Expulsions: Brutality and Complexity in the Global Economy*. Cambridge, MA: Harvard University Press.

Sassen, S. 2015. "Digitization and Work: Potentials and Challenges in Low-Wage Labor Markets." Position paper. <http://www.saskiasassen.com/PDFs/publications/digitization-and-work.pdf> accessed June 2016.

Savulescu, J. and Bostrom, N. (eds.). 2011. *Human Enhancement*. Oxford: Oxford University Press.

Sayer, A. 2011. *Why Things Matter to People: Social Science, Values and Ethical Life*. Cambridge: Cambridge University Press.

Schawbel, D. 2014. "Work Life Integration: The New Norm." *Forbes*. <http://www.forbes.com/sites/danschawbel/2014/01/21/work-life-integration-the-new-norm/> accessed June 2016.

Scheuerman, W. 2004. *Liberal Democracy and the Social Acceleration of Time*. Baltimore and London: Johns Hopkins University Press.

Schivelbusch, W. 1987. *The Railway Journey: The Industrialization and Perception of Time and Space*. Berkeley: California University Press.

Schull, N. 2012. *Addiction by Design*. Princeton, NJ: Princeton University Press.

Schulte, B. 2015. *Overwhelmed: How to Work, Love, and Play When No One Has the Time*. New York: Picador.

Schwartz, B. 1974. "Waiting, Exchange, and Power: The Distribution Of Time in Social Systems." *American Journal of Sociology* 79: 841–70.

Scott, W. R. 2014. *Institutions and Organizations: Ideas, Interests, and Identities*. Thousand Oaks, CA: Sage Publications.

Sharma, S. 2009. "Baring Life and Lifestyle in the Non-Place." *Cultural Studies* 23(1): 129–48.

Sharma, S. 2014. *In the Meantime: Temporality and Cultural Politics*. Durham, NC: Duke University Press.

Sharon, T. and Frank, A. J. 2000. "Utilizing Multimedia Technologies for Interactive Telesonography." Department of Mathematics and Computer Science, Bar-Ilan University. <http://xenia.media.mit.edu/~taly/publications/riao00.pdf> accessed June 2016.

Simmel, G. 1923. "Rodin," in *Philosophische Kultur*. Potsdam: Kiepenhauer, pp. 168–86.

Simmel, G. 1950. *The Sociology of Georg Simmel*, trans. Kurt H. Wolff. New York: Free Press.

Simmel, G. 1991. "Money in Modern Culture." *Theory, Culture and Society* 8: 17–31.

Simmel, G. 2002. "The Metropolis and Mental Life," in G. Bridge and S. Watson (eds.), *The Blackwell City Reader*. Oxford and Malden, MA: Wiley-Blackwell, pp. 11–19.

Simmel, G. 2004. *The Philosophy of Money*. Third Enlarged Edition. London: Routledge.

Sinclair, U. 2008. *Oil!* London: Penguin.

Singer, N. 2014. "In the Sharing Economy, Workers Find Both Freedom and Uncertainty." *New York Times*. <http://www.nytimes.com/2014/08/17/technology/in-the-sharing-economy-workers-find-both-freedom-and-uncertainty.html> accessed June 2016.

Slim, W. 2009. *Defeat Into Victory*. London: Pan Books.

Smith, A. 1979. *An Inquiry into the Nature and Causes of the Wealth of Nations*. Oxford: Clarendon Press.

Snyder, B. H. 2013. "From Vigilance to Busyness: A Neo-Weberian Approach to Clock Time." *Sociological Theory* 31: 243–66.

Son, H. 2015. "The History of Western Future Studies: An Exploration of the Intellectual Traditions and Three-Phase Periodization." *Futures* 66: 120–37.

Sorrell, S. and Dimitropoulos, J. 2008. "The Rebound Effect: Microeconomic Definitions, Limitations and Extensions." *Ecological Economics* 65: 636–49.

Star, S. L. 1991. "Power, Technologies, and the Phenomenology of Conventions: On Being Allergic to Onions," in J. Law (ed.), *A Sociology of Monsters: Essays on Power, Technology and Domination*. London: Routledge.

Star, S. L. 1999. "The Ethnography of Infrastructure." *American Behavioral Scientist* 43(3): 377–91.

Star, S. L. and Ruhleder, K. 1996. "Steps Toward an Ecology of Infrastructure: Design and Access for Large Information Spaces." *Information Systems Research* 7(1): 111–34.

Star, S. L. and Strauss, A. 1999. "Layers of Silence, Arenas of Voice: The Ecology of Visible and Invisible Work." *Computer Supported Cooperative Work CSCW* 8(1): 9–30.

Starwarz, K., Cox, A. L., Bird, J., and Benedyk, R. 2013. "'I'd sit at home and do work emails': How Tablets Affect the Work-Life Balance of Office Workers." *CHI '13 Extended Abstracts on Human Factors in Computing Systems.*

Steiner, C. 2010. "Wall Street's Speed War." *Forbes*, September 27. <http://www.forbes.com/forbes/2010/0927/outfront-netscape-jim-barksdale-daniel-spivey-wall-street-speed-war.html> accessed June 2016.

Stinchcombe, A. 2001. *When Formality Works: Authority and Abstraction in Law and Organizations.* Chicago: University of Chicago Press.

Stivers, T., Enfield, N. J., Brown, P., Englert, C., Hayashi, M., Heinemann, T., Hoymann, G. et al. 2009. "Universals and Cultural Variation in Turn-Taking in Conversation." *Proceedings of the National Academy of Sciences* 106(26): 10587–92.

Stoler, A. 2008. "Imperial Debris." *Cultural Anthropology* 23(2): 191–219.

Strauss, A. and Corbin, J. M. 1998. *Basics of Qualitative Research: Techniques and Procedures for Developing Grounded Theory.* Thousand Oaks, CA: Sage Publications.

Strebel, I. 2011. "The Living Building: Towards a Geography of Maintenance Work." *Social and Cultural Geography* 12(3): 243–62.

Sullivan, J. 2013. "Speed Doesn't Kill ... Slow Kills Organizations." *ERE Media.* <http://www.eremedia.com/ere/speed-doesnt-kill-slow-kills-organizations/> accessed June 2016.

Tainter, J. 1988. *The Collapse of Complex Societies.* Cambridge: Cambridge University Press.

Takeuchi, Y. 2014. "Towards Habitable Bits: Digitizing the Built Environment." ACM International Conference on Interactive Tabletops and Surfaces, 209–18, ACM, New York.

Taylor, S. 1995. "The Effects of Filled Waiting Time and Service Provider Control over the Delay of Evaluations of Service." *Journal of the Academy of Marketing Science* 23(1): 38–48.

Tennant, E. W. 2007. "Locating Transnational Activists: Solidarity with and beyond Propinquity," in S. Sassen (ed.), *Deciphering the Global: Its Spaces, Scales and Subjects.* New York and London: Routledge, pp. 119–38.

Thompson, E. P. 1967. "Time, Work, Discipline and Industrial Capitalism." *Past and Present* 38: 56–97.

Thompson, E. P. 2002. *The Making of the English Working Class.* Harmondsworth: Penguin.

Thrift, N. 2002. "Performing Cultures in the New Economy," in P. du Gay and M. Pryke (eds.), *Cultural Economy.* London: Sage, pp. 201–34.

Thrift, N. 2005. *Knowing Capitalism.* Thousand Oaks, CA: Sage.

Thucydides. 2009. *The Peloponnesian War.* Oxford: Oxford University Press.

Tiku, N. 2015. "Living in the Disneyland Version of Startup Life." *Buzzfeed*, August 3. <http://www.buzzfeed.com/nitashatiku/silicon-valley-coliving#.hpb9zqAkd> accessed June 2016.

Toffler, A. 1970. *Future Shock.* London: Bodley Head.

Tomlinson, J. 2007. *The Culture of Speed: The Coming of Immediacy.* London: Sage.

Towers, I., Duxbury, L., Higgins, C., and Thomas, J. 2006. "Time Thieves and Space Invaders: Technology, Work and the Organization." *Journal of Organizational Change Management* 19: 593–618.

Trahair, R. C. S. 2005/1984. *Elton Mayo: The Humanist Temper*, foreword by Abraham Zaleznik. New Brunswick and London: Transaction Publishers.

Tronto, J. 1993. *Moral Boundaries: A Political Argument for an Ethic of Care*. New York: Routledge.

Tyfield, D. and Urry, J. 2014. "Energy and Society." Special issue of *Theory, Culture and Society* 31: 3–226.

Urry, J. 2000. *Sociology Beyond Societies: Mobilities for the Twenty-First Century*. London: Routledge.

Urry, J. 2007. *Mobilities*. Cambridge: Polity Press.

Urry, J. 2011. *Climate Change and Society*. Cambridge: Polity Press.

Urry, J. 2013. *Societies Beyond Oil*. London: Zed Books.

Urry, J. 2014. "The Problem of Energy." *Theory, Culture and Society* 31: 3–20.

Urry, J. 2016. *What is the Future?* Cambridge: Polity Press.

Valukas, A. 2010. "United States Bankruptcy Court Southern District of New York in re Lehman Brothers Holdings Inc., et al., Debtors. Chapter 11 case no. 08-13555 (JMP) (Jointly Administered)" Report of Anton R. Valukas, Examiner, March 11, 2010, Jenner and Block LLP 353 n. Clark Street Chicago, IL, USA.

Virilio, P. 1986. *Speed and Politics*, 2nd edition. New York: Semiotext(e).

Wajcman, J. 2002. "Special Issue: Information Technologies and the Social Sciences." *Current Sociology* 50(3).

Wajcman, J. 2008. "Life in the Fast Lane? Towards a Sociology of Technology and Time." *The British Journal of Sociology* 59: 59–77.

Wajcman, J. 2015. *Pressed for Time: The Acceleration of Life in Digital Capitalism*. Chicago: University of Chicago Press.

Warkentin, C. 2001. *Reshaping World Politics: NGOs, the Internet, and Global Civil Society*. Lanham, MD: Rowman and Littlefield.

Waters, R. and Kuchler, H. 2014. "Technology Groups in a War to Dominate the World of Work." *The Financial Times*.

Weber, M. 1994. *Political Writings*, edited by P. Lassman and R. Speirs. Cambridge: Cambridge University Press.

Wells, H. G. 1914. *An Englishman Looks at the World*. London: Cassel.

West, C. and Zimmerman, D. 1983. "Small Insults: A Study of Interruptions in Cross-Sex Conversations between Unacquainted Persons," in B. Thorne, C. Kramarae, and N. Henley (eds.), *Language, Gender and Society*. Rowley, MA: Newbury House, pp. 103–17.

Westbrook, R. B. 2005. *Democratic Hope: Pragmatism and the Politics of Truth*. Ithaca, NY: Cornell University Press.

Wilson, R. 2004. "Discussion," in W. G. Runciman (ed.), *Hutton and Butler: Lifting the Lid on the Workings of Power*. Oxford: Oxford University Press and British Academy, pp. 82–6.

Wittchen, H.-U. and Jacobi, F. 2006. "Epidemiologie," in G. Stoppe, A. Bramesfeld, and F. W. Schwartz (eds.), *Volkskrankheit Depression. Bestandsaufnahme und Perspektiven*. Berlin: Springer, pp. 15–37.

Wynne, B. 2010. "Strange Weather, Again: Climate Science as Political Art." *Theory, Culture and Society* 27: 289–305.

Young, M. 1988. *Metronomic Society: Natural Rhythms and Human Timetables.* Cambridge, MA: Harvard University Press.

Zaloom, C. 2003. "Ambiguous Numbers: Trading Technologies and Interpretation in Financial Markets." *American Ethnologist* 30(2): 258–72.

Zaloom, C. 2010. *Out of the Pits: Traders and Technology from Chicago to London.* Chicago: University of Chicago Press.

Zerubavel, E. 1979. "Private Time and Public Time: The Temporal Structure of Social Accessibility and Professional Commitments." *Social Forces* 58(1): 38–58.

Zerubavel, E. 1980. "The Benedictine Ethic and the Modern Spirit of Scheduling: On Schedules and Social Organization." *Sociological Inquiry* 50: 157–69.

Zerubavel, E. 1982. "The Standardization of Time: A Sociohistorical Perspective." *The American Journal of Sociology* 88: 1–23.

# Index

Note: Italic number indicates figure and table.